# PowerPoint® 2003 FOR DUMMIES®

## by Doug Lowe

WILEY

Wiley Publishing, Inc.

**PowerPoint® 2003 For Dummies®**

Published by
**Wiley Publishing, Inc.**
111 River Street
Hoboken, NJ 07030
www.wiley.com

Copyright © 2003 by Wiley Publishing, Inc., Indianapolis, Indiana

Published by Wiley Publishing, Inc., Indianapolis, Indiana

Published simultaneously in Canada

# PowerPoint® 2003 For Dummies®

## Formatting Commands

| Command | Keys |
|---|---|
| Bold | Ctrl+B |
| Italic | Ctrl+I |
| Underline | Ctrl+U |
| Center | Ctrl+E |
| Left Align | Ctrl+L |
| Right Align | Ctrl+R |
| Justify | Ctrl+J |
| Normal | Ctrl+Spacebar |

## Editing Commands

| Command | Keys |
|---|---|
| Undo | Ctrl+Z |
| Cut | Ctrl+X |
| Copy | Ctrl+C |
| Paste | Ctrl+V |
| Select All | Ctrl+A |
| Find | Ctrl+F |
| Replace | Ctrl+H |
| Duplicate | Ctrl+D |

## Commonly Used Commands

| Command | Keys |
|---|---|
| New | Ctrl+N |
| Open | Ctrl+O |
| Save | Ctrl+S |
| Print | Ctrl+P |
| Help | F1 |
| New Slide | Ctrl+M |

## The PowerPoint Window

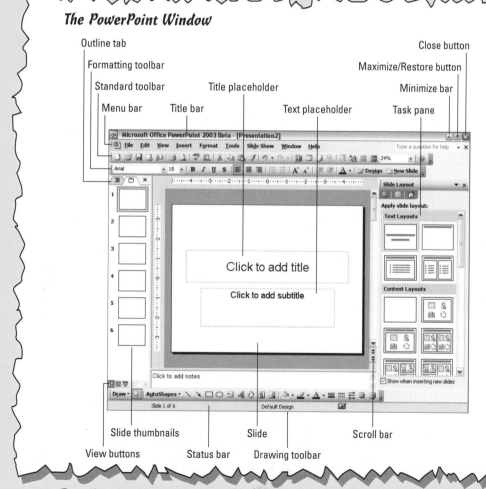

For Dummies: Bestselling Book Series for Beginners

# PowerPoint® 2003 For Dummies®

*Cheat Sheet*

## Slide Show Shortcuts

| To Do This... | Use This... |
| --- | --- |
| Start a slide show | F5 |
| Advance to the next slide | N |
| Perform the next animation | Enter, Page Down, right arrow, down arrow, or spacebar |
| Go back to the previous slide | P |
| Repeat the previous animation | Page Up, left arrow, up arrow, or backspace key |
| Go to a specific slide | Type the slide number and then press Enter |
| Display a black screen | B |
| Display a white screen | W |
| End a slide show | Escape |
| Go to the next hidden slide | H |
| Display a pen pointer | Ctrl+P |
| Display an arrow pointer | Ctrl+A |
| Hide the pointer | Ctrl+H |

### The Standard toolbar

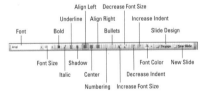

### Drawing toolbar

### Formatting toolbar

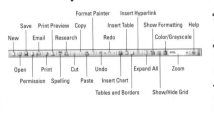

Copyright © 2003 Wiley Publishing, Inc.
All rights reserved.

Item 3908-6.

For more information about Wiley Publishing,
call 1-800-762-2974.

## For Dummies: Bestselling Book Series for Beginners

# About the Author

**Doug Lowe** has written enough computer books to line all the birdcages in California. His most recent books (other than this one, of course) are *Office 2002 Quick Reference For Dummies, Internet Explorer 5.5 For Dummies,* and *Networking For Dummies,* Fifth Edition.

Although Doug has yet to win a Pulitzer Prize, he remains cautiously optimistic. He is hopeful that George Lucas will pick up the film rights to this book and suggests *PowerPoint Episode 1: The Phantom Presentation* as a working title.

Doug lives in sunny Fresno, California, where the motto is "Give Us Electricity or Give Us . . . Uh, No . . . Just Give Us Electricity!" with his wife Debbie, a trio of daughters (Rebecca, Sarah, and Bethany), and a pair of female golden retrievers (Nutmeg and Ginger, the original Spice Girls).

# Dedication

To Debbie, Rebecca, Sarah, and Bethany.

# Author's Acknowledgments

I'd like to thank everyone at Wiley who helped this new edition come together: Melody Layne for getting the project rolling, project editor Kala Schrager for seeing it through, copy editor Rebekah Mancilla for dotting all the *t*'s and crossing all the *i*'s, technical editor Doug Sahlin for making sure it works the way I say it does, and everyone else who pitched in.

I'd also like to thank everyone who helped out with previous editions of this book: Andrea Boucher, Garret Pease, Steve Hayes, Kel Oliver, Nancy DelFavero, Grace Jasmine, Rev Mengle, Tina Sims, Pam Mourouzis, Leah Cameron, Jim McCarter, Kezia Endsley, Becky Whitney, and Michael Partington.

## Publisher's Acknowledgments

We're proud of this book; please send us your comments through our online registration form located at www.dummies.com/register/.

Some of the people who helped bring this book to market include the following:

*Acquisitions, Editorial, and Media Development*

**Project Editor:** Kala Schrager

**Acquisitions Editor:** Melody Layne

**Copy Editor:** Rebekah Mancilla

**Technical Editor:** Doug Sahlin

**Editorial Manager:** Kevin Kirschner, Carol Sheehan

**Media Development Manager:** Laura VanWinkle

**Media Development Supervisor:** Richard Graves

**Editorial Assistant:** Amanda Foxworth

**Cartoons:** Rich Tennant (www.the5thwave.com)

*Production*

**Project Coordinator:** Kristie Rees

**Layout and Graphics:** Seth Conley, Michael Kruzil, Barry Offringa, Lynsey Osborn

**Proofreaders:** John Tyler Connoley, Carl William Pierce, TECHBOOKS Production Services

**Indexer:** Joan Griffitts

---

**Publishing and Editorial for Technology Dummies**

    **Richard Swadley,** Vice President and Executive Group Publisher

    **Andy Cummings,** Vice President and Publisher

    **Mary C. Corder,** Editorial Director

**Publishing for Consumer Dummies**

    **Diane Graves Steele,** Vice President and Publisher

    **Joyce Pepple,** Acquisitions Director

**Composition Services**

    **Gerry Fahey,** Vice President of Production Services

    **Debbie Stailey,** Director of Composition Services

# Contents at a Glance

# Table of Contents

# Introduction

· · · · · · · · · · · · · · · · · · · · · · · · · · · · · · · · · · · · · · · · · · · · · · · · ·

**W**elcome to *PowerPoint 2003 For Dummies,* the book written especially for those who are lucky enough to use this latest and greatest version of PowerPoint and want to find out just enough to finish that presentation that was due yesterday.

Do you ever find yourself in front of an audience, no matter how small, flipping through flip charts or shuffling through a stack of handwritten transparencies? You need PowerPoint! Have you always wanted to take your notebook computer with you to impress a client at lunch, but you don't know what to do with it between trips to the salad bar? Have you ever spent an entire afternoon stuck in an airport, realizing that weather conditions were making you miss a major meeting and that if you could phone in your presentation, you would finally get that promotion you have deserved for the past year? You *really* need PowerPoint!

Or maybe you're one of those unfortunate folks who bought Microsoft Office because it was such a bargain and you needed a Windows word processor and spreadsheet anyway, and hey, you're not even sure what PowerPoint is, but it was free. Who can resist a bargain like that?

Whichever way, you're holding the perfect book right here in your formerly magic-marker-stained hands. Help is here, within these humble pages.

This book talks about PowerPoint in everyday — and often irreverent — terms. No lofty prose here; the whole thing checks in at about the fifth-grade reading level. I have no Pulitzer expectations for this book. My goal is to make an otherwise dull and lifeless subject at least tolerable, and maybe even kind of fun.

## About This Book

This isn't the kind of book that you pick up and read from start to finish as though it were a cheap novel. If I ever see you reading it at the beach, I'll kick sand in your face. This book is more like a reference — the kind of book you can pick up, turn to just about any page, and start reading. It has 27 chapters, each one covering a specific aspect of using PowerPoint — such as printing, changing colors, or using clip art.

Each chapter is divided into self-contained chunks, all related to the major theme of the chapter.

For example, the chapter on using clip art contains nuggets like these:

- ✔ Dropping in some clip art
- ✔ Moving, sizing, and stretching pictures
- ✔ Boxing, shading, and shadowing a picture
- ✔ Editing a clip art picture
- ✔ Getting clip art from the Internet

You don't have to memorize anything in this book. It's a "need-to-know" book: You pick it up when you need to know something. Need to know how to create an organization chart? Pick up the book. Need to know how to override the Slide Master? Pick up the book. Otherwise, put it down and get on with your life.

# How to Use This Book

This book works like a reference. Start with the topic that you want to find out about: To get going, look for it in the Table of Contents or in the Index. The Table of Contents is detailed enough that you should be able to find most of the topics that you look for. If not, turn to the Index, where you find even more detail.

When you find your topic in the Table of Contents or the Index, turn to the area of interest and read as much or as little as you need or want. Then close the book and get on with it.

This book is loaded with information, of course, so if you want to take a brief excursion into your topic, you're more than welcome. If you want to know all about Slide Masters, read the chapter on templates and masters. If you want to know all about color schemes, read the chapter on color schemes. Read whatever you want. This is *your* book — not mine.

On occasion, this book directs you to use specific keyboard shortcuts to get things done. When you see something like Ctrl+Z, this instruction means to hold down the Ctrl key while pressing the Z key and then release both together. Don't type the plus sign.

Sometimes I tell you to use a menu command, like this: Choose File➪Open. This means to use the keyboard or mouse to open the File menu and then choose the Open command.

Whenever I describe a message or information that you see on-screen, it looks like this:

```
Are we having fun yet?
```

Anything you are instructed to type appears in bold like so: Type **a:setup** in the Run dialog box. You type exactly what you see, with or without spaces.

Another nice feature of this book is that whenever I discuss a certain button that you need to click in order to accomplish the task at hand, the button appears in the margin. This way, you can easily locate it on your screen.

# What You Don't Need to Read

Some parts of this book are skippable. I carefully place extra-technical information in self-contained sidebars and clearly mark them so that you can give them a wide berth. Don't read this stuff unless you just gots to know. Don't worry; I won't be offended if you don't read every word.

# Foolish Assumptions

I make only three assumptions about you:

- ✔ You use a computer.
- ✔ It's a Windows computer — not a Macintosh.
- ✔ You use or are thinking about using PowerPoint 2003.

Nothing else. I don't assume that you're a computer guru who knows how to change a controller card or configure memory for optimal use. These types of computer chores are best handled by people who like computers. Hopefully, you are on speaking terms with such a person. Do your best to stay there.

# How This Book Is Organized

Inside this book are chapters arranged in six parts. Each chapter is broken down into sections that cover various aspects of the chapter's main subject. The chapters have a logical sequence, so it makes sense to read them in order if you want. But you don't have to read the book that way; you can flip it open to any page and start reading.

Here's the lowdown on what's in each of the five parts:

# Part I: Basic PowerPoint 2003 Stuff

In this part, you review the basics of using PowerPoint. This is a good place to start if you're clueless about what PowerPoint is, let alone how to use it.

# Part II: Making Your Presentations Look Mahvelous

The chapters in this part show you how to make presentations that look good. Most important are the chapters about templates and masters, which control the overall look of a presentation. Get the template right, and everything else falls into place.

# Part III: PowerPoint Gone Wild

The chapters in this part show you how to spice up an otherwise dreary presentation with drawings, graphs, animations, sealing wax, and other fancy stuff. Not so wild that you would only want to show it on late-night TV, but pretty wild nonetheless.

# Part IV: PowerPoint and the Net

The chapters in this part show you how to use PowerPoint's many Internet features, including how to save and retrieve presentations from a Web site, how to create Web pages with PowerPoint, and how to use PowerPoint's collaborate features.

# Part V: The Part of Tens

This wouldn't be a *For Dummies* book without lists of interesting snippets: the ten PowerPoint commandments, ten tips for creating readable slides, ten ways to keep your audience awake, ten things that often go wrong, and my all-time favorite: ten things that didn't fit anywhere else.

# Icons Used in This Book

As you're reading all this wonderful prose, you occasionally see the following icons. They appear in the margins to draw your attention to important information. They are defined as follows:

Watch out! Some technical drivel is just around the corner. Read it only if you have your pocket protector firmly attached.

Pay special attention to this icon — it tells you that some particularly useful tidbit is at hand, perhaps a shortcut or a way of using a command that you may not have considered.

Danger! Danger! Danger! Stand back, Will Robinson!

Did I tell you about the memory course I took?

# Where to Go from Here

Yes, you can get there from here. With this book in hand, you're ready to charge full speed ahead into the strange and wonderful world of desktop presentations. Browse through the Table of Contents and decide where you want to start. Be bold! Be courageous! Be adventurous! Above all else, have fun!

# Part I
# Basic PowerPoint 2003 Stuff

The 5th Wave          By Rich Tennant

"No, it's not a pie chart, it's just a corn chip that got scanned into the document."

# In this part . . .

*O*nce upon a time, the term *presentation software* meant poster board and marker pens. Now, however, programs such as Microsoft PowerPoint enable you to create spectacular presentations on your computer.

The chapters in this part comprise a bare-bones introduction to PowerPoint. You learn exactly what PowerPoint is and how to use it to create simple presentations. More advanced stuff such as adding charts or using fancy text fonts is covered in later parts. This part is just the beginning. As a great king once advised, it is best to begin at the beginning and go on until you come to the end; then stop.

# Chapter 1

# Opening Ceremonies

- - - - - - - - - - - - - - - - - - - - - - - - - - - - - - - - - - - - - - - -

- - - - - - - - - - - - - - - - - - - - - - - - - - - - - - - - - - - - - - - -

*T*his chapter is a grand and gala welcoming ceremony for PowerPoint. In fact, this chapter is kind of like the opening ceremony for the Olympics, in which all the athletes march in and parade around the track waving their flags and famous people (who you've never heard of) make speeches in French. In this chapter, I parade the features of PowerPoint around the track so you can see what they look like. I may even make a few speeches. Let the games begin!

## What in Sam Hill Is PowerPoint?

PowerPoint is a program that comes with Microsoft Office (although you can buy it separately, as well). Most people buy Microsoft Office because it's a great bargain: You get Word and Excel for less than it would cost to buy them separately. As an added bonus, you get a bunch of extra stuff thrown in: Outlook, Access, PowerPoint, a complete set of Ginsu knives, and a Binford VegaPneumatic Power Slicer and Dicer (always wear eye protection).

You know what Word is — it's the world's most loved and most hated word processor — perfect for concocting letters, term papers, and great American novels. Excel is a spreadsheet program used by bean counters the world over. But what the heck is PowerPoint? Does anybody know or care? (And as long as we're asking questions, who in Sam Hill was Sam Hill?)

PowerPoint is a *presentation* program, and it's one of the coolest programs I know. If you've ever flipped a flip chart, headed over to an overhead projector, or slipped on a slide, you're going to love PowerPoint. With just a few clicks of the mouse, you can create presentations that bedazzle your audience and instantly sway them to your point of view, even if you're selling real estate on Mars, season tickets for the Mets, or a new Medicare plan to Congress.

Here are some of the many uses of PowerPoint:

- **Business presentations:** PowerPoint is a great timesaver for anyone who makes business presentations, whether you've been asked to speak in front of hundreds of people at a shareholders' convention, a group of sales reps at a sales conference, or your own staff or coworkers at a business planning meeting.

- **Sales presentations:** If you're an insurance salesman, you can use PowerPoint to create a presentation about the perils of not owning life insurance, and then show it to hapless clients on your laptop computer.

- **Lectures:** PowerPoint is also great for teachers or conference speakers who want to back up their lectures with slides or overheads.

- **Homework:** PowerPoint is a great program to use for certain types of homework projects, such as big history reports that count for half your grade.

- **Church:** PowerPoint is also used at churches to display song lyrics on big screens at the front of the church so everyone can sing or to display sermon outlines so everyone can take notes. If your church still uses hymnals or prints the outline in the bulletin, tell the minister to join the twenty-first century.

- **Information stations:** You can use PowerPoint to set up a computerized information kiosk that people can walk up to and use. For example, you can create a museum exhibit about the history of your town or set up a trade-show presentation to provide information about your company and products.

- **Internet presentations:** PowerPoint can even help you to set up a presentation that you can broadcast over the Internet so people can join in on the fun without having to leave the comfort of their own homes or offices.

# *Introducing PowerPoint Presentations*

PowerPoint is similar to a word processor like Word, except that it's geared toward creating *presentations* rather than *documents*. A presentation is kind of like those Kodak Carousel slide trays that your father used to load up with 35mm slides of your family trip to the Grand Canyon. The main difference is that you don't have to worry about dumping all the slides in your PowerPoint presentation out of the tray and onto the floor.

Word documents consist of one or more pages, and PowerPoint presentations consist of one or more *slides*. Each slide can contain text, graphics, and other information. You can easily rearrange the slides in a presentation, delete slides that you don't need, add new slides, or modify the contents of existing slides.

You can use PowerPoint both to create your presentations as well as to actually present them.

You can use several different types of media to actually show your presentations:

- ✔ **Computer monitor:** Your computer monitor, either a tabletop CRT monitor or the LCD display on a laptop computer, is a suitable way to display your presentation when you are showing it to just one or two other people.

- ✔ **Computer projector:** A computer projector projects an image of your computer monitor onto a screen so larger audiences can view it.

- ✔ **Web pages:** Web pages on the Internet or on a company intranet can allow you to display your presentation to a larger audience.

- ✔ **Overhead transparencies:** Overhead transparencies can be used to show your presentation using an overhead projector.

- ✔ **Printed pages:** Printed pages allow you to distribute a printed copy of your entire presentation to each member of your audience. (When you print your presentation, you can print one slide per page, or you can print several slides on each page to save paper.)

- ✔ **35mm slides:** For a fee, you can have your presentation printed onto 35mm slides either by a local company or over the Internet. Then, your presentation really is like a Kodak Carousel slide tray! (For more information, refer to Chapter 27.)

# Presentation files

A presentation is to PowerPoint what a document is to Word or a worksheet is to Excel. In other words, a presentation is a file that you create with PowerPoint. Each presentation that you create is saved on disk as a separate file.

PowerPoint presentations have the special extension `.ppt` added to the end of their file names. For example, `Sales Conference.ppt` and `History Day.ppt` are both valid PowerPoint filenames. When you type the filename for a new PowerPoint file, you don't have to type the `.ppt` extension because PowerPoint automatically adds the extension for you. PowerPoint often hides the `.ppt` extension, so a presentation file named `Conference.ppt` often appears as just `Conference`.

PowerPoint is set up initially to save your presentation files in the My Documents folder, but you can store PowerPoint files in any folder of your choice on your hard drive. You can store a presentation on a diskette if you want to take it home with you to work on it over the weekend or if you want to give the presentation to other people so they can use it on their computers. (If the presentation is too large to squeeze onto a diskette, you can store it on a CD-ROM if your computer has a CD-RW drive.)

# What's in a slide?

PowerPoint presentations are comprised of one or more slides. Each slide can contain text, graphics, and other elements. A number of PowerPoint features work together to help you easily format attractive slides:

✓ **Slide layouts:** Every slide has a slide layout that controls how information is arranged on the slide. A slide layout is simply a collection of one or more placeholders, which set aside an area of the slide to hold information. Depending on the layout that you choose for a slide, the placeholders can hold text, graphics, clip art, sound or video files, tables, charts, graphs, diagrams, or other types of content.

✓ **Background:** Every slide has a background, which provides a backdrop for the slide's content. The background can be a solid color; a blend of two colors; a subtle texture, such as marble or parchment; a pattern, such as diagonal lines, bricks, or tiles; or an image file. Each slide can have a different background, but you usually want to use the same background for every slide in your presentation to provide a consistent look.

✓ **Color scheme:** PowerPoint has built-in color schemes that make it easy for anyone to create attractive slides that don't clash. You can stray from the color schemes if you want, but you should do so only if you have a better eye that the design gurus that work for Microsoft.

✔ **Slide Master:** The Slide Master controls the basic design and formatting options for slides in your presentation. The Slide Master includes the position and size of basic title and text placeholders; the background and color scheme used for the presentation; and font settings, such as typefaces, colors, and sizes. In addition, the Slide Master can contain graphic and text objects that you want to appear on every slide.

You can edit the Slide Master to change the appearance of all the slides in your presentation at once. This helps to ensure that the slides in your presentation have a consistent appearance.

✔ **Design template:** A design template is simply a presentation file that contains a pre-designed Slide Master that you can use to create presentations that look like a professional graphic artist designed them. When you create a new presentation, you can base it on one of the presentations that comes with PowerPoint. PowerPoint comes with a collection of design templates that you can use, and you can get additional templates from the Microsoft Web site. You can also create your own design templates.

All the features described in the previous list work together to control the appearance of your slides in much the same way that style sheets and templates control the appearance of Word documents. You can customize the appearance of individual slides by adding any of the following elements:

✔ **Title and body text:** Most slide layouts include placeholders for title and body text. You can type any text that you want into these placeholders. By default, PowerPoint formats the text according to the Slide Master, but you can easily override this formatting to use any font, size, style, or text color that you want.

✔ **Text boxes:** You can add text anywhere on a slide by drawing a text box and then typing text. Text boxes allow you to add text that doesn't fit conveniently in the title or body text placeholders.

✔ **Shapes:** You can use PowerPoint's drawing tools to add a variety of shapes on your slides. You can use predefined AutoShapes, such as rectangles, circles, stars, arrows, and flowchart symbols; or you can create your own shapes by using basic line, polygon, and freehand drawing tools.

✔ **Pictures:** You can insert pictures onto your slides that you have scanned into your computer or downloaded from the Internet. PowerPoint also comes with a large collection of clip art pictures that you can use.

✔ **Diagrams:** PowerPoint includes a diagramming feature that enables you to create several common types of diagrams: Organization Charts, Venn Diagrams, Stacked Pyramid Diagrams, and others.

✔ **Media files:** You can also add sound clips or video files to your slides.

# Starting PowerPoint

Here's the procedure for starting PowerPoint:

1. **Get ready.**

   Light some votive candles. Take two Tylenol. Put on a pot of coffee. If you're allergic to banana slugs, take an allergy pill. Sit in the lotus position facing Redmond, Washington, and recite the Windows creed three times:

   *Bill Gates is my friend. Resistance is futile. No beer and no TV make Homer something something . . .*

2. **Click the Start button.**

   The Start button is ordinarily found at the lower-left corner of the Windows display. When you click it, the famous Start menu appears. The Start menu works pretty much the same, no matter which version of Windows you're using.

   If you can't find the Start button, try moving the mouse pointer all the way to the bottom edge of the screen and holding it there a moment. With luck on your side, you see the Start button appear. If not, try moving the mouse pointer to the other three edges of the screen: top, left, and right. Sometimes the Start button hides behind these edges.

3. **Point to All Programs on the Start menu.**

   After you click the Start button to reveal the Start menu, move the mouse pointer up to the word *Programs* and hold it there a moment. Yet another menu appears, revealing a bevy of commands. (On versions of Windows prior to Windows XP, All Programs is called simply "Programs.")

4. **Click Microsoft Office on the All Programs menu, and then click Microsoft Office PowerPoint 2003.**

   Your computer whirs and clicks and possibly makes other unmentionable noises while PowerPoint comes to life.

   If you use PowerPoint frequently, it may appear in the *Frequently Used Program List* directly on the Start menu so you don't have to choose All Programs➪Microsoft Office to get to it. If you want PowerPoint to always appear at the top of the Start menu, choose Start➪All Programs➪ Microsoft Office. Then, right-click Microsoft Office PowerPoint 2003 and choose the Pin to Start Menu command.

# Customizing Your Settings

Before you get too deep into PowerPoint, I suggest that you change a couple of settings. You can use PowerPoint just fine without making these changes, but your life will be easier if you make them now. Just follow these simple steps:

1. **Choose Tools⇨Options and click the Save tab.**

   This summons the Save options in the Options dialog box.

2. **Uncheck the Allow Fast Saves option.**

   This option has long been a thorn in PowerPoint's side, and is best left turned off.

3. **Click OK.**

   The Options dialog box vanishes.

4. **Choose Tools⇨Customize and click the Options tab.**

   This displays the Options in the Customize dialog box.

5. **If it's not already checked, check the Always Show Full Menus option.**

   This short-circuits PowerPoint's annoying habit of showing you only some of the commands on each of its menus.

6. **Check the Show Standard And Formatting Toolbars On Two Rows option.**

   By default, PowerPoint jams the Standard and Formatting toolbars onto one row. Unfortunately, this hides half of the buttons on each toolbar. By displaying the toolbars on separate rows, you'll be able to see all of the buttons on both toolbars.

7. **Click OK.**

   That's all there is to it. We now return you to our originally scheduled programming.

# Navigating the PowerPoint Interface

When you start PowerPoint, it greets you with a screen that's so cluttered with stuff that you're soon ready to consider newsprint and markers as a viable alternative for your presentations. The center of the screen is mercifully blank, but all around the edges and tucked into every corner are little icons and buttons and menus and whatnot. What is all that stuff?

Figure 1-1 shows the basic PowerPoint screen in all its cluttered glory. The following list points out the more important parts of the PowerPoint screen:

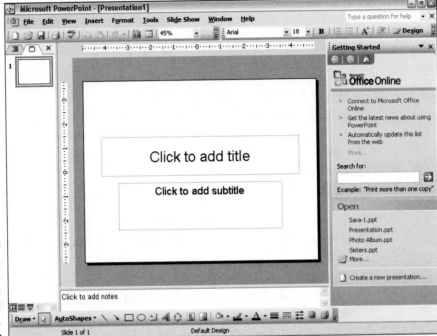

Figure 1-1:
Power-
Point's
cluttered
screen.

✔ **Menu bar:** Across the top of the screen, just below the Microsoft PowerPoint title, is the *menu bar*. The deepest and darkest secrets of PowerPoint are hidden on the menu bar. Wear a helmet when exploring it.

PowerPoint has an annoying "feature" that tries to simplify menus by showing only those commands that you frequently use on the menus. If this feature has been enabled on your computer, the menus start out by showing only those commands that the programmers at Microsoft think you'll use most often. The less frequently used commands are hidden beneath the double down arrow that appears at the bottom of each menu. As you work with PowerPoint, the commands that you use most often show up on the menus, so you don't have to click the down arrow to access them.

Here's the bottom line: If you can't find a menu command, don't give up. Just click the double down arrow at the bottom of the menu. Or, just stare at the menu for a few seconds. Eventually, PowerPoint realizes that you can't find what you're looking for, and the missing menu commands magically appear.

Better yet, turn back a few pages to the section "Customizing Your Settings" and check the Always Show Full Menus option.

✔ **Toolbars:** Just below the menu bar are two of the many *toolbars* that PowerPoint offers you in an effort to make its most commonly used features easy to use. Each toolbar consists of a bunch of buttons that you can click to perform common functions. The toolbar on the top is the Standard toolbar; immediately beneath it is the Formatting toolbar.

Down near the bottom of the screen is the Drawing toolbar. It has buttons that let you draw pictures on your slides.

If you ignored my advice in the section "Customizing Your Settings," the two toolbars pictured below the menu bar may be jammed together on one line on your computer. If so, refer back to that section to learn how to put them on separate lines.

If you're not sure about the function of one of the billions and billions of buttons that clutter the PowerPoint screen, place the mouse pointer on the button in question. After a moment, the name of the button appears in a box just below the button.

✔ **Current slide:** Right smack in the middle of the screen is where your current slide appears.

✔ **Outline tab and Slide tab:** On the left side of the slide is an area that has two tabs, labeled Outline and Slides. The Outline tab shows your presentation arranged as an outline. You can switch between the Slides tab and the Outline tab by clicking the tab you want to view. (For more information on working in Outline View, see Chapter 3.) The Slides tab, shown in Figure 1-1, shows little thumbnail images of your slides.

✔ **Notes Pane:** Beneath the slide is a small area called the *Notes Pane,* which you can use to add notes to your slides. For more information on using this feature, see Chapter 5.

✔ **Task Pane:** To the right of the slide is an area called the *Task Pane.* The Task Pane is designed to help you complete common tasks quickly. When you first start PowerPoint, the Task Pane appears with the New Presentation options, which let you create a new presentation or open an existing presentation. As you work with PowerPoint, you'll encounter other options in the Task Pane for common tasks, such as searching, changing the slide design, or setting animation options.

✔ **Status bar:** At the very bottom of the screen is the *status bar,* which tells you the slide that is currently displayed (for example, Slide 1 of 1).

✔ **Salad bar:** The salad bar is located . . . well, actually, there is no salad bar. You have to pay extra for that.

You'll never get anything done if you feel that you have to understand every pixel of the PowerPoint screen before you can do anything. Don't worry about the stuff that you don't understand; just concentrate on what you need to know to get the job done and worry about the bells and whistles later.

Lots of stuff is crammed onto the PowerPoint screen — enough stuff that the program works best if you let it run in *Full Screen* mode. If PowerPoint doesn't take over your entire screen, look for the boxy-looking Maximize button near the top-right corner of the PowerPoint window (it's the middle of the three buttons clustered in the top-right corner — the box represents a window maximized to its largest possible size). Click it to maximize the PowerPoint screen. Click it again to restore the PowerPoint screen to its smaller size.

# The View from Here Is Great

On the bottom-left edge of the PowerPoint window is a series of View buttons. These buttons enable you to switch among the various *views,* or ways of looking at your presentation. Table 1-1 summarizes what each View button does.

| Table 1-1 | View Buttons |
|---|---|
| **Button** | **What It Does** |
| ▦ | Switches to Normal View, which shows your slide, outline, and notes all at once. This view is how PowerPoint normally appears. |
| ▦ | Switches to Slide Sorter View, which enables you to easily rearrange slides and add slide transitions and other special effects. |
| ▽ | Switches to Slide Show View, which displays your slides in an on-screen presentation. |

# Creating a New Presentation

When you first start PowerPoint, the Getting Started page appears in the Task Pane on the right side of the screen (refer to Figure 1-1). The Getting Started page provides different ways for you to get started by opening an existing presentation or creating a new one:

 ✔ **The Open section of the Getting Started task pane:** The Open section of the Getting Started task pane lists the four presentations that you have most recently worked on, plus a More option that lets you open any existing presentation. If the presentation that you want to work on is listed, just click it to open the presentation. Otherwise, click More to locate your presentation. (For more information, see the section "Opening a Presentation" later in this chapter.)

✔ **Create a New Presentation:** Click this link to bring up the New Presentation pane.

The New Presentation pane has three sections that list additional ways to create new presentations:

✔ **New:** This section has several options for creating new presentations:

- **Blank Presentation:** Click Blank Presentation to start a new presentation from scratch.

- **From Design Template:** Click From Design Template to choose one of the templates that comes with PowerPoint as a starting point.

- **From AutoContent Wizard:** Click From AutoContent Wizard to start a wizard that actually creates a skeleton presentation for you.

- **From Existing Presentation:** Click From Existing Presentation to create a new presentation based on an existing one. Use this option if you want to create a presentation that is similar to a presentation that you have previously created.

- **Photo Album:** Click Photo Album to create presentations that consist mostly of pictures.

✔ **Templates:** This section provides a search box in which you can type a key word to search for an appropriate template on Microsoft's Web site.

✔ **Recently Used Templates:** This section simply lists the four templates that you've used most recently. (The first time you use PowerPoint, this section won't be visible. After you begin to work with presentations, however, templates will appear in this section.).

## Using the AutoContent Wizard

An easy way to get started with PowerPoint is to use the AutoContent Wizard. This wizard asks you for some pertinent information, such as your name, the title of your presentation, and the type of presentation that you want to create. Then it automatically creates a skeleton presentation that you can modify to suit your needs.

The marketing folks at Microsoft want you to believe that the AutoContent Wizard writes your presentation for you, as if you just click the button and then go play a round of golf while PowerPoint does your research, organizes your thoughts, writes your text, and throws in a few good lawyer jokes to boot. Sorry. All the AutoContent Wizard does is create an outline for a number of common types of presentations. It doesn't do your thinking for you. The more proficient you become at using PowerPoint, the less you'll want to use the AutoContent Wizard.

To create a presentation using the AutoContent Wizard, follow these steps:

1. **Start PowerPoint.**

   PowerPoint comes to life, as shown in Figure 1-1.

2. **Click Create a New Presentation at the bottom of the Getting Started pane, then click From AutoContent Wizard.**

   The AutoContent Wizard takes over and displays the dialog box shown in Figure 1-2. You may also notice your office assistant saying something pithy about the AutoContent Wizard; ignore him for now by right-clicking and choosing Hide.

**Figure 1-2:**
The
AutoContent
Wizard gets
under way.

3. **Click Next.**

4. **Select the type of presentation that you want to create by clicking one of the presentation types.**

   A variety of presentation types exist in six different categories. Click the category that you find most useful and select a presentation type.

5. **Click Next.**

   When you click Next, the AutoContent Wizard advances to the dialog box shown in Figure 1-3.

6. **Indicate the type of output that you want to create.**

   Choose On-Screen Presentation if you are going to use a computer projector to display your slides.

7. **Click Next.**

**Figure 1-3:**
The wizard
asks what
kind of
output
you are
creating.

8. **Type the title of your presentation and footer information, such as your name or company.**

   Note that you get the last-updated presentation by default as well as a slide number. (You can click the check box if you don't feel like having these default settings.)

9. **Click Next.**

10. **Click Finish.**

    The AutoContent Wizard creates a presentation for you. After the presentation is finished, you can use the editing and formatting techniques described in the rest of this chapter and throughout the book to personalize the presentation.

## Zooming in

PowerPoint automatically adjusts its zoom factor so that Slide View displays each slide in its entirety. You can change the size of your slide by choosing View⇨Zoom or by using the Zoom control in the Standard toolbar. This allows you to zoom in close to work on a detailed drawing.

## Editing text

In PowerPoint, slides are blank areas that you can adorn with various types of objects. The most common types of objects are *text objects,* which are rectangular areas that are specially designated for holding text. Other types of objects include shapes, such as circles or triangles, pictures imported from clip art files, and graphs.

Most slides contain two text objects: one for the slide's title, the other for its body text. However, you can add additional text objects if you want, and you can remove the body text or title text object. You can even remove both to create a slide that contains no text.

Whenever you move the mouse cursor over a text object, the cursor changes from an arrow to the *I-beam,* which you can use to support bridges or build aircraft carriers. Seriously, when the mouse cursor changes to an I-beam, you can click the mouse button and start typing text.

When you click a text object, a box appears around the text and an insertion pointer appears right at the spot where you clicked. PowerPoint then becomes like a word processor. Any characters that you type are inserted into the text at the insertion pointer location. You can use the Delete or Backspace keys to demolish text, and you can use the arrow keys to move the insertion pointer around in the text object. If you press the Enter key, a new line of text begins within the text object.

When a text object contains no text, a placeholder message appears in the object. For a title text object, the message `Click to add title` appears. For other text objects, the placeholder message reads `Click to add text`. Either way, the placeholder message magically vanishes when you click the object and begin typing text.

If you start typing without clicking anywhere, the text that you type is entered into the title text object — assuming that the title text object doesn't already have text of its own. If the title object is not empty, any text that you type (with no text object selected) is simply ignored.

After you finish typing text, press the Esc key or click the mouse anywhere outside the text object.

In Chapter 2, you find many details about playing with text objects, so hold your horses. You have more important things to attend to first.

## Moving from slide to slide

You have several ways to move forward and backward through your presentation, from slide to slide:

  ✔ **Click one of the double-headed arrows at the bottom of the vertical scroll bar.** Doing so moves you through the presentation one slide at a time.

✔ **Use the Page Up and Page Down keys on your keyboard.** Using these keys also moves one slide at a time.

✔ **Use the scroll bar.** When you drag the box in the scroll bar, a little box appears to display the number and title of the current slide. Dragging the scroll bar is the quickest way to move directly to any slide in your presentation. You can also click the arrows at the top or bottom of the scroll bar to move one slide at a time.

✔ **Click the thumbnail for the slide that you want to display in the list of slides on the left side of the screen.** If the thumbnails are not visible, click the Slides tab above the outline.

## Adding a new slide

The slides created by the AutoContent Wizard may not be adequate for your presentation. Although you may be able to adapt some of the prebuilt slides by editing their titles and text objects, eventually you'll need to add slides of your own.

You're in luck! PowerPoint gives you about 50 ways to add new slides to your presentation. You see only three of them here:

✔ Click the New Slide button on the standard toolbar.

✔ Choose Insert➪New Slide.

✔ Press Ctrl+M.

In all three cases, PowerPoint displays the Slide Layout Pane alongside the new slide. This pane enables you to pick from 27 different types of slide layouts. Just click the mouse on the one that you want to use and PowerPoint sets the new slide to the layout of your choosing.

Each slide layout has a name, which you can see by hovering the mouse pointer over the layout for a moment. The layout that's highlighted in Figure 1-4 is called *Title and Text.* The layout name tells you which types of objects are included in the layout. For example, the Text layout includes a text object. *Title, Text & Clip Art* layout includes two objects; one for text, the other for a picture from the PowerPoint clip art gallery.

You'll probably use the Text layout most. It's the best format for presenting a topic along with several supporting points. For example, Figure 1-4 shows a typical bulleted list slide, in which a list of bulleted items describes signs that your son is headed down the road toward moral decay.

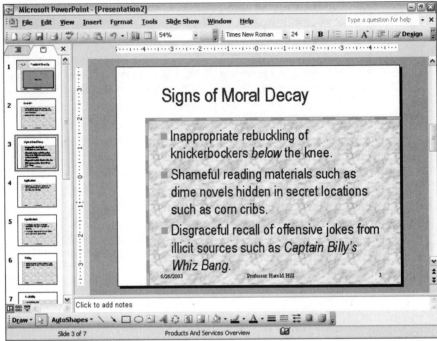

One of the layouts available in the AutoLayout section of the New Slide dialog box is named *Blank.* This layout doesn't include any objects; it is a blank slate that you can use to create a slide that doesn't fit any of the predefined layouts. All slide layouts except Blank include a single-line text object that serves as a title for the slide. This title is formatted consistently from slide to slide in order to give your presentation a professional look.

# Displaying Your Presentation!

When your masterpiece is ready, you can show it on the screen. Just follow these steps:

**1. Choose Slide Show➪View Show.**

There are several shortcuts to this command. You can also start the show by pressing F5 or by clicking the Slide Show button, located with the other view buttons in the lower-left corner of the screen.

2. **Behold the first slide.**

   The slide fills the screen. Isn't it pretty?

3. **Press Enter to advance to the next slide.**

   You can keep pressing Enter to call up each slide in the presentation. If you don't like the Enter key, you can use the spacebar instead.

   If you want to go back a slide, press the Page Up key.

4. **Press Esc when you're done.**

   You don't have to wait until the last slide is shown. If you find a glaring mistake in a slide, or if you just get bored, you can press Escape at any time to return to PowerPoint.

For the complete lowdown on showing your presentation, kindly turn to Chapter 7.

# Printing Your Presentation

After you finish your masterpiece, you may want to print it. I say more about printing in Chapter 6. But for now, here's the quick procedure for printing all the slides in your presentation:

1. **Make sure that your printer is turned on and ready to print.**

   Make sure that the *select* or *on-line* light is on. If it isn't, press the Select or On-line button to make it so. Check the paper supply while you're at it.

2. **Click the Print button on the Standard toolbar.**

   If you prefer, choose File⇨Print or press Ctrl+P or Ctrl+Shift+F12. Whichever way you do it, you see the Print dialog box. The Print dialog box has a myriad of options that you can fiddle with to print your presentation just so, but you can leave them alone if you just want to print all the slides in your presentation.

3. **Click OK or press the Enter key.**

   Make sure that you say "Engage" in a knowing manner, pointing at your printer as you do so. The secret is to fool your printer into thinking that you know what you're doing.

# Saving Your Work

Now that you've spent hours creating the best presentation since God gave Moses the Ten Commandments, it's time to save your work to a file. If you make the rookie mistake of turning off your computer before you've saved your presentation, *poof!* Your work will vanish as if David Copperfield were in town.

Like everything else in PowerPoint, you have at least four ways to save a document:

- ✔ Click the Save button on the Standard toolbar.
- ✔ Choose File⇨Save.
- ✔ Press Ctrl+S.
- ✔ Press Shift+F12.

If you haven't yet saved the file to your hard drive, the magical Save As dialog box appears. Type the name that you want to use for the file in the Save As dialog box and click OK to save the file. After you save the file once, subsequent saves update the disk file with any changes that you made to the presentation since the last time you saved it.

Some notes to keep in mind when saving files:

- ✔ Put on your Thinking Cap when assigning a name to a new file. The filename is how you can recognize the file later on, so pick a meaningful name that suggests the file's contents.
- ✔ After you save a file for the first time, the name in the presentation window's title area changes from *Presentation* to the name of your file. This is simply proof that the file has been saved.

- ✔ Don't work on your file for hours at a time without saving it. I've learned the hard way to save my work every few minutes. After all, I live in California so I never know when a rolling blackout will hit my neighborhood. Get into the habit of saving every few minutes, especially after making a significant change to a presentation, such as adding a covey of new slides or making a gaggle of complicated formatting changes. It's also a good idea to save your work before printing your presentation.

# *Opening a Presentation*

After you save your presentation to your hard drive, you can retrieve it later when you want to make additional changes or to print it. As you may guess, PowerPoint gives you about 2,037 ways to accomplish the retrieval. Here are the four most common:

- ✔ Click the Open button on the Standard toolbar.
- ✔ Choose File➪Open.
- ✔ Press Ctrl+O.
- ✔ Press Ctrl+F12.

All four retrieval methods pop up in the Open dialog box, which gives you a list of files to choose from. Click the file that you want, and then click OK or press the Enter key.

The Open dialog box has controls that enable you to rummage through the various folders on your hard drive in search of your files. If you know how to open a file in any Windows application, you know how to do it in PowerPoint (because the Open dialog box is pretty much the same in any Windows program).

If you seem to have lost a file, rummage around in different folders to see whether you can find it. Perhaps you may have saved a file in the wrong folder by accident. Also, check the spelling of the filename. Maybe your fingers weren't on the home row when you typed the filename, so instead of `River City.ppt`, you saved the file as `Eucwe Xurt`.ppt. I hate it when that happens. If all else fails, you can use Windows' built-in Search feature. Click the Start button, and then click Search and follow the instructions that appear in the Search Results window.

The fastest way to open a file from the Open dialog box is to double-click the file that you want to open. This spares you from having to click the file once and then clicking OK. Double-clicking also exercises the fast-twitch muscles in your index finger.

PowerPoint keeps track of the last four files that you've opened and displays them on the File menu. To open a file that you've recently opened, click the File menu and inspect the list of files at the bottom of the menu. If the file that you want is in the list, click it to open it.

The last four files you opened are also listed on the Getting Started task pane, so you can open them quickly if the Getting Started task pane is visible.

# Closing a Presentation

Having finished your presentation and printed it just right, you have come to the time to close it. Closing a presentation is kind of like gathering up your papers, putting them neatly in a file folder, and returning the folder to its proper file drawer. The presentation disappears from your computer screen. Don't worry: It's tucked safely away on your hard drive where you can get to it later if you need to.

To close a file, choose File⇨Close. You also can use the keyboard shortcut Ctrl+W, but you need a mind like a steel trap to remember that Ctrl+W stands for Close.

You don't have to close a file before exiting PowerPoint. If you exit PowerPoint without closing a file, PowerPoint graciously closes the file for you. The only reason that you may want to close a file is that you want to work on a different file and you don't want to keep both files open at the same time.

If you've made changes since the last time you saved the file, PowerPoint offers to save the changes for you. Click Yes to save the file before closing or click No to abandon any changes that you've made to the file.

If you close all the open PowerPoint presentations, you may discover that most of the PowerPoint commands have been rendered useless (they are grayed on the menu). Fear not. Open a presentation, or create a new one, and the commands return to life.

# Exiting PowerPoint

Had enough excitement for one day? Use any of these techniques to shut PowerPoint down:

- ✔ Choose File⇨Exit.
- ✔ Click the X box at the top-right corner of the PowerPoint window.
- ✔ Press Alt+F4.

Bam! PowerPoint is history.

You should know a couple things about exiting PowerPoint (or any application):

- ✔ PowerPoint doesn't let you abandon ship without first considering if you want to save your work. If you've made changes to any presentation files and haven't saved them, PowerPoint offers to save the files for you. Lean over and plant a fat kiss right in the middle of your monitor — PowerPoint just saved you your job.

- ✔ Never, never, never, ever, never turn off your computer while PowerPoint or any other program is running. Bad! Always exit PowerPoint and all other programs that are running before you turn off your computer.

# Chapter 2

# Editing Slides

## In This Chapter

▶ Moving around in a presentation

▶ Working with objects

▶ Editing text

▶ Undoing a mistake

▶ Deleting slides

▶ Finding and replacing text

▶ Rearranging slides

*I*f you're like Mary Poppins ("Practically Perfect in Every Way"), you can skip this chapter. Perfect people never make mistakes, so everything that they type in PowerPoint comes out right the first time. They never have to press the Backspace key to erase something they typed incorrectly, or go back and insert a line to make a point they left out, or rearrange their slides because they didn't add them in the right order to begin with.

If you're more like Jane ("Rather Inclined to Giggle; Doesn't Put Things Away") or Michael ("Extremely Stubborn and Suspicious"), you probably make mistakes along the way. This chapter shows you how to go back and correct those mistakes.

Reviewing your work and correcting it if necessary is called *editing*. It's not a fun job, but it has to be done. A spoonful of sugar usually helps.

This chapter focuses mostly on editing text objects. Many of the techniques apply to editing other types of objects, such as clip art pictures or drawn shapes. For more information about editing other types of objects, see Part III.

# Moving from Slide to Slide

The most common way to move around in a PowerPoint presentation is to press the Page Up and Page Down keys on your keyboard:

- **Page Down:** Press Page Down to move forward to the next slide in your presentation.

- **Page Up:** Press Page Up to move backward to the preceding slide in your presentation.

You can also use the vertical scroll bars to navigate through your presentation:

- **Double-headed arrows:** You can move forward or backward through your presentation one slide at a time by clicking the double-headed arrows at the bottom of the vertical scroll bar on the right edge of the presentation window.

- **Single-headed arrows:** You can also scroll forward or backward through your presentation by clicking and holding the single-headed arrow at the top or bottom of the vertical scroll bar.

- **Scroll box:** Another way to move quickly from slide to slide is to click the scroll box within the vertical scroll bar on the right side of the window and drag it up or down by holding down the left mouse button. As you drag the box, a little text box pops up next to the slide bar to tell you which slide will be displayed if you release the button at that position.

# Working with Objects

*In the beginning, the User created a slide. And the slide was formless and void, without meaning or content. And the User said, "Let there be a Text Object." And there was a Text Object. And there was evening and there was morning, one day. Then the User said, "Let there be a Picture Object." And there was a Picture Object. And there was evening and there was morning, a second day. This continued for forty days and forty nights, until there were forty objects on the slide, each after its own kind. And the User was laughed out of the auditorium by the audience who could read the slide not.*

I present this charming little parable solely to make the point that PowerPoint slides are nothing without objects. *Objects* are items such as text, pictures, and charts that give meaning and content to otherwise formless and empty slides. When it comes to objects, however, sometimes less is more. Don't overdo it by cluttering up your slides with so many objects that the main point of the slide is obscured.

Most of the objects on your slides will be text objects, which let you type text on your slides. For more information about working with text objects, see the section "Editing a Text Object" later in this chapter.

Every slide has a slide layout that consists of one or more *placeholders*. A placeholder is simply an area on a slide that is reserved for text, clip art, a graph, or some other type of object. For example, a slide that uses the Title layout has two placeholders for text objects: one for the title and the other for the subtitle. You use the Slide Layout task pane to choose the layout when you create new slides. You can change the layout later, and you can add more objects to the slide. You can also delete objects, move them around, or resize them if you want. For more information about slide layouts, see Chapter 1.

You can add many different types of objects, such as clip art, charts, graphs, shapes, and so on. You can add additional objects to your slide by using one of the tools that appears on the Drawing toolbar at the bottom of the screen. For more information about adding additional objects to your slides, see Chapters 10, 14, 15, and 16.

Each object occupies a rectangular region on the slide. The contents of the object may or may not visually fill the rectangular region, but you can see the outline of the object when you select it (see the section "Selecting objects" later in this chapter).

Objects can overlap. Usually, you don't want them to, but sometimes doing so creates a jazzy effect. You may lay some text on top of some clip art, for example.

## Selecting objects

Before you can edit anything on a slide, you have to select the object that contains whatever it is that you want to edit. For example, you can't start typing away to edit text on-screen. Instead, you must first select the text object that contains the text that you want to edit. Likewise, you must select other types of objects before you can edit their contents.

Here are some guidelines to keep in mind when selecting objects:

- **The arrow cursor:** Before you can select anything, make sure that the cursor is shaped like an arrow. If it isn't, click the arrow button on the Drawing toolbar. (This button is officially called the *Select Objects button*, but it sure looks like an arrow to me.)

- **Text objects:** To select a text object so that you can edit its text, move the arrow pointer over the text that you want to edit and click the left mouse button. A rectangular box appears around the object, and the background behind the text changes to a solid color to make the text easier to read. A text cursor appears so that you can start typing away.

✔ **Non-text objects:** Other types of objects work a little differently. Click an object, and the object is selected. The rectangular box appears around the object to let you know that you have hooked it. After you have hooked the object, you can drag it around the screen or change its size, but you can't edit it. To edit a nontext object, you must double-click it. (Selecting the object first is not necessary. Just point to it with the arrow pointer and double-click.)

✔ **Click and drag:** Another way to select an object — or more than one object — is to use the arrow pointer to drag a rectangle around the objects that you want to select. Point to a location above and to the left of the object or objects that you want to select, and then click and drag the mouse down and to the right until the rectangle surrounds the objects. When you release the button, all the objects within the rectangle are selected.

✔ **The Tab key:** Also, you can press the Tab key to select objects. Press Tab once to select the first object on the slide. Press Tab again to select the next object. Keep pressing Tab until the object that you want is selected.

✔ **The Shift key:** You can select more than one object by selecting the first object and then holding down the Shift key while clicking to select additional objects.

Pressing Tab to select objects is handy when you can't easily point to the object that you want to select. This problem can happen if the object that you want is buried underneath another object or if the object is empty or otherwise invisible and you're not sure of its location.

## Resizing or moving an object

When you select an object, an outline box appears around it. If you look closely at the box, you can see that it has *love handles,* one on each corner and one in the middle of each edge. You can use these love handles to adjust the size of an object. You can also grab the box between the love handles to move the object around on the slide.

In addition, a green dot called the *rotate handle* appears, floating above the object. You can rotate the object by grabbing this handle and dragging it around in a circle.

To change the size of an object, click it to select it and then grab one of the love handles by clicking it with the arrow pointer. Hold down the mouse button and move the mouse to change the object's size.

The various handles on an object give you different ways to change the object's size:

 ✔ The handles at the corners allow you to change both the height and the width of the object.

 ✔ The handles on the top and bottom edges allow you to change just the object's height.

 ✔ The handles on the right and left edges change just the width of the object.

If you hold down the Ctrl key while you drag one of the love handles, the object stays centered at its current position on the slide. Try it, and you can see what I mean. Also, try holding down the Shift key as you drag an object using one of the corner love handles. This combination maintains the object's proportions as you resize it.

Changing a text object's size doesn't change the size of the text in the object; it changes only the size of the "frame" that contains the text. Changing the width of a text object is equivalent to changing margins in a word processor: It makes the text lines wider or narrower. To change the size of the text within a text object, you must change the font size. Chapter 9 has the exciting details.

To move an object, click anywhere on the outline box except on a love handle, and then drag the object to its new locale.

The outline box can be hard to see if you have a fancy background on your slides. If you select an object and have trouble seeing the outline box, try squinting or cleaning your monitor screen. Or, in severe weather, try choosing the View➪Color/Grayscale command or clicking the Color/Grayscale View button in the Standard toolbar. This brings up a menu that lets you choose one of three color modes for viewing your slides:

 ✔ **Color mode:** Displays slides in full color

 ✔ **Grayscale mode:** Displays colors as shades of gray

 ✔ **Pure Black and White mode:** Shows the slides in black and white

Viewing the slide in Grayscale mode or Pure Black and White mode may make the love handles easier to spot. To switch back to full-color view, use the Color/Grayscale command or button again and choose Color from the menu that appears.

# *Editing a Text Object*

When you select a text object for editing, PowerPoint transforms itself into a baby word processor. If you're familiar with just about any other Windows word-processing software, including Microsoft Word or even WordPad (the free word processor that comes with Windows), you'll have no trouble editing text in PowerPoint. This section presents some of the highlights for you, though — just in case.

PowerPoint automatically wraps text so that you don't have to press Enter at the end of every line. Press Enter only when you want to begin a new paragraph.

Text in a PowerPoint presentation is usually formatted with a *bullet character* at the beginning of each paragraph. The default bullet character is usually a simple square box, but you can change it to just about any shape that you can imagine (see Chapter 9). The point to remember here is that the bullet character is a part of the paragraph format, and not a character that you have to type in your text.

Most word processing software enables you to switch between *Insert mode* and *Typeover mode* by pressing the Insert key on the right side of your keyboard. In Insert mode, any characters that you type are inserted at the cursor location; in Typeover mode, each character that you type replaces the character at the cursor location. However, PowerPoint always works in Insert mode, so any text that you type is inserted at the cursor location. Pressing the Insert key has no effect on the way text is typed.

You can move around within a text object by pressing the arrow keys or by using the mouse. You can also use the End and Home keys to take you to the start or end of the line that you're on. Additionally, you can use the arrow keys in combination with the Ctrl key to move around even faster. For example, press the Ctrl key and the left or right arrow key to move left or right an entire word at a time.

You delete text by pressing the Delete or Backspace key. To delete from the cursor location to the start or end of a word, use the Ctrl key along with the Delete or Backspace key. If you first select a block of text, the Delete and Backspace keys delete the entire selection. (The next section, "Selecting Text," has some tips for selecting text.)

# Selecting Text

Some text-editing operations — such as amputations and transplants — require that you first select the text on which you want to operate. The following list shows you the methods for selecting blocks of text:

- ✔ When you use the keyboard, hold down the Shift key while you press any of the cursor movement keys to move the cursor.

- ✔ When you use the mouse, point to the beginning of the text that you want to mark and then click and drag the mouse over the text. Release the button when you reach the end of the text that you want to mark.

PowerPoint has an automatic word selection option that tries to guess when you intend to select an entire word. If you use the mouse to select a block of text that includes at least one full word, you notice that the selected text jumps to include entire words as you move the mouse. If you don't like this feature, you can disable it by using the Tools⇨Options command (click the Edit tab and then uncheck the check box labeled When Selecting, Automatically Select Entire Word).

You can use the following tricks to select different amounts of text:

- ✔ **A single word:** To select a single word, point the cursor anywhere in the word and double-click.

- ✔ **An entire paragraph:** To select an entire paragraph, point anywhere in the paragraph and triple-click.

After you have selected text, you can edit it in the following ways:

- ✔ **Delete text:** To delete the entire block of text that you've selected, press the Delete key or the Backspace key.

- ✔ **Replace text:** To replace an entire block of text, select it and then begin typing. The selected block vanishes and is replaced by the text that you're typing.

- ✔ **Cut, Copy, and Paste:** You can use the Cut, Copy, and Paste commands from the Edit menu with selected text blocks. The following section describes these commands.

# Using Cut, Copy, and Paste

Like any good Windows program, PowerPoint uses the standard Cut, Copy, and Paste commands. These commands work on text that you've selected or, if you've selected an entire object, the commands work on the object itself. In other words, you can use the Cut, Copy, and Paste commands with bits of text or with entire objects.

Cut, Copy, and Paste all work with one of the greatest mysteries of Windows, the *Clipboard.* The Clipboard is where Windows stashes stuff so that you can get to it later. The Cut and Copy commands add stuff to the Clipboard, and the Paste command copies stuff from the clipboard to your presentation.

PowerPoint uses a relatively new clipboard feature called the Office Clipboard, which lets you store not just one bit of information, but as many as 24 bits. For more information about using the Office Clipboard, see the section "Using the Office Clipboard" later in this chapter.

The keyboard shortcuts for Cut, Copy, and Paste are the same as they are for other Windows programs: Ctrl+X for Cut, Ctrl+C for Copy, and Ctrl+V for Paste. Because these three keyboard shortcuts work in virtually all Windows programs, memorizing them pays off.

The Copy and Paste commands are often used together to duplicate information. If you want to repeat an entire sentence, for example, you copy the sentence to the Clipboard, place the cursor where you want the sentence duplicated, and then use the Paste command. Or, if you want to create a slide that has five identical rectangles on it, start by drawing one rectangle. Then, copy the rectangle to the Clipboard and paste it to the slide four times. You'll end up with five rectangles; the original one you drew, plus the four copies that you pasted.

The Cut and Paste commands are used together to move stuff from one location to another. To move a sentence from one slide to another, for example, select the sentence and cut it to the Clipboard. Then move to the slide on which you want to place the sentence, click where you want the sentence moved, and choose the Paste command.

## Cutting a text block

When you cut a block of text, the text is removed from the slide and placed on the Clipboard where you can retrieve it later if you want. Copying a text block stores the text in the Clipboard but doesn't remove it from the slide.

To cut a block, first mark the block that you want to cut by using the keyboard or the mouse. Then conjure up the Cut command by using any of these three methods:

✔ Choose the Edit⇨Cut command from the menu bar.

✔ Click the Cut button on the Standard toolbar.

✔ Press Ctrl+X.

Using any method causes the text to vanish from your screen. Don't worry, though. It's safely nestled away on the Clipboard.

## Copying a text block

To copy a block of text, select the text and invoke the Copy command by using one of these methods:

✔ Choose the Edit⇨Copy command.

✔ Click the Copy button on the Standard toolbar.

✔ Press Ctrl+C.

The text is copied to the Clipboard, but the text doesn't vanish from the screen. To retrieve the text from the Clipboard, use the Paste command, as described in the following section.

## Pasting text

To paste text from the Clipboard, first move the cursor to the location where you want to insert the text. Then invoke the Paste command by using whichever of the following techniques suits your fancy:

✔ Choose the Edit⇨Paste command from the menu bar.

✔ Click the Paste button on the Standard toolbar.

✔ Press Ctrl+V.

When you paste text into a PowerPoint presentation, PowerPoint automatically reformats the text to match the formatting of the text object that you pasted the text into. If you want to retain the formatting of the original text, click the Paste Options button that appears next to the pasted text, and then choose Keep Source Formatting from the menu that appears.

In some cases, PowerPoint will have to adjust the slide layout to accommodate pasted text. When it does, an Automatic Layout Options button appears next to the pasted text. If you don't like the layout change that PowerPoint made, you can reverse it by clicking the Automatic Layout Options button, and then choosing Undo Automatic Layout from the menu that appears.

# *Cutting, copying, and pasting entire objects*

The use of Cut, Copy, and Paste isn't limited to text blocks; the commands also work with entire objects. Just select the object, copy or cut it to the Clipboard, move to a new location, and paste the object from the Clipboard.

To move an object from one slide to another, select the object and cut it to the Clipboard. Then move to the slide where you want the object to appear and paste the object from the Clipboard.

To duplicate an object on several slides, select the object and copy it to the Clipboard. Then move to the slide that you want the object duplicated on and paste the object.

You can duplicate an object on the same slide by selecting the object, copying it to the Clipboard, and then pasting it. The only glitch is that the pasted object appears on top of the original object, but you can just grab the newly pasted object with the mouse and move it to another location on the slide.

An easier way to duplicate an object is to use the Edit⇨Duplicate command. (The keyboard shortcut for the Edit⇨Duplicate command is Ctrl+D.) It combines the functions of Copy and Paste but doesn't disturb the Clipboard. The best thing about the Edit⇨Duplicate command is that if you duplicate an object once, and then move the duplicate object to a new location on the slide, PowerPoint automatically positions any subsequent duplicate objects that you create based on where you moved the first duplicate. This makes it easy to create a series of objects that are all lined up nice and neat.

Try this to see what I mean: On a blank slide, draw a little rectangle. (If you're not sure how to create a rectangle, refer to Chapter 14.) Select the rectangle and press Ctrl+D to duplicate the rectangle. Then, grab the duplicate rectangle with the mouse and move it to a position that's next to the original rectangle instead of on top of it. Now press Ctrl+D again and watch PowerPoint put a third rectangle next to the second rectangle! PowerPoint determines the position of the third rectangle based on where you put the second rectangle relative to the first one.

An even easier way to duplicate an object is to hold down the Ctrl key and drag the object to a new location on the slide. When you release the mouse button, a duplicate copy of the object is created.

If you want to blow away an entire object permanently, select it and press the Delete key or the Backspace key or use the Edit⇨Clear command. This step removes the object from the slide but doesn't copy it to the Clipboard. It's gone forever. Well, sort of — you can still get it back by using the Undo command, but only if you act fast. See the section, "Oops! I Didn't Mean It (The Marvelous Undo Command)" for more information.

To include the same object on each of your slides, you can use a better method than copying and pasting: Add the object to the *Slide Master,* which governs the format of all the slides in a presentation (see Chapter 12).

## Using the Office Clipboard

The Office Clipboard is a useful feature shared by all Office programs. It lets you gather up to 24 items of text or graphics from any Office program, and then selectively paste them into an Office document. The Office Clipboard appears in the task pane at the right side of the screen, where it lists all the items you have copied or cut to the Office clipboard. In Figure 2-1, you can see the Office Clipboard in the task bar at the right side of the window.

To paste an item from the Office Clipboard, first summon the Office Clipboard task pane by choosing Edit⇨Office Clipboard. Then, click the item in the Office Clipboard that you want to insert.

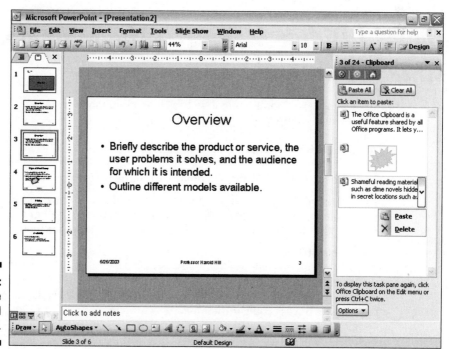

**Figure 2-1:** The Office Clipboard in action.

Items that you cut or copy are added to the Office Clipboard only if the Office Clipboard is active. You have several ways to activate the Office Clipboard:

- Choose Edit⇨Office Clipboard.
- Press Ctrl+C twice.
- Copy or cut two items consecutively, without doing anything else in between.

A special Office Clipboard icon appears in the Windows taskbar whenever the Office Clipboard is active. As long as this icon appears, any items that you cut or copy are added to the Office Clipboard — even if the Office Clipboard is not visible in the taskbar in the program that you're working in.

To remove an item from the Office Clipboard, right-click the item and choose Delete from the contextual menu that appears. You can remove all items from the Office Clipboard by clicking the Clear All button that appears at the top of the Office Clipboard task pane.

After you are finished working with the Office Clipboard, you can hide it by clicking the Close button (marked by an "X"), which is located at the top-right corner of the Office Clipboard task pane.

# Oops! 1 Didn't Mean 1t (The Marvelous Undo Command)

Made a mistake? Don't panic. Use the Undo command. Undo is your safety net. If you mess up, Undo can save the day.

You have three ways to undo a mistake:

- Choose the Edit⇨Undo command from the menu bar.
- Click the Undo button on the Standard toolbar. (If you can't find the Undo button, use the down arrow on the standard toolbar to access it the first time: It will then become a customized toolbar feature.)
- Press Ctrl+Z.

Undo reverses whatever you did last. If you deleted text, Undo adds it back in. If you typed text, Undo deletes it. If you moved an object, Undo puts it back where it was. You get the idea.

Undo is such a useful command that committing the Ctrl+Z keyboard short-cut to memory is a good idea. If you want, think of the word "Zip!" to help you remember how to zip away your mistakes.

Undo remembers up to 20 of your most recent actions. You can undo each action one at a time by repeatedly choosing the Undo command. Or, you can click the down arrow next to the Undo icon in the Standard toolbar and choose the actions you want to undo from the list that appears. However, as a general rule, you should correct your mistakes as soon as possible. If you make a mistake, feel free to curse, kick something, or fall on the floor in a screaming tantrum if you must, *but don't do anything else on your computer!* If you use the Undo command immediately, you can reverse your mistake and get on with your life.

PowerPoint also offers a Redo command, which is sort of like an Undo for Undo. In other words, if you undo what you thought was a mistake by using the Undo command and then decide that it wasn't a mistake after all, you can use the Redo command. Here are three ways to use the Redo command:

- Choose the Edit⇨Redo command from the menu bar.
- Click the Redo button on the Standard toolbar.
- Press Ctrl+Y.

# Deleting a Slide

Want to delete an entire slide? No problem. Simply move to the slide that you want to delete and use the Edit⇨Delete Slide command. Zowie! The slide is history. (If the Delete Slide command doesn't show up on your Edit menu, click the double-headed down arrow at the bottom of the Edit menu.)

Another way to delete a slide is to click the miniature of the slide in the Slide Preview Pane (on the left side of the screen), and then press the Delete key or the Backspace key.

Deleted the wrong slide, eh? No problem. Just press Ctrl+Z or choose the Edit⇨Undo command to restore the slide.

# Duplicating a Slide

PowerPoint sports a Duplicate Slide command that lets you duplicate an entire slide; text, formatting, and everything else included. That way, after you toil over a slide for hours to get its formatting just right, you can create a duplicate to use as the basis for another slide.

To duplicate a slide, move to the slide that you want to duplicate. Then choose the Insert⇨Duplicate Slide. A duplicate of the slide is inserted into your presentation.

If you're a keyboard shortcut fanatic, all you have to do is select the slide that you want to duplicate in the Slide Preview Pane (located on the left side of the screen), and then press Ctrl+D.

# Finding Text

You know that buried somewhere in that 60-slide presentation is a slide that lists the options available on the Vertical Snarfblat, but where is it? This sounds like a job for the PowerPoint Find command!

The Find command can find text buried in any text object on any slide. These steps show you the procedure for using the Find command:

**1. Think of what you want to find.**

   *Snarfblat* will suffice for this example.

**2. Choose Edit⇨Find or use the keyboard shortcut Ctrl+F.**

   The Find dialog box appears, as shown in Figure 2-2, which contains the secrets of the Find command.

**Figure 2-2:**
The Find
dialog box.

| Find | ? ☒ |
|------|-----|
| Find what: | Find Next |
| ┃ ▾ | Close |
| ☐ Match case | |
| ☐ Find whole words only | Replace... |

**3. Type the text that you want to find.**

   It shows up in the Find What box.

**4. Press the Enter key.**

   Or click the Find Next button. Either way, the search begins.

If the text that you type is located anywhere in the presentation, the Find command zips you to the slide that contains the text and highlights the text. You can then edit the text object or search for the next occurrence of the text within your presentation. If you edit the text, the Find dialog box stays on-screen to make it easy to continue your quest.

Here are some facts to keep in mind when using the Find command:

- ✔ **Find the next occurrence:** To find the next occurrence of the same text, press Enter or click the Find Next button again.

- ✔ **Edit the text:** To edit the text you found, click the text object. The Find dialog box remains on-screen. To continue searching, click the Find Next button again.

- ✔ **Start anywhere:** You don't have to be at the beginning of your presentation to search the entire presentation. When PowerPoint reaches the end of the presentation, it automatically picks up the search at the beginning and continues back to the point at which you started the search.

- ✔ **Give up:** You may receive the following message:

  ```
  PowerPoint has finished searching the presentation. The
            search item wasn't found.
  ```

  This message means that PowerPoint has given up. The text that you're looking for just isn't anywhere in the presentation. Maybe you spelled it wrong, or maybe you didn't have a slide about Snarfblats after all.

- ✔ **Match case:** If the right mix of uppercase and lowercase letters is important to you, check the Match Case box before beginning the search. This option is handy when you have, for example, a presentation about Mr. Smith the Blacksmith.

- ✔ **Find whole words:** Use the Find Whole Words Only check box to find your text only when it appears as a whole word. If you want to find the slide on which you discuss Smitty the Blacksmith's mitt, for example, type **mitt** for the Find What text and check the Find Whole Words Only box. That way, the Find command looks for *mitt* as a separate word. It doesn't stop to show you the *mitt* in *Smitty.*

- ✔ **Replace text:** If you find the text that you're looking for and decide that you want to replace it with something else, click the Replace button. This step changes the Find dialog box to the Replace dialog box, which is explained in the following section.

- ✔ **Close the Find dialog box:** To make the Find dialog box go away, click the Close button or press the Esc key.

# Replacing Text

Suppose that the Rent-a-Nerd company decides to switch to athletic consulting, so it wants to change the name of its company to Rent-a-Jock. Easy. Just use the handy Replace command to change all occurrences of the word *Nerd* to *Jock.* The following steps show you how:

1. **Choose Edit⇨Replace or use the keyboard shortcut Ctrl+H.**

   The Replace dialog box, shown in Figure 2-3, appears.

2. **In the Find What box, type the text that you want to find.**

   Enter the text that you want to replace with something else (*Nerd,* in this example).

3. **Type the replacement text in the Replace With box.**

   Enter the text that you want to use to replace the text that you typed in the Find What box (*Jock,* in this example).

4. **Click the Find Next button.**

   PowerPoint finds the first occurrence of the text.

5. **Click the Replace button to replace the text.**

   Read the text first to make sure that it found what you were looking for.

6. **Repeat the Find Next and Replace sequence until you're finished.**

   Click Find Next to find the next occurrence, click Replace to replace it, and so on. Keep going until you have finished.

If you're absolutely positive that you want to replace all occurrences of your Find What text with the Replace With text, click the Replace All button. This step dispenses with the Find Next and Replace cycle. The only problem is that you're bound to find at least one spot where you didn't want the replacement to occur. Replacing the word *mitt* with *glove,* for example, results in *Sglovey* rather than *Smitty.* Don't forget that you can also use the Find Whole Words Only option to find and replace text only if it appears as an entire word.

If you totally mess up your presentation by clicking Replace All, you can use the Undo command to restore sanity to your presentation.

# *Rearranging Your Slides in Slide Sorter View*

Normal View is the view that you normally work in to edit your slides, move things around, add text or graphics, and so on. However, Normal View has one serious limitation: It doesn't give you a big picture of your presentation. You can see the details of only one slide at a time, and the Slide Preview Pane lets you see snapshots of only a few slides. To see an overall view of your presentation, you need to work in Slide Sorter View.

You can switch to Slide Sorter View in two easy ways:

✔ Click the Slide Sorter View button in the bottom-left corner of the screen.

✔ Choose the View⇨Slide Sorter command.

The PowerPoint Slide Sorter View is shown in Figure 2-4.

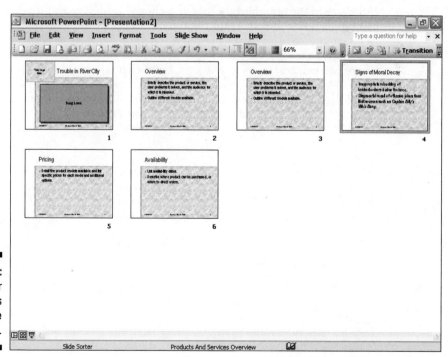

**Figure 2-4:**
Slide Sorter View lets you see the big picture.

The following list tells you how to rearrange, add, or delete slides from Slide Sorter View:

- ✔ **Move a slide:** To move a slide, click and drag it to a new location. Point to the slide and then press and hold down the left mouse button. Drag the slide to its new location and release the button. PowerPoint adjusts the display to show the new arrangement of slides.

- ✔ **Delete a slide:** To delete a slide, click the slide to select it and then press the Delete key or the Backspace key. This works only in Slide Sorter View. You also can use the Edit⇨Delete Slide command.

- ✔ **Add a new slide:** To add a new slide, click the slide that you want the new slide to follow and then click the New Slide button. The Slide Layout task pane appears so that you can choose the layout for the new slide. To edit the contents of the slide, return to Slide or Outline View by using the view buttons (located at the bottom-left corner of the screen) or the View command.

If your presentation contains more slides than can fit on-screen at one time, you can use the scroll bars to scroll through the display. Or you can change the zoom factor to make the slides smaller. Click the down arrow next to the zoom size in the Standard toolbar and choose a smaller zoom percentage, or just type a new zoom size into the toolbar's Zoom Control box.

Slide Sorter View may seem kind of dull and boring, but it's also the place where you can add jazzy transitions, build effects, or add cool animation effects to your slides. For example, you can make your bullets fall from the top of the screen like bombs and switch from slide to slide by using strips, wipes, or blinds. Chapter 17 describes all this cool stuff.

# Chapter 3

# Outlining Your Presentation

*Y*ou've probably already noticed that most presentations consist of slide after slide of bulleted lists. You may see a chart here or there and an occasional bit of clip art thrown in for comic effect, but the bread and butter of presentations is the bulleted list. It sounds boring, but it's often the best way to make sure that your message gets through.

For this reason, presentations lend themselves especially well to outlining. Presentations are light on prose but heavy in the point and subpoint department — and that's precisely where outlines excel. The Outline tab that appears to the left of your slides in Normal View lets you focus on your presentation's main points and subpoints. In other words, it enables you to focus on content without worrying about appearance.

## Calling Up the Outline

In Normal View, the left side of the screen shows little thumbnail previews of the slides in your presentation. Above these thumbnails is a pair of tabs that enables you to switch between the thumbnails and an outline of your presentation. The Outline tab shows your presentation as an outline; each slide appears as a separate heading at the highest level of the outline, and the text on each slide appears as lower-level headings subordinate to the slide headings.

To summon the outline, click the Outline tab that is located above the thumbnails. The outline appears, as shown in Figure 3-1.

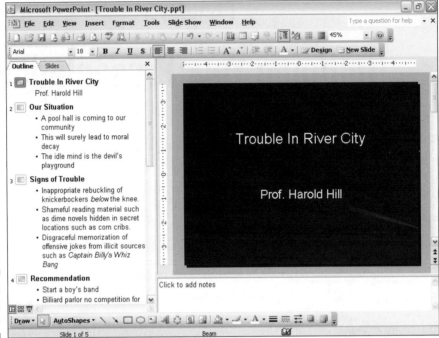

**Figure 3-1:**
Viewing
the outline.

You can expand the area devoted to the outline by clicking and dragging the border of the Outline Pane.

The following list highlights a few important things to notice about the outline:

- ✔ **The outline is comprised of the titles and body text of each slide.** Any other objects that you add to a slide — such as pictures, charts, and so on — are not included in the outline. Also, if you add any text objects to the slide in addition to the basic title and body text objects that are automatically included when you create a new slide, the additional text objects are not included in the outline.

- ✔ **Each slide is represented by a high-level heading in the outline.** The text of this heading is drawn from the slide's title, and an icon that represents the entire slide appears next to the heading. Also, the slide number appears to the left of the slide icon.

- ✔ **Each text line from a slide's body text appears as an indented heading.** This heading is subordinate to the slide's main title heading.

- ✔ **An outline can contain subpoints that are subordinate to the main points on each slide.** PowerPoint enables you to create as many as five heading levels on each slide, but your slides will probably get too complicated if you go beyond two headings. You can find more about working with heading levels in the section "Promoting and Demoting Paragraphs" later in this chapter.

# Using the Outlining Toolbar

PowerPoint includes a special Outlining toolbar that contains special buttons for working with outlines. This toolbar is not normally displayed, but you can summon it by choosing View⇨Toolbars⇨Outlining. The Outlining toolbar appears to the left of the outline.

Table 3-1 summarizes what each button does.

| Table 3-1 | Buttons on the Outlining Toolbar | |
|---|---|---|
| *Button* | *Name* | *What It Does* |
| ← | Promote | Promotes the paragraph to a higher outline level |
| → | Demote | Demotes the paragraph to a lower outline level |
| ↑ | Move Up | Moves the paragraph up |
| ↓ | Move Down | Moves the paragraph down |
| — | Collapse | Collapses the selected slide or slides |
| ✚ | Expand | Expands the selected slide or slides |
| ≡ | Collapse All | Collapses an entire presentation |
| ≡ | Expand All | Expands an entire presentation |
| ▣ | Summary Slide | Creates a summary slide |
| A/A | Show Formatting | Shows or hides text formatting |

# Selecting and Editing an Entire Slide

When you work in Outline View, you often have to select an entire slide. PowerPoint provides three ways to do that:

- ✔ Click the slide's Slide icon.
- ✔ Click the slide's number.
- ✔ Triple-click anywhere in the slide's title text.

When you select an entire slide, the slide title and all its body text are highlighted. In addition, any extra objects, such as graphics, that are on the slide are also selected, even though those objects don't appear in the outline.

You can delete, cut, copy, or duplicate an entire slide:

- ✔ **Delete:** To delete an entire slide, select it and then press the Delete key or choose the Edit⇨Delete command. Or, right-click the slide and choose Delete Slide from the menu that appears.

- ✔ **Cut or copy:** To cut or copy an entire slide to the Clipboard, select it and then press Ctrl+X (Cut) or Ctrl+C (Copy) or use the Edit⇨Cut or Edit⇨ Paste command. You can then move the cursor to any location in the outline and press Ctrl+V or use the Edit⇨Paste command to paste the slide from the Clipboard. (You can also cut or copy a slide by right-clicking the slide and choosing Cut or Copy from the menu that appears.)

- ✔ **Duplicate:** To duplicate a slide, select it and then invoke the Edit⇨ Duplicate command or press Ctrl+D. This step places a copy of the selected slide immediately after the selected slide. (Actually, you don't have to select the entire slide to duplicate it. Just click anywhere in the slide's title or body text.)

# Selecting and Editing One Paragraph

You can select and edit an entire paragraph along with all its subordinate paragraphs. Just click the bullet next to the paragraph that you want to select or triple-click anywhere in the text. To delete an entire paragraph along with its subordinate paragraphs, select it and then press the Delete key.

To cut or copy an entire paragraph to the Clipboard along with its subordinates, select it and then press Ctrl+X (Cut) or Ctrl+C (Copy). You can then press Ctrl+V to paste the paragraph anywhere in the presentation.

# Promoting and Demoting Paragraphs

To *promote* a paragraph means to move it up one level in the outline. If you promote the "Disgraceful recall of jokes from illicit sources such as *Captain Billy's Whiz Bang*" line in Figure 3-1, for example, that line becomes a separate slide rather than a bullet paragraph under "Signs of Moral Decay."

To promote a paragraph, place the cursor anywhere in the paragraph and then press Shift+Tab or click the Promote button on the Outlining toolbar. Alternately, you can just click and drag the paragraph's bullet to the left.

To *demote* a paragraph is just the opposite: The paragraph moves down one level in the outline. If you demote the "Shameful reading material such as dime novels . . ." paragraph in Figure 3-1, it becomes a subpoint under "Inappropriate rebuckling of knickerbockers *below* the knee" rather than a separate main point.

To demote a paragraph, place the cursor anywhere in the paragraph and then either press the Tab key or click the Demote button in the Outlining toolbar. Alternately, you can click and drag the paragraph's bullet to the right.

Note that you can't promote a slide title. Slide title is the highest rank in the outline hierarchy. If you demote a slide title, the entire slide is *subsumed* into the preceding slide. In other words, the slide title becomes a main point in the preceding slide.

You can promote or demote paragraphs by using the mouse, but the technique is a little tricky. When you move the mouse pointer over a bullet (or the slide button), the pointer changes from a single arrow to a four-cornered arrow. This arrow is your signal that you can click the mouse to select the entire paragraph (and any subordinate paragraphs). Then, you can use the mouse to promote or demote a paragraph along with all its subordinates by dragging the selected paragraph left or right.

Be sensitive when you demote paragraphs. Being demoted can be an emotionally devastating experience.

# Adding a New Paragraph

To add a new paragraph to a slide by using the outline that appears in the Outline tab, move the cursor to the end of the paragraph that you want the new paragraph to follow and then press Enter. PowerPoint creates a new paragraph at the same outline level as the preceding paragraph. (If the slide has only a title paragraph, this will create a new slide.)

If you position the cursor at the beginning of a paragraph and press Enter, the new paragraph is inserted to the left of the cursor position. If you position the cursor in the middle of a paragraph and press Enter, the paragraph is split in two.

After you add a new paragraph, you may want to change its level in the outline. To do that, you must promote or demote the new paragraph. To create a subpoint for a main point, for example, position the cursor at the end of the main point and press Enter. Then demote the new paragraph by pressing the Tab key.

# Adding a New Slide

You can add a new slide in many ways when you're working with the outline. This list shows the most popular methods:

- ✔ **Promote existing text:** Promote an existing paragraph to the highest level. This method splits a slide into two slides.

- ✔ **Promote new text:** Add a new paragraph and then promote it to the highest level.

- ✔ **Press Enter:** Place the cursor in a slide's title text and press Enter. This method creates a new slide before the current slide. Whether the title text stays with the current slide, goes with the new slide, or is split between the slides depends on the location of the cursor within the title when you press Enter.

- ✔ **Press Ctrl+Enter:** Place the cursor anywhere in a slide's body text and press Ctrl+Enter. This method creates a new slide immediately following the current slide. The position of the cursor within the existing slide doesn't matter; the new slide is always created after the current slide. (The cursor must be in the slide's body text, however, in order for this method to work. If you put the cursor in a slide title and press Ctrl+Enter, the cursor jumps to the slide's body text without creating a new slide.)

- ✔ **Insert a new slide:** Place the cursor anywhere in the slide and invoke the Insert⇨New Slide command. Or, if you prefer, use the keyboard shortcut Ctrl+M, or click the New Slide button.

- ✔ **Duplicate an existing slide:** Select an existing slide by clicking the slide's icon or triple-clicking the title and then duplicate it by using the Edit⇨Duplicate command or its keyboard shortcut, Ctrl+D.

Because the outline focuses on slide content rather than on layout, new slides receive the basic Bulleted List layout, which includes title text and body text formatted with bullets. If you want to change the layout of a new slide, you must call up the Slide Layout task pane by choosing the Format⇨Slide Layout command. (The Slide Layout task pane automatically appears if you create the slide by using the Insert⇨New Slide command, the Ctrl+M keyboard shortcut, or the New Slide button.)

# Moving Text Up and Down

The outline is a handy way to rearrange your presentation. You can easily change the order of individual points on a slide, or you can rearrange the order of the slides.

You can rearrange your presentation by selecting the paragraphs that you want to move and then clicking the Move Up or Move Down buttons in the Outlining toolbar to move the selected paragraphs. Or, you can point to the bullet next to the paragraph that you want to move. Then, when the mouse pointer changes to the four-cornered arrow, click and drag the paragraph up or down. A horizontal line appears, showing the horizontal position of the selection. Release the mouse when the horizontal line is positioned where you want the text.

Be careful when you're moving text in a slide that has more than one level of body text paragraphs. Notice the position of the horizontal line as you drag the selection; the entire selection is inserted at that location, which may split up subpoints. If you don't like the result of a move, you can always undo it by pressing Ctrl+Z or clicking the Undo button.

# Expanding and Collapsing the Outline

If your presentation has many slides, you may find that grasping its overall structure is difficult, even when looking at the outline. Fortunately, PowerPoint enables you to *collapse* the outline so that only the slide titles are shown. Collapsing an outline doesn't delete the body text; it merely hides the body text so that you can focus on the order of the slides in your presentation.

*Expanding* a presentation restores the collapsed body text to the outline so that you can once again focus on details. You can collapse and expand an entire presentation, or you can collapse and expand one slide at a time.

To collapse the entire presentation, click the Collapse All button in the Outlining toolbar or use the keyboard shortcut Alt+Shift+1. To expand the presentation, click the Expand All button or press Alt+Shift+9.

To collapse a single slide, position the cursor anywhere in the slide that you want to collapse. Then click the Collapse button or press Alt+Shift+– (the minus sign). If you prefer, right-click the slide title and choose Collapse from the menu that appears.

To expand a single slide, click anywhere in the slide title, and then click the Expand button or press Alt+Shift++ (the plus sign). Or, right-click the slide title and choose Expand from the menu.

# Creating a Summary Slide

The Summary Slide button is a nifty feature. It automatically creates a summary slide that shows the titles of some or all the slides in your presentation. To use the Summary Slide feature, follow these steps:

1. **Select the slides whose titles you want to appear on the summary slide.**

   To include the entire presentation, press Ctrl+A to select all the slides.

2. **Click the Summary Slide button. You can find the Summary Slide button on the Outlining toolbar.**

   If the Outlining toolbar is not visible, summon it by choosing View➪Toolbars➪Outlining.

   A summary slide is created at the beginning of the selected slides, as shown in Figure 3-2.

3. **Change the title of the summary slide.**

   Unless, of course, you like the boring title "Summary Slide."

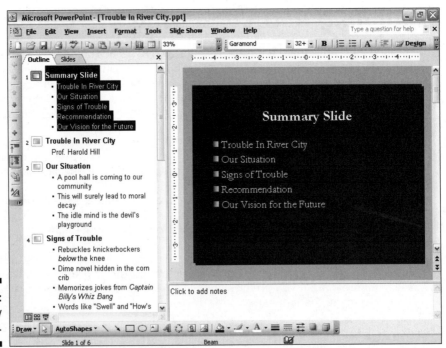

**Figure 3-2:**
A summary
slide.

# Chapter 4

# Doing It with Style

. . . . . . . . . . . . . . . . . . . . . . . . . . . . . . . . . . . . . . . . .

## In This Chapter

▶ Checking your spelling

▶ Using the Thesaurus

▶ Capitalizing and punctuating correctly

▶ Checking your presentation for embarrassing stylistic mistakes

▶ Using the AutoCorrect feature

. . . . . . . . . . . . . . . . . . . . . . . . . . . . . . . . . . . . . . . . .

*I* was voted "Worst Speller" in the sixth grade. Not that being "Worst Speller" qualifies me to run for president or anything, but it shows how much I appreciate computer spell checkers. Spelling makes no sense to me. I felt a little better after watching *The Story of English* on public television. Now at least I know whom to blame for all the peculiarities of English spelling — the Anglos, the Norms (including the guy from *Cheers*), and the Saxophones.

Fortunately, PowerPoint 2003 has a pretty decent spell checker. In fact, the spell checker in PowerPoint is so smart that it knows that you've made a spelling mistake almost before you make it. The spell checker watches over your shoulder as you type and helps you to correct your spelling errors as you work.

PowerPoint also has a nifty style checker that helps catch innocent typographical errors before you show your presentation to a board of directors. The style checker can fix your capitalization (capital idea, eh?), make sure that you punctuate your bullet points consistently, warn you about using too many fonts, and catch other embarrassing style gaffes.

## Checking Spelling As You Go

Spelling errors in a word-processing document are bad, but at least they're small. In a PowerPoint presentation, spelling errors are small only until you use a projector to throw your presentation onto a 30-foot screen. Then they get all blown out of proportion. Nothing is more embarrassing than a 3-foot-tall spelling error. And if you're like me, you probably try to look for mistakes in other people's presentations just for kicks. Thank goodness for PowerPoint's on-the-fly spell checker.

The PowerPoint spell checker doesn't make you wait until you finish your presentation and run a special command to point out your spelling errors. It boldly points out your mistakes right when you make them by underlining any mistake that you make with a wavy red line, as shown in Figure 4-1.

In Figure 4-1, three words have been marked as misspelled: *Snickerbockers* (isn't that a kind of cookie?), *Shamfull,* and *memorizashun.* When you see the telltale wavy red line, you have several options:

✔ **Make the correction:** You can retype the word using the correct spelling.

✔ **Let PowerPoint help:** You can click the word with the right mouse button to call up a menu that lists suggested spellings for the word. In most cases, PowerPoint can figure out what you meant to type and suggests the correct spelling. To replace the misspelled word with the correct spelling, just click the correctly spelled word in the menu.

✔ **Ignore the misspelling:** Sometimes, you want to misspell a word on purpose (for example, if you run a restaurant named "The Koffee Kup"). More likely, the word is correctly spelled, but PowerPoint just doesn't know about the word.

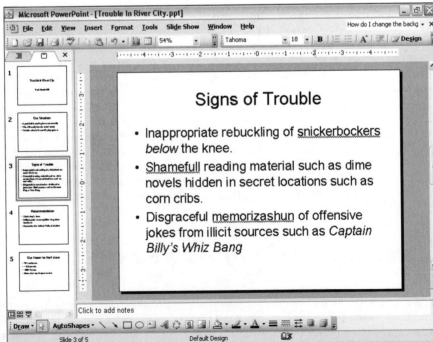

**Figure 4-1:** PowerPoint usually knows before you do that you've misspelled a word.

The spell checker can't tell you when you've used the wrong word but spelled it correctly. For example, the second bullet point in Figure 4-1 mentions *dime navels* instead of *dime novels*. Cheap literature may be a bad thing, but cheap citrus certainly is not.

# Spell Checking After-the-Fact

If you prefer to ignore the constant nagging by PowerPoint about your spelling, you can always check your spelling the old-fashioned way: by running the spell checker after you have finished your document. The spell checker works its way through your entire presentation, looking up every word in its massive list of correctly spelled words and bringing any misspelled words to your attention. It performs this task without giggling or snickering. As an added bonus, the spell checker even gives you the opportunity to tell it that you're right and it's wrong and that it should discern how to spell words the way you do.

The following steps show you how to check the spelling for an entire presentation:

1. **If the presentation that you want to spell check is not already open, open it.**

2. **Fire up the spell checker.**

   Click the Spelling button on the Standard toolbar, press F7, or choose Tools➪Spelling.

3. **Tap your fingers on your desk.**

   PowerPoint is searching your presentation for embarrassing spelling errors. Be patient.

4. **Don't be startled if PowerPoint finds a spelling error.**

   If PowerPoint finds a spelling error in your presentation, it switches to the slide that contains the error, highlights the offensive word, and displays the misspelled word along with a suggested correction, as shown in Figure 4-2.

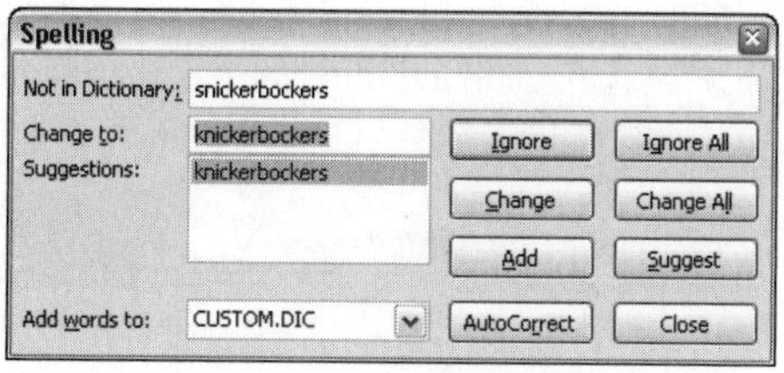

**Figure 4-2:**
The PowerPoint spell checker points out a boo-boo.

| Spelling | |
|---|---|
| Not in Dictionary: | snickerbockers |

Change to: knickerbockers
Suggestions: knickerbockers

Ignore | Ignore All
Change | Change All
Add | Suggest

Add words to: CUSTOM.DIC | AutoCorrect | Close

**5. Choose the correct spelling or laugh in PowerPoint's face.**

If you agree that the word is misspelled, scan the list of corrections that PowerPoint offers and select the one that you like. Then click the Change button.

If you like the way that you spelled the word in the first place (maybe it's an unusual word that isn't in the PowerPoint spelling dictionary, or maybe you like to spell like Chaucer did), click the Ignore button. Watch as PowerPoint turns red in the face.

If you want PowerPoint to ignore all occurrences of a particular misspelling, click the Ignore All button. Likewise, if you want PowerPoint to correct all occurrences of a particular misspelling, click the Change All button.

**6. Repeat Steps 4 and 5 until PowerPoint gives up.**

When you see the following message, you're finished:

```
The spelling check is complete
```

PowerPoint always checks spelling in the entire presentation, beginning with the first slide — unless you specify a single word or group of words by highlighting them first. PowerPoint checks the spelling of titles, body text, notes, and text objects added to slides. It doesn't check the spelling for embedded objects, however, such as charts or graphs.

---

## Don't make me tell you about the custom dictionary

The PowerPoint spell checker uses two spelling dictionaries: a standard dictionary, which contains untold thousands of words that were all reviewed for correctness by Noah Webster himself (just kidding), and a custom dictionary, which contains words that you have added by clicking the Add button when the spell checker found a spelling error.

The custom dictionary is shared by other Microsoft programs that use spell checkers — most notably Microsoft Word. So if you add a word to the custom dictionary in Word, the PowerPoint spell checker knows about the word, too.

What if you accidentally add a word to the dictionary? Then you have a serious problem. You have two alternatives. You can petition Noah Webster to have your variant spelling officially added to the English language, or you can edit the Custom.dic file, search through the file until you find the bogus word, and then delete it. The easiest way to edit the Custom.dic file is to go into Microsoft Word, choose Tools⇨ Options, click the Spelling & Grammar tab, and then click the Custom Dictionaries button. You can then select the Custom.dic file and click Modify to edit its contents.

If PowerPoint can't come up with a suggestion or if none of its suggestions are correct, you can type your own correction and click the Change button. If the word that you type isn't in the dictionary, PowerPoint asks whether you're sure that you know what you're doing. Double-check and click OK if you really mean it.

If you get tired of PowerPoint always complaining about a word that's not in its standard dictionary, click Add to add the word to the custom dictionary. If you can't sleep at night until you know more about the custom dictionary, read the sidebar titled "Don't make me tell you about the custom dictionary."

The speller can't tell the difference between *your* and *you're, ours* and *hours, angel* and *angle,* and so on. In other words, if the word is in the dictionary, PowerPoint passes it by regardless of whether you used the word correctly. The PowerPoint spell checker, however, is no substitute for good, old-fashioned proofreading. Print your presentation, sit down with a cup of cappuccino, and *read* it.

# Using the Thesaurus

One of the nifty new features of PowerPoint 2003 is a built-in thesaurus that can quickly show you synonyms for a word that you've typed. Using it is easy:

1. **Right-click a word that you've typed and choose Synonyms from the menu that appears.**

   A menu listing synonyms for the word appears. (Sometimes PowerPoint throws an antonym into the list just to be contrary.)

2. **Select the word that you want to use to replace your word.**

   PowerPoint replaces the original word with your selection.

If you choose Thesaurus from the Synonyms menu, the Thesaurus section of the Research task pane will appear with the synonyms listed, as shown in Figure 4-3. The Thesaurus lets you look up words to find even more synonyms. For example, if you select *shocking* from the list of synonyms, you get another set of words. You can keep clicking words to find other synonyms as long as you'd like, until you're ready to get back to real work.

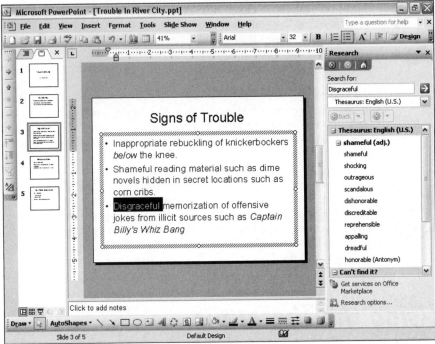

Figure 4-3:
The
Thesaurus.

# Capitalizing Correctly

The PowerPoint Change Case command enables you to capitalize the text in your slides properly. These steps show you how to use it:

**1. Select the text that you want to capitalize.**

**2. Choose Format➪Change Case.**

The Change Case dialog box appears, as shown in Figure 4-4.

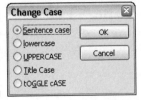

Figure 4-4:
The Change
Case dialog
box.

**3. Study the options for a moment and then click the one that you want.**

The case options follow:

- **Sentence case:** The first letter of the first word in each sentence is capitalized. Everything else is changed to lowercase.

- **lowercase:** Everything is changed to lowercase.

- **UPPERCASE:** Everything is changed to capital letters.

- **Title Case:** The first letter of each word is capitalized. PowerPoint is smart enough to leave certain words, such as "a" and "the" lowercase, but you should double-check to ensure that it worked properly.

- **tOGGLE cASE:** This option turns capitals into lowercase and turns lowercase into capitals, for a ransom-note look.

4. **Click OK or press Enter and check the results.**

Always double-check your text after using the Change Case command to make sure that the result is what you intended.

Slide titles should almost always use title case. The first level of bullets on a slide can use title or sentence case. Lower levels usually should use sentence case.

Avoid uppercase if you can. It's hard to read and LOOKS LIKE YOU'RE SHOUTING.

# Using Style Checker Options

PowerPoint's spell checker does more than check your spelling: It also checks your style, letting you know if you've used punctuation and capitalization consistently, warning you about slides that contain too many bullets or text that's too small, and so on.

Unfortunately, PowerPoint's style checking features are turned off by default. But you can activate them by following these steps:

1. **Choose Tools⇨Options.**

   The dialog box shown in Figure 4-5 appears.

2. **Select the Spelling and Style tab.**

3. **Check the Check Style option.**

   If this option is not already checked, click it to select it.

   The style checker uses the Office Assistant to let you know about any style problems that it may find. As a result, you have to enable the Office Assistant to use the style checker. If the Office Assistant isn't already enabled, a dialog box appears, offering to enable it. Click the Enable Assistant button to enable the Office Assistant.

**Figure 4-5:**
The Options dialog box contains the settings for the spelling and style checker.

4. **Click the Style Options button and adjust the style settings to your liking.**

   The Style Options dialog box has two tabs with options for checking the following style elements:

   • **Case and End Punctuation:** These settings, shown in Figure 4-6, make sure that your capitalization and punctuation are consistent.

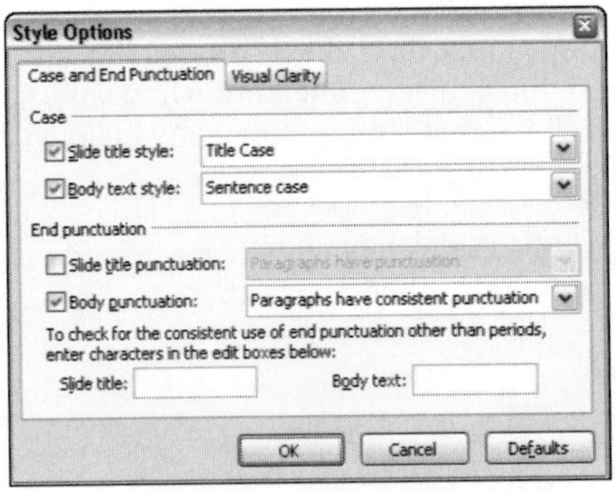

**Figure 4-6:**
The Case and End Punctuation settings.

   • **Visual clarity:** These options, shown in Figure 4-7, check for visual clarity and warn you about slides that have too many fonts, titles, and body text that is too small to read or too long; slides that have too many bullets; or slides that have text that runs off the page. Note the default numbers used here. It's up to you if you prefer to change maximum font sizes or whatever, but realize that these defaults usually work pretty well.

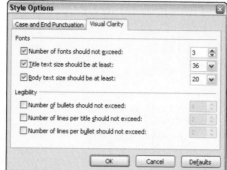

**Figure 4-7:**
The Visual
Clarity
settings.

**5. Click OK if you like all this stuff and move on!**

Now, whenever PowerPoint detects a style problem, a light-bulb icon appears next to the text with questionable style. Click this icon to call up the Office Assistant, who cheerfully explains the problem and offers several possible solutions.

The style checker works only if you have the Office Assistant turned on and if it is configured to display tips. For more information, refer to Chapter 8.

# Using the AutoCorrect Feature

PowerPoint includes an AutoCorrect feature that can automatically correct spelling errors and style errors as you type them. For example, if you accidentally type `teh`, PowerPoint automatically changes your text to `the`. And if you forget to capitalize the first word of a sentence, PowerPoint automatically capitalizes it for you.

Any time PowerPoint makes a correction that you don't like, just press Ctrl+Z (or choose Edit⇨Undo) to undo the correction. For example, if you really intended to type `teh`, press Ctrl+Z immediately after PowerPoint corrects it to `the`.

If you move the insertion pointer back to a word that has been corrected (or if you click the word), a small blue line appears beneath the first letter of the word. Point the mouse at this blue line and the button with a lightning bolt in it appears. You can then click this button to bring up a menu that enables you to undo the correction that was made, tell PowerPoint to stop making that type of correction, or summon the AutoCorrect options dialog box to adjust your AutoCorrect settings.

To control PowerPoint's AutoCorrect feature, choose Tools⇨AutoCorrect Options. This brings forth the dialog box shown in Figure 4-8.

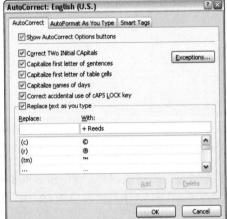

**Figure 4-8:**
The
AutoCorrect
Options
dialog box.

As you can see, the AutoCorrect Options dialog box contains check boxes for a variety of options that govern how AutoCorrect works:

- ✔ **Show AutoCorrect Options buttons:** This option displays the AutoCorrect button beneath words that were changed by the AutoCorrect feature, which allows you to undo the change or tell PowerPoint to stop making that particular type of correction.

- ✔ **Correct TWo INitial CApitals:** Looks for words with two initial capitals and changes the second one to lowercase. For example, if you type BOther, PowerPoint changes it to Bother. However, if you type three or more capitals in a row, PowerPoint assumes that you did it on purpose, so no correction is made.

- ✔ **Capitalize first letter of sentences:** Automatically capitalizes the first word of a new sentence if you forget.

- ✔ **Capitalize first letter of table cells:** Automatically capitalizes the first word in table cells.

- ✔ **Capitalize names of days:** You know, Monday, Tuesday, Wednesday, and so forth.

- ✔ **Correct accidental use of the cAPS LOCK key:** This is an especially cool feature. If PowerPoint notices that you're capitalizing everything backwards, it assumes that you accidentally pressed the Caps Lock key. So it turns off Caps Lock and corrects the words that you capitalized backwards.

✔ **Replace text as you type:** This option is the heart of the AutoCorrect feature. It consists of a list of words that are frequently typed wrong, along with the replacement word. For example, `teh` is replaced by `the` and `adn` is replaced by `and`. The AutoCorrect list also contains some shortcuts for special symbols. For example, `(c)` is replaced by the copyright symbol (©) and `(tm)` is replaced by the TradeMark symbol (™).

TIP

You can add your own words to this list. Type the word that you want PowerPoint to watch for in the Replace text box and the word that you want PowerPoint to substitute for the first word in the With text box, and then click the Add button.

The AutoCorrect feature also includes several formatting options that can automatically apply formats as you type. To set these options, click the AutoFormat As You Type tab. The options shown in Figure 4-9 appear. These options let you control formatting options, such as automatically converting straight quotes to curly quotes, changing fractions, such as 1/2 to actual fraction symbols such as ½, and so on.

**Figure 4-9:**
The AutoFormat As You Type options.

# Using Smart Tags

Smart Tags are a feature that identifies certain text and marks it as special. For example, if PowerPoint recognizes a company's financial symbol, it marks the symbol as a financial symbol Smart Tag. Then, you can get a current stock quote for the company directly from PowerPoint with just a few mouse clicks. Smart Tags have been available in Word and Excel since Office XP, but have just now crept their way into PowerPoint. Whoopie!

If you want to activate Smart Tags, choose Tools➪AutoCorrect and click the Smart Tags tab. This displays the Smart Tags options, shown in Figure 4-10. You can then indicate which types of Smart Tags that you want PowerPoint to find. The list includes dates, times, names, phone numbers, and financial symbols.

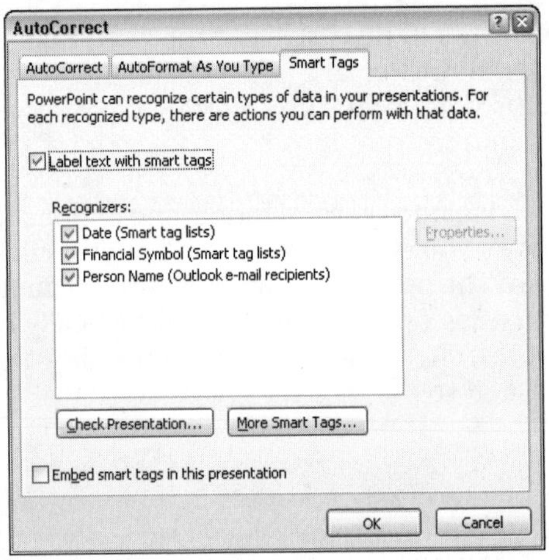

**Figure 4-10:**
The Smart
Tags
options.

If you enable Smart Tags and PowerPoint detects one in your presentation, the Smart Tag will be underlined with a little dotted purple line. Then, when you point at the Smart Tag text, a special Smart Tag button appears next to the text. You can click this button to reveal a menu of options for the Smart Tag. For example, the menu for a financial symbol includes commands that let you get a stock quote, a company report, or recent news about the company.

# Chapter 5

# Don't Forget Your Notes!

*E*ver had the fear — or maybe the actual experience — of showing a beautiful slide, complete with snappy text and perhaps an exquisite chart, and suddenly forgetting why you included the slide in the first place? You stumble for words. "Well, as you can see, this is a beautiful chart, and, uh, this slide makes the irrefutable point that, uh, well, I'm not sure — are there any questions?"

Fear not! One of the slickest features in PowerPoint 2003 is its ability to create speaker notes to help you get through your presentation. You can make these notes as complete or as sketchy as you want or need. You can write a complete script for your presentation or just jot down a few key points to refresh your memory.

The best part about speaker notes is that you're the only one who sees them. They don't actually show up on your slides for all the world to see. Instead, notes pages are printed separately. One notes page is allocated for each slide in the presentation, and each notes page includes a reduced version of the slide so that you can keep track of which notes page belongs to which slide.

One great feature of PowerPoint is that, assuming your computer has the hardware to pull it off, you can display your slides on a computer projector and your notes on a separate monitor so only you can see them. For more information about this feature, see the section "Displaying Notes on a Separate Monitor" later in this chapter.

Don't you think that it's about time for a short chapter? Although notes pages are one of the slickest features in PowerPoint, creating notes pages isn't all that complicated — hence the brevity of this chapter.

# Understanding Notes

Notes are like an adjunct attachment to your slides. They don't appear on the slides themselves, but are displayed separately. Each slide in your presentation has its own page of notes.

In Normal View, the notes are hidden at the bottom of the screen in a separate Notes pane. To work with notes in Normal View, you must first enlarge the Notes pane to give yourself some room to work. For more information, see the section "Adding Notes to a Slide" later in this chapter.

PowerPoint also has a separate view designed for working with notes pages, called (you guessed it) Notes Page View. To call up Notes Page View, choose View➪Notes Page. Figure 5-1 shows a slide in Notes Page View. Each notes page consists of a reduced version of the slide and an area for notes.

Of course, these notes are too small to see or work with in Notes Page View unless you increase the zoom setting. If you want to work in Notes Page View, you'll need to zoom in so you can see your work.

Unfortunately, no keyboard shortcut is available to switch directly to Notes Page View. Earlier versions of PowerPoint included a button for this alongside the other view buttons in the lower-left corner of the screen. But for some mysterious reason, Microsoft decided to omit this button in recent versions of PowerPoint. So the only way to get to Notes Page View now is to choose View➪Notes Page.

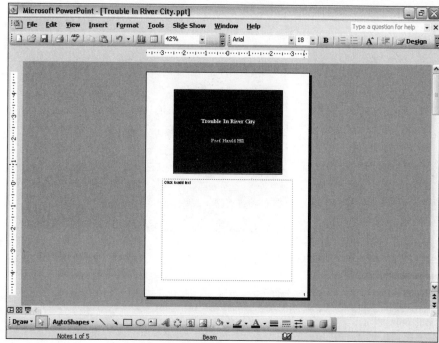

**Figure 5-1:**
Notes Page
View lets
you see
your notes.

# Adding Notes to a Slide

To add notes to a slide, follow this procedure:

1. **In Normal View, move to the slide to which you want to add notes.**

2. **Click and drag the Notes pane border, if necessary, to bring the notes text into view.**

3. **Click the notes text object, where it reads** Click to add notes.

4. **Type away.**

The text that you type appears in the notes area. As you create your notes, you can use any of the PowerPoint standard word-processing features, such as cut, copy, and paste. Press Enter to create new paragraphs.

Figure 5-2 shows a slide with the Notes pane enlarged to a comfortable size and some notes typed.

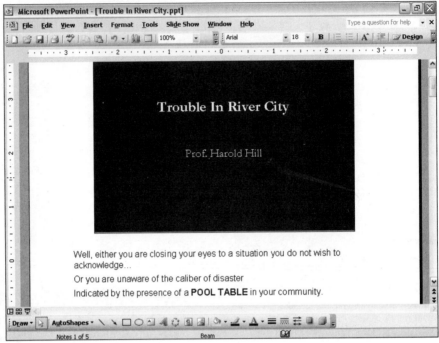

**Figure 5-2:**
A slide
with notes.

# Adding an Extra Notes Page for a Slide

PowerPoint doesn't provide a way to add more than one page of notes for each slide. However, these steps show you a trick that accomplishes essentially the same thing:

1. **Create a duplicate slide immediately following the slide that requires two pages of notes.**

   To duplicate the slide, move to the slide that you want to duplicate in Normal View, and then choose Insert⇨Duplicate Slide.

2. **Switch to the Notes Page View.**

   The notes page for the new duplicate slide appears.

3. **Delete the slide object at the top of the duplicate notes page.**

   To do so, click the slide object at the top of the page and press Delete.

4. **Extend the notes text area up so that it fills the page.**

   To extend the notes area, just drag the top-center love handle of the notes text area up.

5. **Type the additional notes for the preceding slide on this new notes page.**

   Add a heading, such as "Continued from slide 23," at the top of the text to help you remember that this portion is a continuation of notes from the preceding slide.

6. **Return to Normal View.**

   Click the Normal View button or choose View➪Normal.

7. **Choose Slide Show➪Hide Slide to hide the slide.**

   The Hide Slide command hides the slide, which means that it isn't included in an on-screen slide show.

The result of this trick is that you now have two pages of notes for a single slide, and the second notes page doesn't have an image of the slide on it and is not included in your slide show.

If you're printing overhead transparencies, you may want to uncheck the Print Hidden Slides check box in the Print dialog box. This way, the hidden slide isn't printed. Be sure to recheck the box when you print the notes pages, though. Otherwise, the notes page for the hidden slide isn't printed either — and the reason you created the hidden slide in the first place was to print a notes page for it!

Think twice before creating a second page of notes for a slide. Do you really have that much to say about a single slide? Maybe the slide contains too much to begin with and should be split into two slides.

# Adding a New Slide from Notes Page View

If you're working in Notes Page View and realize that you want to create a new slide, you don't have to return to Normal View. Just click the New Slide button on the Standard toolbar or choose Insert➪New Slide to add the new slide.

If you want to work on the slide's appearance or contents, however, you must switch back to Normal View. You can't modify a slide's appearance or contents from Notes Page View.

# Printing Notes Pages

If you don't have a computer that can show your slides on a projector and your notes on a separate monitor, you can always print your notes on paper, and then use the printed notes while you give your presentation. These steps show you how to print your notes:

1. **Choose File⇨Print.**

   The Print dialog box appears.

2. **Use the Print What list box to choose the Notes Pages option.**

3. **Make sure that the Print Hidden Slides box is checked if you want to print notes pages for hidden slides.**

   The Print Hidden Slides check box is dimmed if the presentation doesn't have any hidden slides. To hide a slide, select the slide and choose Slide Show⇨Hide Slide. (See Chapter 7 for more information.)

4. **Click OK or press Enter.**

If you have just printed slides on overhead transparencies, don't forget to reload your printer with plain paper. You probably don't want to print your speaker notes on transparencies!

You can find more information about printing in Chapter 6.

# Displaying Notes on a Separate Monitor

If you're lucky enough to have a computer that can use two monitors, you can display your notes on one monitor and connect a projector as the other monitor to show your slides. This way, you can see your notes on the monitor while your audience sees only the projected slides.

To enable this feature, choose Slide Show⇨Set Up Show. This summons the Set Up Show dialog box. In the Multiple Monitors section of the dialog box, change the Display Slide Show On: setting to Secondary Monitor. You switch to Notes View on the primary monitor to view your notes, and then start the slide show on the secondary monitor to show the slides on the projector.

# *Random Thoughts about Notes*

This section provides some ideas that may help you make the most of your notes pages.

- If you're giving an important presentation for a large audience, you may want to consider using notes pages to write a complete script for your presentation. For less formal presentations, more succinct notes are probably better.

- Use notes pages to jot down any anecdotes, jokes, or other asides that you want to remember to use in your presentation.

- If you prefer to handwrite your notes, you can print blank notes pages. Don't bother adding notes to your presentation, but you can choose File⇨Print to print notes pages. The resulting notes pages have a reduced image of the slide at the top and a blank space in which you can handwrite your notes later.

- You may also consider providing blank notes pages for your audience. If you choose File⇨Print, you can print audience handouts that contain two, three, or six slides per page, but these handout pages leave no room for the audience members to write notes.

# Chapter 6

# Printing Your Presentation

● ● ● ● ● ● ● ● ● ● ● ● ● ● ● ● ● ● ● ● ● ● ● ● ● ● ● ● ● ● ● ● ● ● ● ●

*In This Chapter*

▶ Printing slides

▶ Printing handouts

▶ Printing speaker notes

▶ Printing an outline

▶ Previewing your output

▶ Troubleshooting

● ● ● ● ● ● ● ● ● ● ● ● ● ● ● ● ● ● ● ● ● ● ● ● ● ● ● ● ● ● ● ● ● ● ● ●

*T*he Print command. The Printmeister. Big presentation comin' up. Printin' some slides. The Printorama. The Mentor of de Printor. Captain Toner of the Good Ship Laseroo.

Don't worry — when you print a PowerPoint presentation, no one's waiting to ambush you with annoying one-liners like that guy who used to be on *Saturday Night Live*. Just a handful of boring dialog boxes with boring check boxes. Point-point, click-click, print-print.

## The Quick Way to Print

The fastest way to print your presentation is to click the Print button found in the Standard toolbar. It's the one with the little picture of a printer in it. Clicking this button prints your presentation without further ado, using the current settings for the Print dialog box, which I explain in the remaining sections of this chapter. Usually, this action results in printing a single copy of all the slides in your presentation. But if you have altered the Print dialog box settings, clicking the Print button uses the altered settings automatically.

# Using the Print Dialog Box

For precise control over how you want your presentation to be printed, you must conjure up the Print dialog box as shown in Figure 6-1. To summon this dialog box, choose File⇨Print or press Ctrl+P.

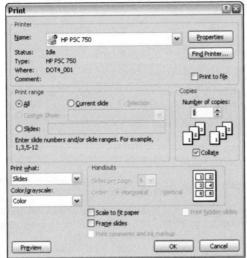

**Figure 6-1:**
Behold
the Print
dialog box.

After you call up the Print dialog box, click OK or press Enter to print all the slides in your presentation. Fiddle around with the settings to print a select group of slides, to print more than one copy, or to print handouts, speaker notes, or an outline. This section shows you the treasures that lie hidden in this dialog box.

Printing can be es-el-oh-double-ewe, so don't panic if your presentation doesn't start printing right away. PowerPoint printouts tend to demand a great deal from the printer, so sometimes the printer has to work for a while before it can produce a finished page. Be patient. The Printer wizard has every intention of granting your request.

## Changing printers

If you're lucky enough to have two or more printers at your disposal, you can use the Name field to pick which printer you want to use. Each printer must first be successfully installed in Windows — a topic that's beyond the reach of this humble book, but that you will find plenty of information about in the appropriate version of Andy Rathbone's *Windows For Dummies* (published by Wiley Publishing, Inc.).

## Printing part of a presentation

When you first use the Print command, the All option is checked so that your entire presentation prints. The other options in the Print Range portion of the Print dialog box enable you to tell PowerPoint to print distinct portions of your presentation:

- ✔ **Current slide**: Prints just the current slide. Before you invoke the Print command, you should move to the slide that you want to print. Then check this option in the Print dialog box and click OK. This option is handy when you make a change to one slide and don't want to reprint the entire presentation.

- ✔ **Selection:** Prints just the portion of the presentation that you selected before invoking the Print command. First, select the slides that you want to print. Then call up the Print command, click the Selection box, and click OK.

- ✔ **Custom Show:** If you have used the Slide Show⇨Custom Shows command to create custom slide shows, you can use this option to select the show that you want to print. Chapter 7 has the scoop on custom shows.

- ✔ **Slides:** Lets you select specific slides for printing. You can print a range of slides by typing the beginning and ending slide numbers, separated by a hyphen, as in *5-8* to print slides 5, 6, 7, and 8. Or you can list individual slides, separated by commas, as in *4,8,11* to print slides 4, 8, and 11. And you can combine ranges and individual slides, as in *4,9-11,13* to print slides 4, 9, 10, 11, and 13.

## Printing more than one copy

The Number of Copies field in the Print dialog box lets you print more than one copy of your presentation. You can click one of the arrows next to this field to increase or decrease the number of copies, or you can type directly in the field to set the number of copies.

Below the Number of Copies field is a check box labeled Collate. If this box is checked, PowerPoint prints each copy of your presentation one at a time. In other words, if your presentation consists of ten slides and you select three copies and check the Collate box, PowerPoint first prints all ten slides of the first copy of the presentation, and then all ten slides of the second copy, and then all ten slides of the third copy. If you don't check the Collate box, PowerPoint prints three copies of the first slide, followed by three copies of the second slide, followed by three copies of the third slide, and so on.

The Collate option saves you from the chore of manually sorting your copies. If your presentation takes forever to print because it's loaded down with heavy-duty graphics, however, you can probably save time in the long run by unchecking the Collate box. Why? Because many printers are fast when it comes to printing a second or third copy of a page. The printer may spend ten minutes figuring out how to print a particularly complicated page, but after it figures it out, the printer can print additional copies in ten seconds each. If you print collated copies, the printer must labor over each page separately for each copy of the presentation that it prints.

## Choosing what to print

The Print What field in the Print dialog box enables you to select which type of output that you want to print. The following choices are available:

- ✔ **Slides:** Prints slides. (Duh.)
- ✔ **Notes pages:** Prints speaker notes pages, which are covered in Chapter 5.
- ✔ **Handouts (With Slides per Page):** Prints audience handout pages. Select the number of slides that you want to appear on each handout page by clicking the Slides per Page box. You can also order the slides to appear horizontally or vertically on the handout.
- ✔ **Outline View:** Prints an outline of your presentation.

Select the type of output that you want to print and then click OK or press Enter. Off you go!

When you're printing slides to be used as overhead transparencies, print a proof copy of the slides on plain paper before committing the output to transparencies. Transparencies are too expensive to print on until you're sure that your output is just right.

To change the orientation of your printed output from Landscape to Portrait mode (or vice versa), choose File⇨Slide Setup.

To print handouts with two, three, or six slides per page, PowerPoint naturally must shrink the slides to make them fit. Because slides usually have outrageously large type, the handout slides are normally still readable, even at their reduced size.

## Exploring the other printing options

The Print command has several additional options, which hide out near the bottom of the dialog box, hoping to slip by unnoticed. This list shows you what they do:

- **Color/grayscale:** This drop-down list box lets you choose whether to print your slides in color, black and white, or with shades of gray.

- **Scale to fit paper:** Adjusts the size of the printed output to fit the paper in the printer. Leave this option unchecked to avoid bizarre printing problems.

- **Frame slides:** Draws a thin border around the slides.

- **Print comments and ink markup:** If you've added comments to your slides, you can print the comments on separate pages by choosing this option. This option is grayed out if the presentation has no comments.

- **Print hidden slides:** You can hide individual slides by choosing Tools⇨Hide Slide. After a slide is hidden, it doesn't print unless you check the Print Hidden Slides option in the Print dialog box. This option is grayed out if the presentation has no hidden slides.

# Using the Print Preview Command

The Print Preview feature lets you see how your pages will appear before committing them to paper (or transparencies). To use the Print Preview feature, choose File⇨Print Preview or click the Print Preview button. Or, you can choose File⇨Print to bring up the Print dialog box, and then click the Preview button. Either way, a preview of the printed page appears, as shown in Figure 6-2.

From the Print Preview screen, you can zoom in to examine the preview more closely by clicking anywhere in the preview area. Or, you can scroll through the pages using the scroll bar, the Page Up and Page Down keys, or the Prev Page and Next Page buttons located at the top-left corner of the screen.

After you're satisfied that the printout will be to your expectations, click the Print button to print the presentation. If you discover a mistake in the preview, click Close to return to PowerPoint so you can correct the mistake before printing your slides.

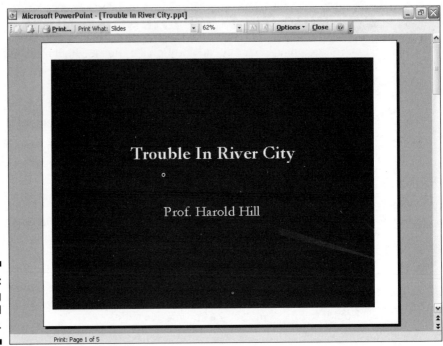

**Figure 6-2:**
Previewing
your printed
output.

# Chapter 7

# Show Time!

*Y*ou can play some really slick tricks during an on-computer slide show with PowerPoint. You can use the mouse (or keyboard) to move from slide to slide, to go back to a slide that you've already shown, or to skip a slide. You can also use the mouse to doodle on your slides, underlining or circling key points as you go. (I call this the "John Madden Effect," in honor of the former football coach who circles game plays with great relish on telecasts.) This chapter shows you how to employ these nifty tricks to dazzle your audience.

Before you go to the play-by-play section of this chapter, however, consider your audience. PowerPoint culture is changing as Internet and intranet broadcasting becomes more common and as projection devices become staples in everyone's office. The following are three ways that you can present an on-computer slide show:

✔ In a one-on-one meeting

✔ In a large group setting with a computer data projector

✔ Over the Internet

These three types of slide shows have many similarities. This chapter focuses on live presentations. For presentations on your intranet or Internet, see Chapter 21. Whichever method you use, however, you first have to set up your show.

# Setting Up a Slide Show

To set up a slide show to present it on your computer, first open the presentation that you want to set up, and then choose Slide Show➪Set Up Show. This action summons the Set Up Show dialog box, which is shown in Figure 7-1. With this dialog box, you can twiddle with the various options that are available for presenting slide shows.

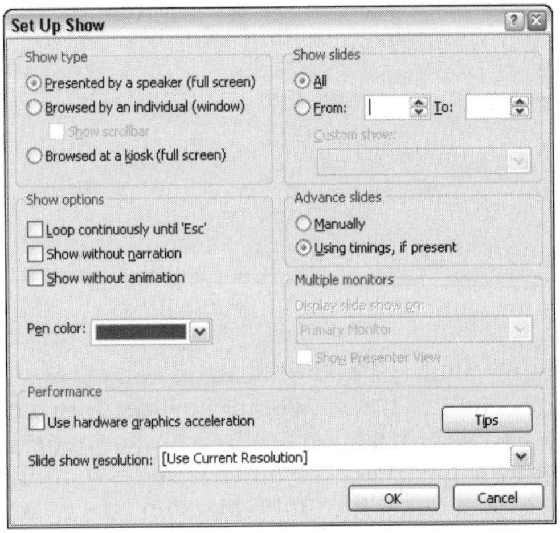

**Figure 7-1:**
The Set Up
Show dialog
box.

With the options on the Set Up Show dialog box, you can do the following:

- ✔ **Configure the presentation:** You can configure the presentation for one of three basic slide show types: Presented by a Speaker (Full Screen), Browsed by an Individual (Window), or Browsed at a Kiosk (Full Screen).

- ✔ **Loop through slides:** Choose Loop Continuously until Esc if you want the show to run indefinitely. If you enable this setting, the show jumps back to the first slide after the last slide is shown, and continues to repeat until you press the Esc key.

- ✔ **Simplify the presentation:** Uncheck the Show Without Narration and Show Without Animation options if you want to simplify the presentation by not playing narrations that you've recorded or animations that you've created.

- ✔ **Select pen color:** Select the color to use for the pen. (See the section "The John Madden Effect" later in this chapter for more information about using the pen.)

- ✔ **Select slides:** Choose All to include all slides in the slide show, or choose From and supply starting and ending slide numbers if you want to display just some of the slides in the presentation.

✔ **Set up custom shows:** Choose Custom Show if you have set up any custom shows within your presentation. (See the section "Using Custom Shows" later in this chapter for more information.)

✔ **Choose to change slides manually:** Choose Manually to advance from slide to slide by pressing Enter, pressing the spacebar, or clicking the mouse button. Or, if you want the show to proceed automatically, choose Using Timings, if this option is present.

✔ **Select a monitor:** If your computer has two monitors, select the monitor to use for the slide show by using the drop-down list in the Multiple Monitors section.

# Starting a Slide Show

When you want to do a slide show in a one-on-one or small group setting without a projector, beginning the show is just a click away. To start a slide show immediately, click the Slide Show button located (along with the other View buttons) in the lower-left corner of the screen. If you have set up a full-screen slide show, PowerPoint fills the entire screen with the first slide of the slide show. To advance to the next slide, click the mouse, or press Enter, the down arrow, the Page Down key, or the spacebar. You can also start a slide show by choosing View⇨Slide Show or Slide Show⇨View Show.

To start the slide show from the first slide, make sure the first slide of the show is selected. (Press Ctrl+Home to call up the first slide before starting the show.)

You can also start a slide show by using the keyboard shortcut F5, or by choosing View⇨Slide Show or Slide Show⇨View Show.

If you've configured PowerPoint to display the slide show on a secondary monitor, the slide show runs on the secondary monitor. The primary monitor still displays the presentation in Normal View. If you want, you can switch to Notes View on the primary monitor to display your notes while the slides are displayed on the secondary monitor. (For more information about displaying notes on one monitor and slides on another, refer to Chapter 5.)

# Setting Up a Projector

If you're going to present your show using a computer projector and a laptop computer, you need to know how to connect the computer to your laptop computer as well as how to set up the projector, turn it on, focus it, and so on. Most of these details vary from one projector to the next, so you'll have to consult the manual that came with the projector or bribe someone to set up the projector for you. The following list provides a few general tips that may help:

- ✔ Most laptop computers have an external video port on the back or the side, and most projectors have a video input connection. A standard VGA monitor cable works to connect the computer to the projector.

- ✔ To use the laptop with a projector, you must first activate the external video port. Some laptops have a key that you can press to accomplish this; others require that you twiddle with the display settings to activate the external video port. If you can't figure out how to make the switch, try right-clicking an empty area of the desktop and choose Properties from the menu that appears. Click the Settings tab, and then click the Advanced button and look for a setting to enable the external video port. (On my Toshiba laptop, this setting is located in the Display Device tab of the dialog box that appears when I click the Advanced button.)

- ✔ When your presentation is finished, be sure to switch your computer back to its normal video port setting *before* you disconnect the projector. It's never a good idea to unplug a video cable while the video port is active. Plus, if your laptop disables its built-in display while the external port is active, you won't be able to see anything!

- ✔ Most projectors can accept input from more than one source. For example, you may be able to connect a computer and a VCR to the projector. The projector should have some buttons or perhaps a menu setting that lets you select the input that is used to display the projected image. If you connect your computer to the projector and everything else seems okay but you still don't get a picture, make sure that the projector is set to the correct input.

- ✔ If you want to use the projector's remote control to operate your presentation, you'll need the appropriate cable to connect the projector to your laptop computer's mouse port. The correct cable should come with the projector.

- ✔ Finally, if your presentation has sound, you'll need to connect your computer's sound outputs to a set of amplified speakers or, if you're showing the presentation in a large auditorium, a PA system. The correct cable to connect to a PA system depends on the PA system, but a cable with a mini-stereo plug on one end and a ¼" plug on the other will probably do the trick.

# Keyboard and Mouse Tricks for Your Slide Show

During an on-screen slide show, you can use the keyboard and mouse to control your presentation. Tables 7-1 and 7-2 list the keys and clicks that you can use.

If the mouse pointer is hidden, you can summon it by jiggling the mouse. Then, when the mouse pointer is visible, a faint menu appears in the lower-left corner of the slide. You can use this menu to activate various slide show features.

| Table 7-1 | Keyboard Tricks for Your Slide Show |
| --- | --- |
| *To Do This* | *Press Any of These Keys* |
| Display next slide | Enter, spacebar, Page Down, or N |
| Display preceding slide | Backspace, Page Up, or P |
| Display first slide | 1+Enter |
| Display specific slide | Slide number+Enter |
| Toggle screen black | B or . (period) |
| Toggle screen white | W or , (comma) |
| Show or hide pointer | A or = (equal sign) |
| Erase screen doodles | E |
| Stop or restart automatic show | S, or + (plus sign) |
| Display next slide even if hidden | H |
| Display specific hidden slide | Slide number of hidden slide+Enter |
| Change pen to arrow | Ctrl+A |
| Change arrow to pen | Ctrl+P |
| End slide show | Esc, Ctrl+Break (the Break key doubles as the Pause key), or – (minus) |

| Table 7-2 | Mouse Tricks for Your Slide Show |
| --- | --- |
| *To Do This* | *Do This* |
| Display next slide or build | Click |
| Move through slides | Roll the wheel on your mouse (if your mouse has a wheel) |
| Call up menu of actions | Right-click |
| Display first slide | Hold down both mouse buttons for two seconds |
| Doodle | Press Ctrl+P to change the mouse arrow to a pen and then draw on-screen like John Madden |

# The John Madden Effect

If you've always wanted to diagram plays on-screen the way John Madden does, try using the pen during a slide show:

1. **Start a slide show.**

2. **When you want to doodle on a slide, press Ctrl+P.**

   The mouse arrow pointer changes to a pen shape.

3. **Draw away.**

   Figure 7-2 shows an example of a doodled-upon slide.

4. **To erase your doodles, press E.**

Drawing doodles like this requires good mouse dexterity. With practice, you can create all kinds of interesting doodles. Work on circling text or drawing exclamation points or question marks, smiley faces, and so on.

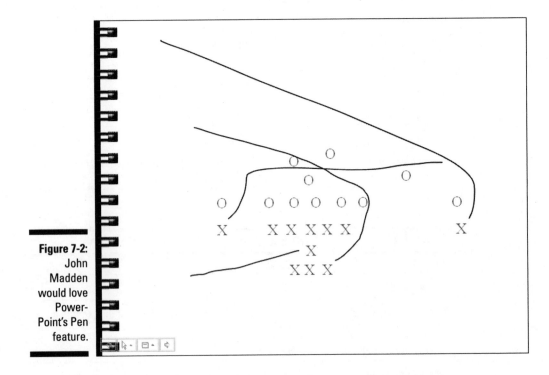

**Figure 7-2:**
John Madden would love Power-Point's Pen feature.

Keep these tasty tidbits in mind when doodling:

- To hide the mouse pointer temporarily during a slide show, press A or the equal sign (=). The pointer returns the moment you move the mouse, or you can press A or the equal sign again to summon it back.

- If you use the pen, be sure to say "Bam" and "Pow" a lot.

- If you don't like the pen color, you can change it by using the faint Show menu that appears in the bottom-left corner of the slide. This menu has four little icons; the second one from the left displays a list of pen options: a ballpoint pen, a felt-tipped pen that draws a somewhat heavier line, and a highlighter, which draws in broad lines that are semi-transparent, just like a real highlighter. (The Show menu disappears after a few seconds if you don't use it, but you can get it to reappear by moving the mouse around a bit.)

You can also right-click the mouse for a floating menu of these choices; however, this may be a little more distracting for your audience than the keystrokes because the audience will suddenly be privy to all your fancy footwork. Do notice, however, that the menu allows you to change pen colors and a few other tricks. You can set up the pen color by choosing Slide Show➪Set Up Show before you begin your presentation so as not to distract your audience. If you have a remote mouse and you won't have access to your keyboard during your presentation, I suggest that you investigate the floating menu method.

# Rehearsing Your Slide Timings

You can use the PowerPoint Rehearsal feature to rehearse your presentation. The Rehearsal lets you know how long your presentation takes, and it can even set slide timings so that the slides automatically advance based on the timings you set during the Rehearsal.

To rehearse a slide show, choose Slide Show➪Rehearse Timings. This starts the slide show, with a special Rehearsal dialog box visible, as shown in Figure 7-3.

**Figure 7-3:**
Rehearsing
a slide
show.

Now rehearse your presentation. Click the mouse or use keyboard shortcuts to advance slides. As you rehearse, the Rehearse dialog box keeps track of how long you display each slide and the total length of your presentation.

When you dismiss the final slide, PowerPoint displays a dialog box that gives you the option of applying the timings recorded during the Rehearsal to the slides in the presentation, or ignoring the rehearsal timings. If you were satisfied with the slide timings during the rehearsal, click Yes.

If you mess up during a Rehearsal, click the Repeat button. Clicking this button restarts the Rehearsal from the beginning.

# Running a Presentation over a Network

PowerPoint allows you to run presentation conferences over a computer network, which basically means that you can run a slide show and invite other network users to view the slide show on their computers. Because this feature uses Web technology to give it its "oomph," the only software needed to view the presentation is a Web browser. For more information about this Presentation Broadcast Web phenomenon, check out Chapter 20.

# Using Custom Shows

The Custom Shows feature in PowerPoint lets you create several similar slide shows stored in a single presentation file. For example, suppose that you're asked to give presentations about company benefits to management and non-management staff. You can create a presentation containing slides for all the company benefits and then create a custom show containing only those slides describing benefits that are available to non-management staff. This custom slide show can leave out slides such as "Executive Washrooms," "Golf Days," and "Boondoggles." You may then show the complete presentation to management, but show the custom show to non-management staff.

A presentation can contain as many custom shows as you want. Each custom show is simply a subset of the complete presentation — comprised of selected slides from the complete presentation.

## Creating a custom show

To create a custom show, follow these steps:

1. **Choose Slide Show⇨Custom Shows.**

   This displays the Custom Shows dialog box.

2. **Click the New button.**

   The Define Custom Show dialog box appears, as shown in Figure 7-4.

**Figure 7-4:** Defining a custom show.

3. **Type a name for the custom show in the Slide Show Name field.**

4. **Add the slides that you want to appear in the custom slide show.**

   All the slides available in the presentation are listed in the list box on the left side of the Define Custom Show dialog box. To add a slide to the custom show, click the slide that you want to add, and then click Add. The slide that you added appears in the list box on the right side of the Define Custom Show dialog box.

   You don't have to add slides to the custom show in the same order that the slides appear in the presentation. Slides for a custom show can appear in any order you want. You can also include a slide from the original presentation more than once in a custom show.

   To remove a slide that you've added by mistake, click the slide that you want to remove in the list box on the right side of the Define Custom Show dialog box, and then click Remove.

   You can use the up or down arrows near the right edge of the Define Custom Show dialog box to change the order of the slides in the custom show.

5. **Click OK.**

   You return to the Custom Shows dialog box.

6. **Click Close to dismiss the Custom Shows dialog box.**

## Showing a custom show

To show a custom show, first open the presentation that contains the custom show. Then, choose Slide Show⇨Custom Shows to summon the Custom

Shows dialog box. Click the custom show that you want, and then click the Show button.

You can also call up a custom show during a slide show by right-clicking the mouse anywhere in the presentation, choosing Go⇨Custom Shows, and clicking the custom show that you want to display.

## Hiding slides

If you don't want to go to all the trouble of creating a custom show, but you want to exclude a few slides from a presentation, you don't have to delete the slides. Instead, you can hide them. To hide a slide, select the slide, and then choose Slide Show⇨Hide Slide. To unhide a slide, select the slide and choose Slide Show⇨Hide Slide again. (You can determine which slides have been hidden by looking at the slide in the Slides tab. If the slide number has a slash through it, the slide is hidden.)

# Packaging Your Presentation on a CD

One of the nifty new features of PowerPoint 2003 is the Package for CD command, which you access by choosing File⇨Package for CD. If your computer has a CD burner, you can use this command to create a self-contained CD with your presentation along with any necessary support files (such as fonts or large sound files) and a special PowerPoint Viewer that lets you view the presentation on any computer, even if the computer doesn't have PowerPoint installed.

To create a CD with your presentation, follow these steps:

1. **Open the presentation in PowerPoint, then choose File⇨Package For CD.**

   The Package for CD dialog box appears, as shown in Figure 7-5.

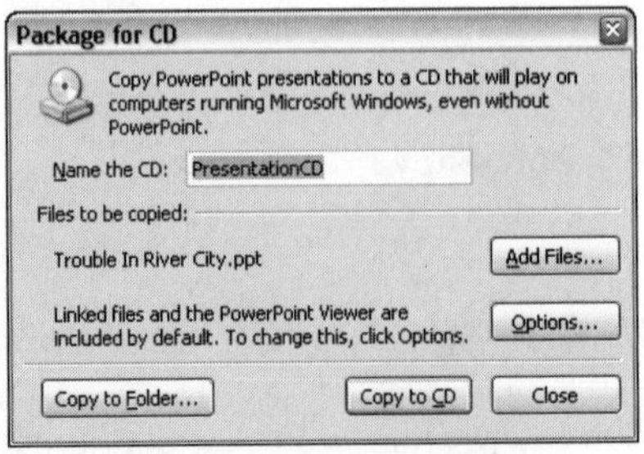

**Figure 7-5:**
The Package for CD dialog box.

| Package for CD | |
|---|---|
| Copy PowerPoint presentations to a CD that will play on computers running Microsoft Windows, even without PowerPoint. | |
| Name the CD: PresentationCD | |
| Files to be copied: | |
| Trouble In River City.ppt | Add Files... |
| Linked files and the PowerPoint Viewer are included by default. To change this, click Options. | Options... |
| Copy to Folder... | Copy to CD    Close |

## 2. Click Options.

This summons the Options dialog box, shown in Figure 7-6.

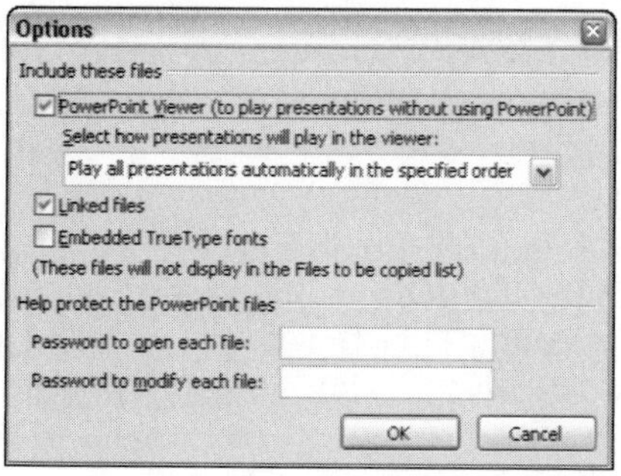

**Figure 7-6:**
The Options
dialog box.

## 3. Study the options and change any that aren't set the way you want.

The following paragraphs describe each of the options that are available:

- **PowerPoint Viewer:** Check this option to include the PowerPoint Viewer on the CD. If you include the viewer, you can use the drop-down list beneath this option to indicate whether you want to play the presentations on the CD automatically or allow the user to choose which presentation to play.

- **Linked Files:** Check this option to include any linked files, such as videos or large audio files.

- **Embedded TrueType fonts:** Check this option to ensure that the fonts you used in your presentation will be available when you show the presentation on another computer.

- **Password to open each file:** Enter a password if the presentation contains top-secret information, such as the true whereabouts of Jimmy Hoffa.

- **Password to modify each file:** Enter a password if you want to prevent unauthorized people from changing the presentation.

## 4. Click OK to return to the Package to CD dialog box.

## 5. If you want to add other presentations to the CD, click Add Files, select the files that you want to add, and then click Add.

You can put as many files as will fit on the CD. You can add other PowerPoint presentations or any other files you'd like to add to the CD, such as Word documents or text files.

## 6. Click Copy to CD.

If you haven't already inserted a blank CD into the drive, you are prompted to insert one now.

7. **Insert a blank CD into your CD-RW drive and click Retry.**

   PowerPoint copies the files to the CD. This may take a few minutes, so now is a good time to catch a few z's. After the CD is finished, the drive spits it out and asks if you want to make another copy.

8. **Remove the CD, and then click Yes if you want to make another copy. Otherwise, click No, and then click Close.**

   You're done!

The CD is set up so that the presentation should start running all by itself when you insert it into a computer. If it doesn't, open a My Computer window, and then open the CD drive and double-click the `pptviewer.exe` link. A list of presentations on the CD appears. Double-click the one that you want to run, and off you go.

# Chapter 8

# Help!

*T*he ideal way to use PowerPoint would be to have a PowerPoint expert sitting patiently at your side, answering your every question with a straightforward answer, gently correcting you when you make silly mistakes, and otherwise minding his or her own business. All you'd have to do is occasionally toss the expert a Twinkie and let him or her outside once a day.

The good news is that PowerPoint has just such an expert built-in. This expert is referred to as the Office Assistant, and he works not just with PowerPoint, but also with other Microsoft Office programs, including Word, Excel, Access, and Outlook. You don't even have to feed the Office Assistant, unlike a real guru.

## Meet the Assistant

Alexander Graham Bell had Watson, Batman had Robin, and Dr. Frankenstein had Igor. Everybody needs an assistant, and Office users are no exception. That's why Microsoft decided to bless Office with the Office Assistant, a handy fellow who offers helpful assistance as you work with Office programs, including PowerPoint.

The Office Assistant is an animated persona who suddenly morphs onto your desktop with sage advice and suggestions and even a little idea light that gives you a clue that you can use a clue! You can also ask the Office Assistant a question when you're not sure what to do, and the Assistant thoroughly searches the PowerPoint online Help database to provide the answer.

The Office Assistant is actually one of several little cartoon characters. Figure 8-1 shows the one I like best. His name is Rocky. See the section "Changing Assistants" later in this chapter for instructions on how to switch to a different Assistant.

**Figure 8-1:**
Meet Rocky,
an Office
Assistant.

The fun thing about the Assistant is that he is animated. Watch the Assistant on-screen as you work. Every once in a while he blinks, and on occasion, he dances or makes a face. The Assistant often responds to commands that you choose in PowerPoint. For example, if you call up the Find command (Edit⇨ Find or Ctrl+F), the Assistant makes a gesture as if he is searching for something. When you print your presentation, the Assistant does some cute little printer schtick. Microsoft went to a lot of trouble to make sure that the Assistant is entertaining, and the results are sometimes amusing. When you ask the Assistant for help, he sits down, plops his feet up on a desk, and takes copious notes — don't you wish real people cared so much!

Notice that the Assistant has a special type of dialog box called a *balloon,* which includes an area for you to type a question and several buttons that you can click. The balloon functions like any other dialog box, but it has a special appearance that's unique to the Assistant.

When you first install PowerPoint, the Assistant is disabled. You can summon him by choosing Help⇨Show the Office Assistant, but he won't pop up automatically to offer help. To enable the Office Assistant, choose Help⇨Show the Office Assistant to display the Assistant. Then, right-click the Assistant, choose Options from the pop-up menu, and then check the Use the Office Assistant option and click OK.

# Summoning the Assistant

You can summon the Assistant in several ways when you need help. In many cases, the Assistant shows up all by himself, so all you need to do to get his attention is click the Assistant. This action pops up the balloon dialog box so that you can ask a question. If the Assistant isn't visible on-screen, you can summon him quickly by choosing Help⇨Show the Office Assistant, by pressing F1, or by clicking the Help button in the Standard toolbar (it's the button with the big question mark in it.)

Sometimes the Assistant figures out that you're struggling with something and offers some helpful assistance all on his own. For example, if you try to select an object that's on the Slide Master (which you can only select in Slide Master View), the Assistant tells you why you can't select the object, as shown in Figure 8-2. The Assistant offers to take you to the Slide Master View so you can select the background object, or to tell you more about masters.

If you click on the option to tell you more about masters, a help screen appears, such as the one shown in Figure 8-3. As you can see, the Help topic in Figure 8-3 explains what masters are and provides information about using them.

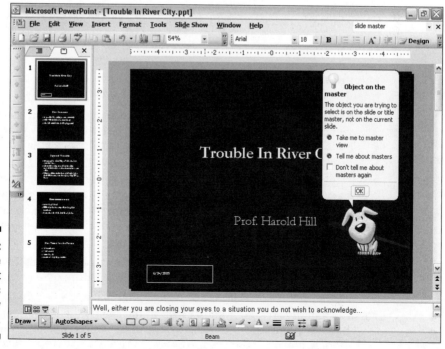

**Figure 8-2:** The Assistant offers friendly advice.

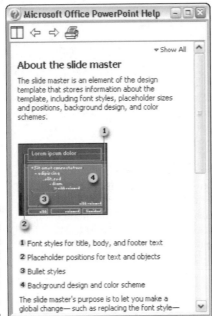

**Figure 8-3:**
A Help
topic about
working
with
masters.

After you get yourself this deep into Help, you need to heed the following
advice to find your way around and get out when you find out what you want
to know:

✔ **Print helpful information:** If you find a Help topic that you consider
uncommonly useful, click the Print button and print the darn thing.

✔ **Navigate from page to page:** If you see an underlined word or phrase,
you can click it to zip to a Help page that describes that word or phrase.
By following these underlined words, you can bounce your way around
from Help page to Help page until you eventually find the help that you
need.

✔ **Get step-by-step instructions:** Sometimes, Help offers several choices
under a heading such as "What do you want to do?" Each choice is pre-
ceded by a little button: Click the button to display step-by-step help for
that choice.

✔ **Retrace your steps:** You can retrace your steps by clicking the Help
window's Back button. You can use the Back button over and over again,
retracing all your steps if necessary.

✔ **Work in PowerPoint and get help at the same time:** Help operates as a
separate program, so you can work within PowerPoint while the Help
window remains on-screen. When you display a help topic, a separate
Help window appears, which you can resize, minimize, or drag as you
choose.

> ✔ **Close Help:** When you've had enough of Help, you can dismiss it by pressing Esc or clicking the close button in the upper-right corner of the Help window.

# Asking a Question

If none of the Help topics offered by the Assistant seem to be what you're looking for, you can type a question right in the Assistant's balloon dialog box to look for help on a specific topic. For example, if you want to know how to change the background color of a slide, type **How do I change the background color of a slide?** in the text box and then click the Search button or press Enter. The Assistant searches Microsoft's extensive Help library, and then displays the results in the Search task pane, as shown in Figure 8-4.

If one of the topics looks promising, click it. Or click Can't Find It to see options for finding additional information.

If none of the topics seem related to the question you asked, try rephrasing the question and click Search again.

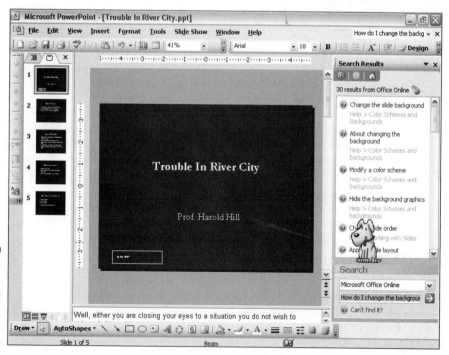

**Figure 8-4:**
The Assistant searches for answers.

You don't actually have to phrase your question as a question. You can eliminate words such as *How do I,* and you can also usually eliminate "noise words" such as *a, an, the, of, in,* and so on. Thus, the brief question "change background color slide" yields exactly the same result as the more verbose "How do I change the background color of a slide?"

# Getting a Tip

As I mentioned earlier, every once in a while, a light bulb appears in the Assistant's word balloon, or even in the middle of your slide. When this light bulb appears, you can click it to see a tip that the Assistant thinks may be useful. If the tip is worthwhile, plant a big fat kiss on the Assistant (not literally!) and be thankful. If not, feel free to roll your eyes and act annoyed.

# Changing Assistants

Rocky, the friendly and loyal cyberpup Assistant, is but one of seven Assistants from which you can choose. The others are a paperclip named ClipIt, a happy face named The Dot, a robot named F1, a puzzle piece named Office Logo, a globe named Mother Nature, and a cat named Links.

To select a different Assistant, summon the Assistant by choosing Help⇨Show Office Assistant. Then click the Options button to display the Office Assistant dialog box. Click the Gallery tab located at the top of this dialog box. The Assistant Gallery is displayed, as shown in Figure 8-5.

To change to a different Assistant, click the Next button. Keep clicking the Next button to work your way through all the Assistants. When you find the one that you want to use, click OK.

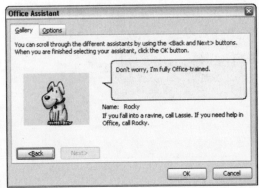

**Figure 8-5:**
The
Assistant
Gallery.

The Assistants differ only in appearance — not in their ability to offer assistance with using PowerPoint features. If I worked for Microsoft, I would have given the Assistants personalities. For example, Rocky would be eager to help. However, you'd have to press F1 five or six times before Links, who happens to be a cat, would even appear on-screen.

You can also click the Options tab on the Office Assistant dialog box to set various options that affect how the Assistant works. In fact, you can use this dialog box to turn the Assistant off altogether if he annoys you.

# Help the Old-Fashioned Way

The Assistant isn't the only way to get help in PowerPoint. You can still get help the old-fashioned Windows way through the traditional Help interface.

To summon old-fashioned Help, first turn off the Assistant by summoning the Assistant Options dialog box and unchecking the Use the Office Assistant check box. Then press F1 or choose Help⇨Microsoft PowerPoint Help. This summons the Help task pane. Next, click the Table of Contents link to summon the Help table of contents, as shown in Figure 8-6.

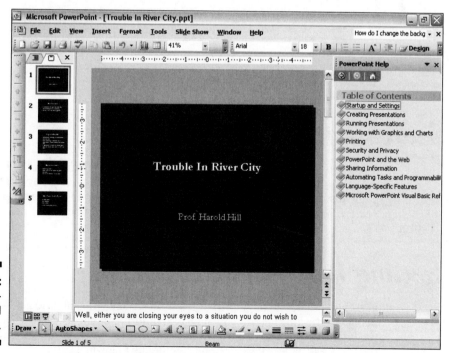

**Figure 8-6:** Good old-fashioned help.

The topics with book icons next to them represent sections that have additional subtopics. You can click one of these sections to reveal the list of subtopics. Each of the actual Help topic pages has an icon that looks like a page with a question mark in it. You can click one of these topics to display the Help page. For example, Figure 8-7 shows the Help page for the topic "Create a Presentation Using Blank Slides."

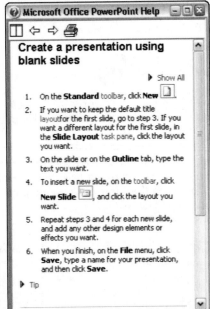

**Figure 8-7:**
A helpful
Help topic.

## Searching for Lost Help Topics

If you can't find help for a nasty problem by browsing through the Help Contents, you can search for Help topics. On the main Help page in the task pane, just type the words that you want to search for in the text box and click Search. With luck, you can quickly find the help you need.

## Getting Help on the Internet

In addition to the help that's built into PowerPoint, you can also get PowerPoint help from the Internet. All you need is an Internet connection. To seek help on the Internet, click one of the options in the Office on Microsoft.com section of the Help task pane. These options include the following:

✔ **Assistance:** This link connects you to the Microsoft Office Assistance home page at Microsoft.com. Here, you can find all kinds of useful information about PowerPoint and other Office programs.

✔ **Training:** This link takes you to the Training home page at Microsoft.com. Here you can find online training tutorials that teach you how to use specific aspects of PowerPoint or other Office programs.

✔ **Communities:** This link takes you a Web page that has links to online forums where you can ask questions.

✔ **Office Update:** This link takes you to the Office Update home page on Microsoft.com, where you can download the latest updates to Office programs.

# Repairing a Broken Office

If PowerPoint doesn't seem to be working right — for example, if it locks up your computer when you use certain commands or if features seem to be missing — you can use the built-in Office repair tool to detect and correct problems. To use the repair tool, first locate your PowerPoint or Office Setup CD. Then, choose Help⇨Detect and Repair. Follow the instructions that appear on-screen. If the repair tool needs to retrieve any files from the installation CD, it asks you to insert the CD in your computer's CD drive.

# Part II
# Making Your Presentations Look Mahvelous

The 5th Wave — By Rich Tennant

"NIFTY CHART, FRANK, BUT NOT ENTIRELY NECESSARY."

# In this part . . .

**1**t is widely believed that Californians indulge in cosmetic surgery more often than Floridians complain about hanging chads. The chapters in this part are all about cosmetic surgery for your presentations. You learn how to perform such procedures as typosuction, clip-art lifts, and color tucks. When you're done, your slides will look simply mahvelous.

# Chapter 9

# Fabulous Text Formats

## In This Chapter

▶ Using bold, italics, underlining, and other character effects

▶ Changing the text font, size, and color

▶ Using bullets and numbers

▶ Lining things up

▶ Tabbing and indenting

▶ Spacing things out

*A* good presentation should be like a fireworks show: At every new slide, the audience gasps, "O-o-o-h. A-a-a-h." The audience is so stunned by the spectacular appearance of your slides that no one really bothers to read them.

This chapter gets you on the road toward ooohs and aaahs by showing you how to format text. If you use PowerPoint's templates as the basis for your presentations, your text is already formatted acceptably. To really pull out the pyrotechnic stops, however, you have to know a few basic formatting tricks.

Many PowerPoint text-formatting capabilities work the same as they do in Microsoft Word. If you want to format text a certain way and you know how to do it in Word, try formatting the same way in PowerPoint. Odds are that it works.

If you find that the Standard and Formatting toolbars are jammed together on one line so that you can't get to the formatting buttons you use often, choose View⇨Toolbars⇨Customize to summon the Customize dialog box. Then click the Options tab to bring up the toolbar options and check the Show Standard and Formatting Toolbars on Two Rows check box.

# Changing the Look of Your Characters

PowerPoint lets you change the look of individual characters in subtle or drastic ways. You can control all character attributes by way of the Font dialog box, shown in Figure 9-1, which you summon by choosing Format➪Font.

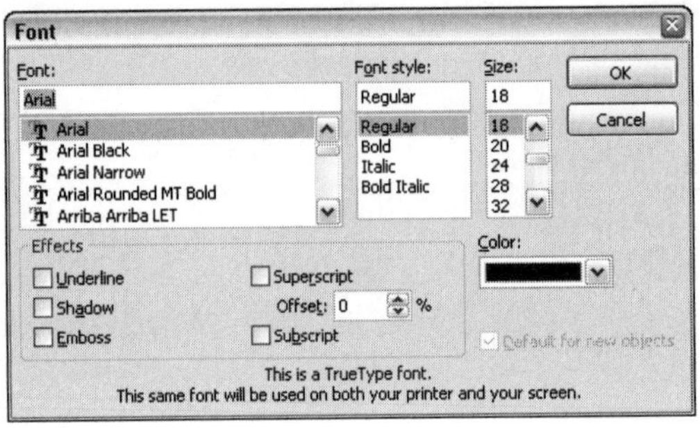

**Figure 9-1:**
The Font
dialog box.

The Font dialog box is a bit cumbersome to use, but fortunately PowerPoint provides an assortment of keyboard shortcuts and toolbar buttons that let you apply the most common formats without summoning the Font dialog box. These shortcuts are listed in Table 9-1.

| Table 9-1 | Character-Formatting Shortcuts | |
|---|---|---|
| *Button* | *Keyboard Shortcut* | *Format* |
|  **B** | Ctrl+B | Bold |
|  *I* | Ctrl+I | Italic |
|  U | Ctrl+U | Underline |
|  S | (none) | Text shadow |
| (none) | Ctrl+spacebar | Normal |
|  Arial | Ctrl+Shift+F | Font |
|  18 | Ctrl+Shift+P | Change font size |
|  A | Ctrl+Shift+> | Increase font size |

| Button | Keyboard Shortcut | Format |
|--------|-------------------|--------|
| A | Ctrl+Shift+< | Decrease font size |
| A | (none) | Font color |

It's true — PowerPoint has many keyboard shortcuts for character formatting. You don't have to learn them all, though. The only ones I know and use routinely are for bold, italic, underline, and normal. Learn these and you'll be in good shape. You get the added bonus that these keyboard shortcuts are the same as the shortcuts that many other Windows programs use. If you are mouse-happy and keyboard-annoyed, then click away for goodness' sakes. What matters most is that you can easily find and use what you need.

## Adding bold, italics, and underlines

If you want, you can instruct these formats to gang-tackle some text. In other words, text can be bold, italic, and underlined for extra, extra emphasis. You can gang-tackle text with any combination of formats that you want.

You also can remove all text formats in one fell swoop by highlighting the text and pressing Ctrl+spacebar.

You can format text in two basic ways. To format existing text, highlight the text that you want to format. Then, click the toolbar button or use the keyboard shortcut for the format that you want. For example, to make existing text bold, highlight it and then click the Bold button or press Ctrl+B.

To type new text using a fancy format, click the toolbar button or use the keyboard shortcut for the format. Then, type away. The text that you type is given the format that you selected. To return to normal formatting, click the button or use the keyboard shortcut again. Or, press Ctrl+Spacebar.

## Changing the size of characters

If text is difficult to read or you simply want to draw attention to it, you can make part of the text bigger than the surrounding text. The easiest way to change the size of your text is to use the Font Size drop-down list that appears next to the font name in the Formatting toolbar. Just choose among the sizes that appear in the Font Size drop-down list, or click in the Font Size box and type whatever size you want to use. Or press Ctrl+Shift+P, then use the Up and Down arrow buttons to select the font size.

You can also change the size of your text by using the Increase Font Size or Decrease Font Size buttons that appear in the Formatting toolbar, or by using the Ctrl+Shift+> or Ctrl+Shift+< keyboard shortcuts. These commands increase or decrease the font size in steps.

## Choosing text fonts

If you don't like the looks of a text font, you can easily switch to a different font. To change the font for existing text, select the text. Then, click the arrow next to the Font control on the Formatting toolbar and choose the font that you want to use. If you're allergic to the mouse, you can get to the font list by pressing Ctrl+Shift+F. Then you can use the Up or Down arrow keys to choose the font you want to use.

If you have set the Formatting and Standard toolbars to display on the same row, you may not see the Font Type dialog box and you won't get any reaction from the keyboard shortcut. Don't forget to look for more buttons by checking the down arrows on the toolbar or by separating the two toolbars when you run PowerPoint. If you read this book in beginning-to-end order, you'll remember that I advised you to separate those toolbars while working through this book.

Here are a gaggle of additional points to ponder concerning fonts:

- ✔ Although you can change the font by choosing Format⇨Font, the Font control on the Formatting toolbar has one major advantage over the Font dialog box. The Formatting toolbar's Font control displays each of your fonts using the font itself, so you can see what each font looks like before you apply it to your text. In contrast, the Font dialog box displays the name of each font using the standard Windows system font.

- ✔ If you want to change the font for all the slides in your presentation, switch to Slide Master View and then change the font. Details on how to do so are covered in Chapter 12.

- ✔ PowerPoint automatically moves the fonts that you use the most to the head of the font list. This feature makes picking your favorite font even easier.

- ✔ Don't overdo it with fonts! Just because you have many different font choices doesn't mean that you should try to use them all on the same slide. Don't mix more than two or three typefaces on a slide, and use fonts consistently throughout the presentation. The PowerPoint Assistant reminds you if you use too many fonts.

## Replacing fonts

PowerPoint has a nifty Replace Fonts command that lets you replace all occurrences of one font with another font in one swift move. For example, suppose that you decide that Garamond is ugly and you'd rather use Book Antiqua. No problem! Just choose the Format➪Replace Fonts command to summon the Replace Fonts dialog box, shown in Figure 9-2. Select the font that you want to get rid of in the Replace drop-down list, and select the font that you want to use in its place in the With drop-down list; then click Replace.

## Adding color to your text

Color is an excellent way to draw attention to text in a slide — that is, if your slides print in color or you can display them on your computer monitor or by using a projector, or if you plan to publish on the Web. To change text color, first select the text whose color you want to change. Then, click the Font Color button on the Formatting toolbar and choose the color that you want to use from the color menu that appears.

If you don't like any color that the Font Color button offers, click where it reads More Font Colors. A bigger dialog box with more color choices appears. If you still can't find the right shade of teal, click the Custom tab and have at it. Check out Chapter 11 if you need further help with colors.

If you want to change the text color for your entire presentation, do so on the Slide Master (see Chapter 12 for details).

## Adding shadows

Adding a shadow behind your text can make the text stand out against its background, which makes the entire slide easier to read. For that reason, many of the templates supplied with PowerPoint use shadows.

You can apply a shadow to any text by first selecting the text, and then clicking the Shadow button, which is located near the right edge of the drawing toolbar. If you want all of the text on a slide to be shadowed, however, you should use the Slide Master to create the shadow format. For more information, peek ahead to Chapter 12.

## Embossing text

Embossed text looks like it has been chiseled in stone. PowerPoint achieves the embossed effect by adding a light shadow above the text rather than the dark shadow that appears below the text when you create shadowed text. Note that you can't create text that is both shadowed and embossed; you can use one or the other effect, but not both at the same time.

When you emboss text, PowerPoint changes the text color to the background color in order to enhance the embossed effect. As a result, the text appears to sink into the background.

Unfortunately, PowerPoint doesn't have a button for creating embossed text. Instead, you have to bring up the Font dialog box by choosing Format⇨Font. Then, you can check the Emboss option and click OK.

Embossed text is difficult to read in smaller font sizes. This effect is best reserved for large titles. Also, embossed text is nearly invisible with some color schemes. You may have to fiddle with the color scheme or switch templates in order to make the embossed text visible.

## Biting the Bulleted List

Most presentations have at least some slides that include a bulleted list, which is a series of paragraphs accented by special characters lovingly known as *bullets*. In the old days, you had to add bullets one at a time. Nowadays, PowerPoint comes with a semiautomatic bullet shooter that is illegal in 27 states.

PowerPoint lets you create fancy bullets that are based on bitmap pictures rather than simple dots and checkmarks. Before you go crazy with picture bullets, take a look at the basic way to bite the bullet.

To add bullets to a paragraph or series of paragraphs:

1. **Highlight the paragraphs to which you want to add bullets.**

   To add a bullet to just one paragraph, you don't have to highlight the entire paragraph. Just place the cursor anywhere in the paragraph.

**2. Click the Bullet button.**

PowerPoint adds a bullet to each paragraph that you select.

The Bullet button works like a toggle: Press it once to add bullets and press it again to remove bullets. To remove bullets from previously bulleted text, therefore, you select the text and click the Bullet button again.

If you don't like the appearance of the bullets that PowerPoint uses, you can select a different bullet character, picture, or even a motion clip by choosing Format➪Bullet. This command displays the Bullets and Numbering dialog box, shown in Figure 9-3. From this dialog box, you can choose a different bullet character, change the bullet's color, or change its size relative to the text size.

**Figure 9-3:**
The Bullets
and
Numbering
dialog box.

The following paragraphs point out some important tidbits to keep in mind when you use bullets:

- ✔ **Customize bullet characters:** You can choose from among several collections of bullet characters that are available. If you don't like any of the bullet characters displayed for you in the dialog box, click Customize in the lower-right corner of the dialog box. This brings up a dialog box that lists a variety of useful alternative bullet characters, such as pointing fingers, a skull and crossbones, and a time bomb. Pick the bullet that you want to use, and then click OK. If you can't find a bullet that suits your fancy, choose a different symbol font in the Font drop-down control.

- ✔ **Change the size of bullet characters:** If the bullet characters don't seem large enough, increase the Size value in the Bullets and Numbering dialog box. The size is specified as a percentage of the text size.

- ✔ **Change the color of bullet characters:** To change the bullet color, use the drop-down Color list box to choose the color that you want to use.

Colors from the current color scheme appear in the drop-down menu that appears when you use the Color list box. (For additional color choices, choose More Colors to call up a dialog box that offers a complete range of color choices. For more information about using colors, see Chapter 11.)

✔ **Use images for your bullet characters:** To use a picture bullet, click the Picture button located in the lower right of the Bullets and Numbering dialog box. This brings up the Picture Bullet dialog box, shown in Figure 9-4. Choose the picture that you want to use for your bullet, and then click OK. (You can use the Import button on this dialog box to use your own bitmap file for a bullet.)

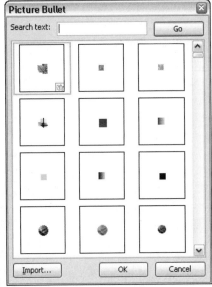

**Figure 9-4:**
Using a
picture
bullet.

You can use certain bullet characters for good comic effect in your presentations. Be creative, but also be careful. A thumbs-down bullet next to the name of your boss may get a laugh, but it may also get you fired. One cool thing to do with bullets when you pitch a product or service is to use your logo as a bullet. It subliminally grinds your image in their brains until they submit to your will.

# Creating Numbered Lists

If you want your slide to include a numbered list, use the Numbering button, which appears next to the Bullets button in the Formatting toolbar. When you click the Numbering button, PowerPoint adds simple numbers to the selected paragraphs.

If you want to change the numbering format, choose Format⇨Bullets and Numbering to bring up the Bullets and Numbering dialog box, and then click the Numbering tab to display the numbering options, shown in Figure 9-5. You can then choose from one of several numbering formats.

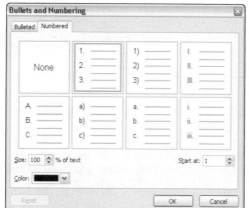

**Figure 9-5:**
Numbering
options.

Normally, the starting number for each list reverts to 1 for each new slide. What if you have a list that has more items than will fit on one slide, such as a David Letterman-style Top Ten list? In that case, you can type the first half of the list on one slide, and then type the second half of the list on a second slide. Next, right-click the first item on the second slide and choose Bullets and Numbering from the menu that appears. Then, change the Start At value to the number at which you want the second part of the list to begin. For example, if the first slide has five numbered items, change the Start At value for the first item on the second slide to 6.

# Lining Things Up

PowerPoint enables you to control the way your text lines up on the slide. You can center text, line it up flush left or flush right, or justify it. You can change these alignments by choosing Format⇨Alignment, or you can use the convenient toolbar buttons and keyboard shortcuts as described in Table 9-2.

| Table 9-2 | Paragraph Alignment Shortcuts | |
|---|---|---|
| *Button* | *Keyboard Shortcut* | *Alignment* |
| | Ctrl+E | Centered |
| | Ctrl+L | Lean to the Left |
| | Ctrl+R | Lean to the Right |
| | Ctrl+J | Stand up, Sit down, Justify! |

Here are some semi-random thoughts on aligning paragraphs:

- *Centered* text lines up right down the middle of the slide. (Actually, down the middle of the text object that contains the text; a text line appears centered on the slide only if the text object is centered on the slide.)

- Bulleted lists look best when left-aligned. Otherwise, the bullets don't line up.

- The Justify option, which lines up text evenly on both the right and left margins, doesn't appear on the Formatting toolbar by default. However, you can add it by choosing Tools⇨Customize.

# Setting Tabs and Indents

PowerPoint enables you to set tab stops to control the placement of text within a text object. For most presentations, you don't have to fuss with tabs. Each paragraph is indented according to its level in the outline, and the template that you use to create the presentation presets the amount of indentation for each outline level.

If you're stubborn about tabs, you can mess with the indent settings and tab stops if you're adventurous and have no real work to do today. Here's how you do it:

1. **Click the Slide button to switch to Normal View.**

   You can't mess with tabs or indents in Notes Page View or Slide Sorter View.

2. **If the Ruler is not visible, summon it by choosing View⇨Ruler.**

Rulers appear above and to the left of the presentation window and show the current tab and indentation settings. If your rulers are missing, you can get them back by choosing View⇨Ruler.

3. **Select the text object whose tabs or indents you want to change.**

   Each text object has its own tabs and indents setting. After you click a text object, the ruler shows that object's tabs and indents.

4. **Click the ruler to add a tab stop.**

   Move the mouse pointer to the ruler location where you want to add a tab stop and then click. A tab stop appears.

5. **Grab the indentation doohickey and drag it to change the indentation.**

   Try dragging the different parts of the indentation doohickey to see what happens. Have fun. Good luck.

Tabs and indents can be pretty testy, but fortunately you don't have to mess with them for most presentations. If you're one of the unlucky ones, keep these pointers in mind:

✔ **Each text object has its own tab settings.** The tab settings for an object apply to all the paragraphs within the object, so you can't change tab settings for individual paragraphs within a text object. This is different from how Word works — in Word, each paragraph has its own tab settings.

✔ **The ruler shows as many as five different indentation levels, one for each outline level.** Only those levels used in the text object are shown, so if the object has only one outline level, only one indent is shown. To see additional indents, demote text within the object by pressing the Tab key.

TECHNICAL STUFF

## Don't even bother with this stuff about tab types

PowerPoint isn't limited to just boring left-aligned tabs. In all, it has four distinct types of tabs: left, right, center, and decimal. The square button that appears at the far-left side of the ruler when you select text tells you which type of tab is added when you click the ruler. Click this button to cycle through the four types of tabs:

✔ **Standard left-aligned tab.** Press Tab to advance the text to the tab stop.

✔ **Right-aligned tab.** Text is aligned flush right with the tab stop.

✔ **Centered tab.** Text lines up centered over the tab stop.

✔ **Decimal tab.** Numbers line up with the decimal point centered over the tab stop.

Each text object is initially set up with default tab stops set at every inch. When you add a tab stop, any default tab stops located to the left of the new tab stop disappear.

To remove a tab stop, use the mouse to drag the stop off the ruler (click the tab stop, drag it off the ruler, and then release the mouse button).

# Spacing Things Out

Feeling a little spaced out? Try tightening the space between text lines. Feeling cramped? Space out the lines a little. These steps show you how to do it all:

1. **Highlight the paragraph or paragraphs whose line spacing you want to change.**

2. **Choose Format⇨Line Spacing.**

   Sorry, PowerPoint has no keyboard shortcut for this step. The Line Spacing dialog box suddenly appears, as shown in Figure 9-6.

**Figure 9-6:**
Changing
the line
spacing.

| Line Spacing |
|---|
| Line spacing |
| 1 ⇕ Lines ⌄ |
| Before paragraph |
| 0.2 ⇕ Lines ⌄ |
| After paragraph |
| 0 ⇕ Lines ⌄ |
| OK    Cancel    Preview |

3. **Change the dialog box settings to adjust the line spacing.**

   *Line spacing* refers to the space between the lines within a paragraph. Before Paragraph adds extra space before the paragraph, and After Paragraph adds extra space after the paragraph.

   You can specify spacing in terms of lines or points. The size of a line varies, depending on the size of the text font. If you specify spacing in terms of points, PowerPoint uses the exact spacing that you specify, regardless of the size of the text font.

4. **Click OK or press Enter.**

You can also increase or decrease the spacing between paragraphs by clicking the Increase Paragraph Spacing or Decrease Paragraph Spacing buttons found in the Formatting toolbar. If you can't find the buttons, remember to try the down arrow.

# Chapter 10

# Working with Pictures and Clip Art

- - - - - - - - - - - - - - - - - - - - - - - - - - - - - - - - - - - - - - - - - - -

- - - - - - - - - - - - - - - - - - - - - - - - - - - - - - - - - - - - - - - - - - -

*F*ace it: Most of us are not born with even an ounce of artistic ability. Some day (soon, we hope), those genetic researchers combing through the billions and billions of genes strung out on those twisty DNA helixes will discover the Artist Gene. Then, in spite of protests from the DaVincis and Monets among us (who fear that their NEA grants will be threatened), doctors will splice the little bugger into our own DNA strands so that we can all be artists. Of course, this procedure won't be without its side effects: Some will develop an insatiable craving for croissants, and others will inexplicably develop French accents and whack off their ears. But artists we shall be.

Until then, we have to rely on clip art, pictures we've found on the Internet, or pictures that we scanned into the computer using a scanner or took with a digital camera.

## Exploring the Many Types of Pictures

The world is awash with many different formats in which pictures can be stored on your computer. Fortunately, PowerPoint works with almost all these formats. The following sections describe the two basic types of pictures that you can work with in PowerPoint: bitmap pictures and vector drawings.

# *Bitmap pictures*

A *bitmap picture* is a collection of small dots that comprise an image. Bitmap pictures are most often used for photographs and for icons and other buttons used on Web pages. You can create your own bitmap pictures with a scanner, a digital camera, or a picture drawing program such as Adobe PhotoShop or Corel PhotoPaint. You can even create crude bitmap pictures with Microsoft Paint, which is the free painting program that comes with Windows.

The dots that comprise a bitmap picture are called *pixels.* The number of pixels in a given picture depends on two factors: the picture's resolution and its size. *Resolution* refers to the number of pixels per inch. Most computer monitors (and projectors) display 72 pixels per inch. At this resolution, a 1" square picture requires 5,184 pixels (72 x 72). Photographs that will be printed on an inkjet or laser printer usually have a much higher resolution, often 300 pixels per inch or more. At 300 pixels per inch, a 4" x 6" photograph requires more than two million pixels.

The amount of color information stored for the picture — also referred to as the picture's *color depth* — affects how many bytes of computer memory the picture requires. The color depth determines how many different colors the picture can contain. Most pictures have one of two color depths: 256 colors or 16.7 million colors. Most simple charts, diagrams, cartoons, and other types of clip art look fine at 256 colors. Photographs usually use 16.7 million colors.

16.7 million color pictures are also known as *TrueColor* pictures or *24-bit color* pictures.

Our 4" x 6" photograph, which has more than two million pixels, requires about 2MB to store with 256 colors. With TrueColor, the size of the picture jumps to a whopping 6.4MB. Fortunately, bitmap pictures can be compressed to reduce their size without noticeably distorting the image. Depending on the actual contents of the picture, a 6MB picture may be reduced to 250KB or less.

Bitmap picture files usually have filename extensions such as `.bmp`, `.gif`, `.jpg`, `.png`, or `.pcx`. Table 10-1 lists the bitmap file formats that PowerPoint supports.

If you have a choice in the matter, I recommend you use JPEG format images for photographs that you want to include in PowerPoint presentations because JPEG's built-in compression saves disk space.

| Table 10-1 | PowerPoint's Bitmap Picture File Formats |
|---|---|
| **Format** | **What It Is** |
| BMP | Garden variety Windows bitmap file, used by Windows Paint and many other programs |
| GIF | Graphics Interchange Format, a format commonly used for small Internet pictures |
| JPEG | JPEG, a common format for photographs that includes built-in compression |
| PCD | Kodak Photo CD format |
| PCT | Macintosh PICT files |
| PCX | A variant type of bitmap file, also used by Windows Paint |
| PNG | Portable Network Graphics file, an image format designed for Internet graphics |
| TGA | Targa files |
| TIFF | Tagged Image Format file, another bitmap program most often used for high-quality photographs |

## Victor, give me a vector

Besides bitmap pictures, the other category of picture files that you can use with PowerPoint are vector drawings. A *vector drawing* is a picture file that contains a detailed definition of each shape that makes up the image. Vector drawings are usually created with high-powered drawing programs such as Corel Draw! or Adobe Illustrator.

PowerPoint supports all the most popular vector drawing formats, as described in Table 10-2.

| Table 10-2 | PowerPoint's Vector File Formats |
|---|---|
| **Format** | **What It Is** |
| CDR | CorelDRAW!, a popular, upper-crust drawing program |
| CGM | Computer Graphics Metafiles |

*(continued)*

**Table 10-2** *(continued)*

| Format | What It Is |
|--------|-----------|
| DRW | Micrografx Designer or Micrografx Draw, two popular ooh-aah drawing programs |
| DXF | AutoCAD, a popular drafting program |
| EMF | An Enhanced Windows MetaFile picture |
| EPS | Encapsulated PostScript, a format used by some high-end drawing programs |
| WMF | Windows MetaFile, a format that many programs recognize |
| WPG | A WordPerfect drawing |

# Using Clip Art

Are you sitting down? Whether you buy PowerPoint by itself or get it as a part of Microsoft Office, you also get a collection of thousands of pictures, sound, and motion clips that you can pop directly into your presentations.

PowerPoint lets you access clip art through a special Clip Art task pane that lets you search for clip art by keyword. The Clip Art task pane makes it easy to find just the right picture to embellish your presentation.

The first time you access the clip art, a dialog box appears offering to search your entire hard disk and create a catalog of all the pictures it contains. I suggest you accept this offer so that you can use it to access your own picture files in addition to the clip art files that come with PowerPoint.

In addition to pictures, PowerPoint can also work sound and video clips. For more information about using sound and video, see Chapter 16.

Don't overdo the pictures. One surefire way to guarantee an amateurish look to your presentation is to load it down with three clip art pictures on every slide that all chime or go "zip" or "boing." Judicious use is much more effective.

# Dropping In Some Clip Art

The following steps explain how to drop clip art into your presentation:

1. **Move to the slide on which you want to plaster the clip art.**

   If you want the same clip art picture to appear on every slide, move to Slide Master View by choosing View➪Master➪Slide Master (or Shift+click the Slide View button).

2. **Choose Insert➪Picture➪Clip Art.**

   Sorry, PowerPoint offers no shortcut key for this command. If you like the mouse, though, you can click the Insert Clip Art button instead. It's the one with the picture of the little cartoon person located near the middle of the Drawing toolbar at the bottom of the screen.

3. **Behold the Insert Clip Art task pane in all its splendor.**

   After a brief moment's hesitation, the Clip Art task pane pops up, as shown in Figure 10-1.

4. **Type a keyword in the Search Text box, then click the Search button.**

   For example, to search for pictures of trombones, type **Trombone** in the Search text box, and then click Search.

   PowerPoint searches through the Clip Organizer to locate the clip art you're looking for, and then displays thumbnails of the pictures it finds in the Clip Art task pane.

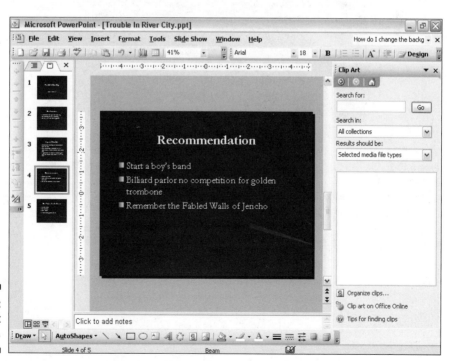

**Figure 10-1:** The Clip Art task pane.

5. **Click the picture that you want to use.**

   The picture is inserted on the current slide, as shown in Figure 10-2.

6. **If you're finished inserting pictures, click the Clip Art task pane's close button (the X in the upper right corner of the taskbar).**

   The task pane vanishes.

You'll probably want to move the picture and change its size. To find out how, see the next section, "Moving, Sizing, and Stretching Clip Art."

If you find a clip art picture you like, you can find other pictures that are drawn in a similar style by right-clicking the picture in the Clip Art task pane (or by clicking the down-arrow on the right side of the picture) and then choosing Find Similar Style.

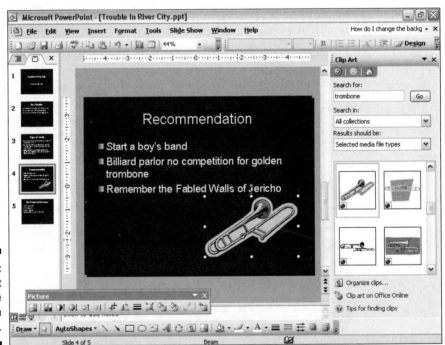

**Figure 10-2:** PowerPoint inserts the picture on the slide.

# Moving, Sizing, and Stretching Clip Art

Because PowerPoint chooses an arbitrary position on the slide to insert clip art, you undoubtedly want to move the clip art to a more convenient location. You probably also want to change the size of the clip art if it is too big or too small for your slide.

Follow these steps to force your inserted clip art into full compliance:

1. **Click the picture and drag it wherever you want.**

   You don't have to worry about clicking exactly the edge of the picture or one of its lines; just click anywhere in the picture and drag it around.

2. **Notice the eight handles. Drag one of them to resize the picture.**

   You can click and drag any of these handles to adjust the size of the picture. When you click one of the corner handles, the proportion of the picture stays the same as you change its size. When you drag one of the edge handles (top, bottom, left, or right) to change the size of the picture in just one dimension, you distort the picture's outlook as you go.

 When you resize a picture, the picture changes its position on the slide. As a result, you can count on moving it after you resize it. If you hold down the Ctrl key while dragging a handle, however, the picture becomes anchored at its center point as you resize it. Therefore, its position is unchanged, and you probably don't have to move it.

Stretching a clip art picture by dragging one of the edge handles can dramatically change the picture's appearance. For example, you can stretch an object vertically to make it look tall and thin or horizontally to make it look short and fat.

# Cropping a Picture

Sometimes, you want to cut off the edges of a picture so that you can include just part of the picture in your presentation. For example, you may have a picture of two people, only one of whom you like. You can use PowerPoint's cropping feature to cut off the other person.

To crop a picture, select the picture and click the Crop button located in the middle of the Picture toolbar. The selection handles change to special crop marks. You can then drag the crop marks around to cut off part of the picture. When you're satisfied, just click outside of the picture.

If you decide later that you don't like the cropping, you can right-click the picture and choose Format Picture from the menu that appears. Then, click the Reset button.

# Adding Embellishments to a Picture

PowerPoint enables you to draw attention to a clip art picture by drawing a box around it, shading its background, or adding a shadow. Figure 10-3 shows what these embellishments can look like.

## Adding borders and shading

To add a border to a picture, first select the picture. This brings up the Picture toolbar, which should appear floating somewhere near the picture. Click the Format Picture button (the one with the image of a bucket and a paintbrush) to summon the Format Picture dialog box. (You can also summon this dialog box by right-clicking the picture and choosing Format Picture from the menu that appears.) Next, click the Colors and Lines tab and play with the fill color and the line color, size, and style options as shown in Figure 10-4 until you're happy. Then click OK to see the results of your efforts.

If you want to draw a border around all four sides of a picture, you can just select the picture, click the Line Style button from the floating Picture toolbar, and then choose a line width from the drop-down menu that appears.

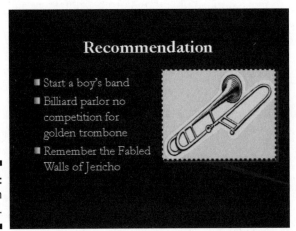

**Figure 10-3:**
Boxing in
a picture.

**Format Picture**

| Colors and Lines | Size | Position | Picture | Text Box | Web |

Crop from

Left: 0"     Top: 0"

Right: 0"     Bottom: 0"

Image control

Color: Automatic

Brightness: ‹ ›  50 %

Contrast: ‹ ›  50 %

Compress...     Recolor...   Reset

OK   Cancel   Preview

**Figure 10-4:**
The Format
Picture
dialog box.

## Adding shadows

To add a shadow, click the Shadow button in the Drawing toolbar at the
bottom of the screen. This brings up a menu of shadow styles. Pick the style
that you want by clicking the style in this menu.

If you apply a shadow to a picture to which you have not applied a fill color,
the shadow is applied to the picture itself, as shown in the trombone on the
right in Figure 10-5. In this slide, both clip art pictures have a shadow. The one
on the right also has a fill color and border, but the one on the left does not.

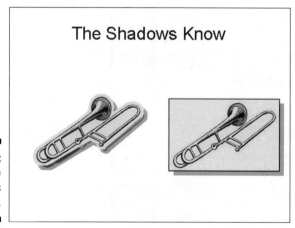

**Figure 10-5:**
The
shadows
know.

You can also apply a shadow by choosing Shadow Settings from the Shadow menu that appears when you click the Shadow button. This brings up a Shadow toolbar that lets you control the size, position, and color of the shadow.

# Editing a Clip Art Picture

Sometimes one of the clip art pictures supplied with PowerPoint is close but not exactly what you want. In that case, you can insert the picture and then edit it to make whatever changes are needed. For example, Figure 10-6 shows two versions of the same clip art picture. One has been edited to show the effects of an earthquake on a famous Seattle landmark.

You can't directly edit a clip art picture. Instead, you must first convert the picture to an equivalent bunch of PowerPoint shape objects. Then you can individually select and edit the objects by using the shape-editing tools described in Chapter 14.

The following steps describe how to edit a clip art picture:

1. **Click the picture that you want to edit, and then click the Draw button on the drawing toolbar and choose the Ungroup command.**

   PowerPoint displays the warning message that indicates you are about to convert a clip art picture to a PowerPoint drawing so that you can edit it. Feel free to ignore this pathetic little warning.

2. **Click Yes to convert the picture.**

   The picture is converted and will now obey your editing commands.

3. **Now ungroup the picture again.**

   Don't ask me why, but PowerPoint isn't smart enough to remember that before it displayed the warning dialog box, you were trying to ungroup the picture. Because PowerPoint forgot to ungroup the picture, you have to do it again. This time it will work.

4. **Now edit the picture.**

   The clip art picture is converted to an equivalent group of PowerPoint shape objects, so you can use the PowerPoint shape-editing tools to change their appearance. You can drag any of the control handles to reshape an object, or you can change colors or add new stuff to the picture. See Chapter 14 for the details on editing PowerPoint shape objects.

After you've ungrouped and edited a picture, you may want to regroup it. You're much less likely to pull the nose off someone's face if the face is a group rather than a bunch of ungrouped ellipse objects.

## Seattle Skew

Before                    After

**Figure 10-6:**
You can edit
a picture to
change its
appearance.

When you convert a picture to PowerPoint objects, you're actually placing a copy of the clip art picture in your presentation. Any changes that you make to the picture are reflected only in your presentation; the original version of the clip art picture is unaffected.

# Colorizing a Clip Art Picture

After inserting a clip art picture into your presentation, you may find that the colors used in the clip art clash with the colors that you've chosen for the presentation's color scheme. Never fear! PowerPoint allows you to selectively change the colors used in a clip art picture. Just follow these steps:

1. **Select the picture that you want to colorize and then click the Recolor Picture button in the floating Picture toolbar that appears when you select the picture.**

   The Recolor Picture dialog box appears, as shown in Figure 10-7.

2. **In the list of Original colors, click the original color you want to change.**

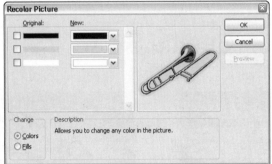

**Figure 10-7:**
Colorizing
your
pictures.

3. **From the drop-down list adjacent to the original color you chose, select a new color to replace the chosen color.**

   The drop-down list displays a standard color menu, with the colors from the color scheme and an Other Color command that brings up a dialog box that allows you to choose a custom color.

   If you want to change the fill color but leave the line color unchanged, click the Fills option button.

4. **Repeat Steps 2 and 3 for any other colors you want to change.**

5. **Click OK when you're finished.**

Unfortunately, you can't recolor bitmap images in this way. To change colors in a bitmap image, you have to use a painting program.

# Getting Clip Art from the Internet

As if the vast collection of clip art that comes with Office and PowerPoint isn't enough, Microsoft also maintains a clip library on the Internet that you can use. If you have access to the Internet, you can access this additional clip art library by clicking Clip Art at Microsoft.com at the bottom of the Clip Art task pane. This opens a separate Internet Explorer window, which you can then use to search for additional clip art images.

If you find a clip art image that you want, you can mark it for later download. Then, after you've found all the images you want to download, you can choose an option that allows you to download the images directly into Clip Organizer. You can then call up the images using the Clip Art task pane as described earlier in this chapter.

# *Inserting Pictures from a File*

If you happen to already have an image file on your computer that you want to insert into a presentation, PowerPoint lets you insert the file by Insert⇨ Picture⇨From File. This bypasses the Clip Art task pane altogether. These steps show you how:

1. **Move to the slide on which you want to splash a picture.**

   If you want the clip art to show up on every slide, conjure up Slide Master View by choosing View⇨Master⇨Slide Master (or Shift+click the Slide View button).

2. **Choose Insert⇨Picture⇨From File.**

   If you prefer, click the Insert Picture button (the one whose icon looks like a pretty mountain sunset). Either way, you are rewarded with the Insert Picture dialog box, shown in Figure 10-8.

**Figure 10-8:** The Insert Picture dialog box.

3. **Dig through the bottom of your hard drive until you find the file that you want.**

   The picture you want may be anywhere. Fortunately, the Insert Picture dialog box has all the controls you need to search high and low until you find the file. Just click the icons at the left side of the box or click the Look In text box, and you are halfway there.

4. **Click the file and then click Insert.**

   You're done!

You also can paste a picture directly into PowerPoint by way of the Clipboard. Anything that you can copy to the Clipboard you can paste into PowerPoint. For example, you can doodle a sketch in Paintbrush, copy it, and then zap over to PowerPoint and paste it. Voilà — instant picture!

If you want to narrow your search to files of a particular type, use the Files of Type drop-down list box, and then choose the type of file that you want to look for.

# Inserting a Picture Directly from a Scanner or Digital Camera

If you have a scanner connected to your computer, you can insert pictures from it directly into PowerPoint. First, put the picture you want to scan into your scanner. Then, call up the Insert➪Picture➪From Scanner or Camera command. This action summons the dialog box shown in Figure 10-9. If you have more than one imaging device connected to your computer, choose the device that you want to use from the drop-down list. Then, click Insert and wait a minute or so for the scanner to scan the picture and insert it into your presentation. You'll probably need to crop and resize the picture to get it just right.

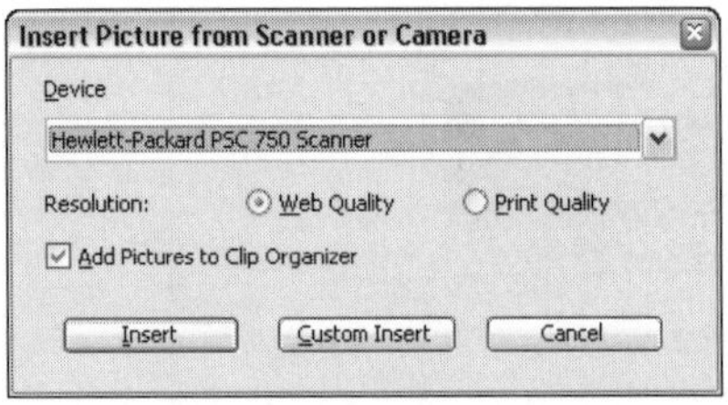

**Figure 10-9:**
The Insert Picture from Scanner or Camera dialog box.

| Insert Picture from Scanner or Camera |
| --- |
| Device |
| Hewlett-Packard PSC 750 Scanner |
| Resolution: ⊙ Web Quality ○ Print Quality |
| ☑ Add Pictures to Clip Organizer |
| [ Insert ] [ Custom Insert ] [ Cancel ] |

If you prefer to crop the picture before you scan it or set other scanning options, click Custom Insert instead. This brings up a dialog box that lets you set various options for the scanner.

You can also use the Custom Insert button to retrieve pictures directly from a digital camera. First, connect the camera to the computer via its USB cable. Then, choose Insert➪Picture➪From Scanner or Camera, select the camera from the list, and click the Custom Insert command. This brings up a dialog box that lets you select the picture that you want to insert.

# Chapter 11

# A Slide of a Different Color

*W*elcome to the Wonderful World of Color. Here is your opportunity to unleash the repressed artist hidden deep within you. Take up your palette, grasp your brush firmly, and prepare to attack the empty canvas of your barren slides.

PowerPoint 2003 enables you to use more than 16 million colors, but you shouldn't feel obligated to use them all right away. Pace yourself. Although now would be a good time to grow a goatee or to cut off your ear.

## Using Color Schemes

The PowerPoint templates come with built-in color schemes, which are coordinated sets of colors chosen by color professionals. Microsoft paid these people enormous sums of money to debate the merits of using mauve text on a teal background. You can use these professionally designed color schemes, or you can create your own if you think that you have a better eye than the Microsoft-hired color guns.

As far as I'm concerned, the PowerPoint color schemes are the best thing to come along since Peanut M&Ms. Without color schemes, people like me are free to pick and choose from among the 16 million or so colors that PowerPoint lets you incorporate into your slides. The resulting slides can easily appear next to Cher and Roseanne in *People* magazine's annual "Worst Dressed of the Year" issue.

Each color scheme has eight colors, with each color designated for a particular use, as shown in this list:

- **Background color:** Used for the slide background.

- **Text-and-lines color:** Used for any text or drawn lines that appear on the slide, with the exception of the title text (described later in this list). This is usually a color that contrasts with the background color. If the background color is dark, the text-and-lines color is generally light, and vice versa.

- **Shadows color:** Used to produce shadow effects for objects drawn on the slide. It is usually a darker version of the background color, unless the background color is very dark. In that case, the shadow color is often a lighter version of the background color.

- **Title text color:** Used for the slide's title text. Like the text-and-lines color, the title text color contrasts with the background color so that the text is readable. The title text usually complements the text-and-lines color to provide an evenly balanced effect. (That sounds like something an artist would say, doesn't it?)

- **Fills color:** When you create an object, such as a rectangle or an ellipse, this color is the default fill color to color the object.

- **Accent colors:** The last three colors in the color scheme. They are used for odds and ends that you can add to your slide. You may use them to color the bars in a bar chart, for example, or the slices in a pie chart. Two of these accent colors are also used to indicate hyperlinks.

Each slide in your presentation can have its own color scheme. The Slide Master also has a color scheme, which is used for all slides that don't specify their own deviant color scheme. To ensure that your slides have a uniform look, simply allow them to pick up the color scheme from the Slide Master. If you want one slide to stand out from the other slides in your presentation, assign it a different color scheme.

PowerPoint picks up the initial color scheme for a presentation from the template on which the presentation is based to serve as a part of the template's Slide Master. However, each template also includes several alternate color schemes, which are designed to complement the main color scheme for the template. You can change the Master scheme later, but if you apply a new template, the new template's scheme overrides any change that you made to the original template's color scheme.

If you find a template that you like but aren't happy with any of its color schemes, you can create your own. The easiest way to do this is to choose a scheme that's close to the colors you want and then modify the scheme's colors. I present the procedure to do so later in this chapter.

You can override the Master color scheme for an individual slide. You can also change the color for any object to any color in the scheme, or to any other color known to science. You can find step-by-step instructions later in this chapter.

Don't get all in a tizzy about color schemes if you plan to print overhead slides on a black-and-white laser printer. The slides look dazzling on-screen, but all those stunning colors are printed in boring shades of gray.

## Using a different color scheme

If you don't like your presentation's color scheme, change it! Here's a simple way:

1. **Switch to Normal View if you aren't already there.**

   Click the Normal View button or choose View⇨Normal.

2. **Choose Format⇨Slide Design.**

   The Slide Design task pane appears to the right of the slide.

3. **Click Color Schemes at the top of the Slide Design task pane.**

   The Color Schemes task pane appears, as shown in Figure 11-1. As you can see, the Color Scheme task pane shows the color schemes that are available for your presentation.

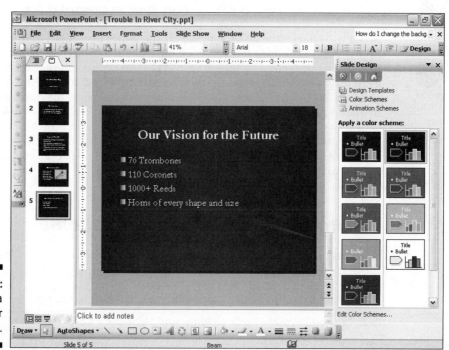

**Figure 11-1:**
Changing a slide's color scheme.

### 4. Click the color scheme that you want to use.

You're done!

For most presentations, you'll want to use the same color scheme for all the slides in the presentation. However, in some cases you may want to use two or more color schemes to draw attention to certain slides in your presentation or to give your audience an immediate visual clue to your slide's contents. For example, if a market-analysis presentation frequently shifts back and forth between current data and last year's data, consider using a different color scheme for the slides that depict last year's data. That way, the audience is less likely to become confused.

You can change the color scheme for a single slide or to just certain slides. To do so, select the slide or slides that you want to recolor in the thumbnail view at the left side of the PowerPoint window, click the down-arrow that appears next to the color scheme you want use, and then choose Apply to Selected Slides.

To change the color of all slides in the presentation, just click the color scheme you want to use or click the down-arrow next to the color scheme and choose Apply to All.

 If only one slide is selected when you click a color scheme, PowerPoint changes the color scheme for all slides in the presentation as if you chose Apply to All. However, if two or more slides are selected, PowerPoint changes just the selected slides as if you clicked Apply to Selected Slides.

 When you change the color scheme for the entire presentation by clicking Apply to All, any slides to which you have applied a custom color scheme are changed as well. For example, suppose that you create a presentation using a color scheme that has a deep blue background, and you highlight certain slides by applying an alternate (light blue) color scheme for those slides. You then decide that you'd rather use a maroon background for the bulk of the slides, so you choose Format➪Slide Color Scheme, select the new color scheme, and click Apply to All. After you do so, you discover that all slides are changed to the maroon background — even the ones that you had highlighted with the light blue color scheme.

## *Changing colors in a color scheme*

To change one or more of the colors in the current color scheme, follow these steps:

### 1. Select the slide whose color scheme you want to change.

### 2. Choose Format➪Slide Design, and then click Color Scheme.

The Color Scheme task pane appears. Refer to Figure 11-1 if you've forgotten what it looks like.

3. **Click Edit Color Schemes at the bottom of the Color Scheme task pane.**

   The Edit Color Scheme dialog box appears, as shown in Figure 11-2.

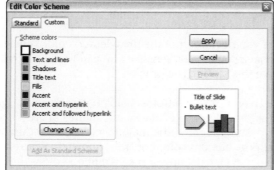

**Figure 11-2:**
Editing a
color
scheme.

4. **Click the color box that you want to change.**

   To change the background color, for example, click the Background color box.

5. **Click the Change Color button.**

   The dialog box shown in Figure 11-3 appears. As you can see, PowerPoint displays what looks like a tie-dyed version of Chinese checkers.

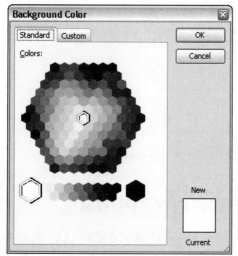

**Figure 11-3:**
Changing
a color.

6. **Click the color that you want and click OK.**

   If you want white or black or a shade of gray, click one of the color hexagons at the bottom of the dialog box. Otherwise, click one of the colored hexagons. After you click OK, you zip back to the Color Scheme dialog box (refer to Figure 11-2).

7. **Choose Apply.**

   The change is applied to the color scheme.

Be warned that after you deviate from the preselected color scheme combinations, you better have some color sense. If you can't tell chartreuse from lime, you better leave this stuff to the pros.

The Standard tab of the Background Color dialog box (shown in Figure 11-3) shows 127 popular colors, plus white, black, and shades of gray. If you want to use a color that doesn't appear in the dialog box, click the Custom tab. This step draws forth the custom color controls, shown in Figure 11-4. From this dialog box, you can construct any of the 16 million colors that are theoretically possible with PowerPoint. You need a Ph.D. in physics to figure out how to adjust the Red, Green, and Blue controls, though. Mess around with this stuff if you want, but you're on your own.

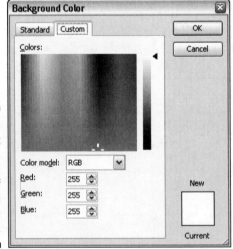

**Figure 11-4:** PowerPoint offers billions and billions of colors from which you can choose.

# *Shading the Slide Background*

You may have noticed that the slide background used in many of the PowerPoint templates is not a solid color. Instead, the color is gradually shaded from top to bottom. This type of shading — called a *gradient fill* — creates an interesting visual effect. For example, look at the slide shown in

Figure 11-5. This slide was based on the templates supplied with PowerPoint, but I modified the color scheme and the background shading to achieve the effect that I wanted.

**Trouble in River City**

Professor Harold Hill

**Figure 11-5:**
Using a
gradient fill
to create an
interesting
background.

Shading for the slide background works much like the color scheme. If you apply it to all slides, the Slide Master is also affected so that any new slides pick up the new shading. Alternatively, you can apply shading to an individual slide. These steps show you how to shade the slide background:

1. **Choose the slide that you want to shade.**

   This step isn't necessary if you want to apply the shading to all slides in the presentation.

2. **Summon Format⇨Background.**

   The Background dialog box appears.

3. **Select Fill Effects from the Background Fill drop-down list.**

   The Background Fill drop-down list is near the bottom of the Background dialog box. When you choose Fill Effects from this list, the Fill Effects dialog box appears, as shown in Figure 11-6.

4. **On the Gradient tab page, choose the shade style that you want.**

   Start by selecting whether you want to use a one-color shade, in which a single color fades to white or black, or a two-color shade, in which one color fades into another. Then play with the controls until you get the fill to look the way you want. You can choose the colors to use for the fill, the transparency level, the direction, and several variants for each option.

   Alternatively, you can select one of several preset shadings by picking the Preset option. The preset shading options include Early Sunset, Nightfall, Rainbow, and several other interesting effects.

5. **Click OK to return to the Background dialog box and then click Apply or Apply To All.**

   Clicking the Apply button applies the shading to just the slide or slides that you chose (in Step 1). Clicking Apply To All applies the shading to all slides.

   You're done! Admire your work. Play with it some more if you don't like it.

When you apply a template, any background shading specified for the template's Masters is applied along with the color scheme.

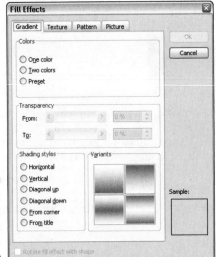

**Figure 11-6:**
The Fill
Effects
dialog box.

# Using Other Background Effects

Besides gradient fills, if you choose Format⇨Background, you can select several other types of interesting background effects. You can access all these effects — Texture, Pattern, and Picture — via the tabs in the Fill Effects dialog box, shown in Figure 11-7.

If you select the Texture tab, the dialog box shown in Figure 11-7 appears. Here you can choose one of 24 textures to give your presentation that polished Formica look.

If you select the Pattern tab, you get another dialog box from which you can choose any of 48 different patterns using your choice of foreground and background colors.

If you click the Picture tab and then click the Select Picture button, a dialog box appears that allows you to select a picture to be used as a background for your slides. You may have to do some searching to find the image that you want.

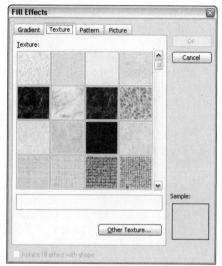

**Figure 11-7:**
Creating a
textured
background.

# Coloring Text and Objects

Normally, the color scheme that you choose for a slide determines the color of the various objects on the slide. If the text color is yellow, for example, all text on the slide is yellow (except the title text, which is controlled by the color scheme's Title Text color). Similarly, if the fill color is orange, any filled objects on the slide are orange.

If you change the colors in the color scheme, all the objects on the slide that follow the scheme are affected. But what if you want to change the color of just one object without changing the scheme or affecting other similar objects on the slide? No problemo. PowerPoint enables you to override the scheme color for any object on a slide. The following sections explain how to do so.

## Applying color to text

To change the color of a text object, first highlight the text whose color you want to change. Then, click the down arrow next to the Font Color button on either the Formatting toolbar or the Drawing toolbar. This action reveals a

Color menu from which you can choose the color for the text. (You can also access this Color menu by summoning the Format⇨Font dialog box and using the Color drop-down list.) If you want to use a color that isn't in the current color scheme, choose More Colors to find a color that you like.

If you use the More Colors option to assign a color, PowerPoint automatically adds the color you chose to the Color menu. You can distinguish your colors from the color scheme colors because your custom colors are always in the bottom line of eight complementary colors.

In addition, if you select a color via the Font Color button, a little color bar at the bottom of the Font Color button changes to the color you select. You can apply this color to additional text simply by clicking the Font Color button.

## Changing an object's fill or line color

When you draw an object such as a rectangle or an ellipse, PowerPoint fills in the object with the color scheme's fill color and draws the object's outline using the color scheme's line color. You can change either of these colors by using the Fill Color and Line Color buttons on the Drawing toolbar. Just follow these steps:

1. **Select the object whose fill color you want to change.**

2. **To change the object's fill color, click the down arrow next to the Fill Color button and choose a color from the menu that appears.**

3. **To change the object's line color, click the down arrow next to the Line Color button and choose a color from the menu that appears.**

   That's all!

To create a transparent object — that is, an object that has no fill color — click the Fill Color button and choose No Fill. To create an object that has no outline, click the Line Color button and choose No Line.

The Fill Color button includes a Fill Effects command that lets you apply gradient fills, patterns, textures, or pictures to any object. The selections for these features are the same as shown in Figures 11-6 and 11-7.

## Creating a semitransparent object

If you like scary movies, you can create a ghostly semitransparent fill for an object. This allows objects behind the semitransparent object to show through. To apply this effect, select the object that you want to turn into a ghost, and then choose the command that appears at the bottom of the

Format menu. The name of this command varies depending on the type of object that you select. For example, if you select a text box, choose Format⇨Text Box. However, if you select an AutoShape object, such as a circle or a rectangle, choose Format⇨AutoShape.

Either way, the dialog box shown in Figure 11-8 appears. You can then slide the Transparency slider to set the amount of transparency for the object. If you move the Transparency slider all the way to the left (0%), the object will be a solid color. Increasing the Transparency value from 0% lets more and more of whatever lies behind the object show through. If you move the slider all the way to the right (100%), the object will be completely transparent, so the object's fill color won't show at all. Click OK when you're done.

**Figure 11-8:**
Making
a ghost.

# Copying color from an existing object

If you want to force one object to adopt the color of another object, you can use a fancy tool called the Format Painter. It sucks up the formatting of one object and then spits it out onto another object at your command. It's a bit messy, but it gets the job done. (You should see it eat.)

To use the Format Painter, follow these steps:

1. **Choose the object whose color you like.**

   You can select a bit of text or an entire object.

2. **Click the Format Painter button on the Standard toolbar.**

   The Format Painter button is the one with the big paintbrush on it. Clicking it sucks up the good color.

**3. Click the object whose color you don't like.**

This step spits out the desirable color onto the object.

In addition to the fill color, the Format Painter also picks up other object attributes, such as shading, textures, optional trim package, and aluminum alloy hubcaps.

If you want to apply one object's format to several objects, select the object whose color you like and then double-click the Format Painter. Now you can click as many objects as you want to apply the first object's format to. When you're done, press the Esc key.

# Chapter 12

# Yes, Master! (Igor's Favorite Chapter)

*W*ant to add a bit of text to every slide in your presentation? Or maybe add your name and phone number at the bottom of your audience handouts? Or place a picture of Rush Limbaugh at the extreme right side of each page of your speaker notes?

*Masters* are the surefire way to add something to every slide. No need to toil separately at each slide. Add something to the Master and it automatically shows up on every slide. Remove it from the Master and — poof! — it disappears from every slide. Very convenient.

Masters govern all aspects of a slide's appearance: its background color, objects that appear on every slide, text that appears on all slides, and more.

## Working with Masters

In PowerPoint, a Master governs the appearance of all the slides or pages in a presentation. Each presentation has at least four Masters:

 ✔ **Slide Master:** Dictates the format of your slides. You work with this Master most often as you tweak your slides to cosmetic perfection.

 ✔ **Title Master:** Prescribes the layout of the presentation's title slide. This Master allows you to give your title slides a different look from the other slides in your presentation.

 ✔ **Handout Master:** Controls the look of printed handouts.

 ✔ **Notes Master:** Determines the characteristics of printed speaker notes.

Each Master specifies the appearance of text (font, size, and color, for example), the slide's background color, the layout of placeholders on the slide, and any additional text or other objects that you want to appear on each slide or page.

Masters are not optional. Every presentation has them. You can, however, override the formatting of objects contained in the Master for a particular slide. This capability enables you to vary the appearance of slides when necessary.

PowerPoint allows you to create more than one Slide or Title Master in a single presentation, so you can mix two or more slide designs in your presentations. That's why I said a presentation has *at least* four masters. If you have more than one Slide or Title Master, a presentation will have more than four masters altogether. Note, however, that you can still have only one Handout or Notes Master in each presentation. For more information about using more than one Slide or Title Master, see the section "Yes, You Can Serve Two Masters" at the end of this chapter.

# Modifying the Slide Master

If you don't like the layout of your slides, call up the Slide Master and do something about it, as shown in these steps:

1. **Choose View⇨Master⇨Slide Master or hold down the Shift key while clicking the Slide View button.**

   If you choose View⇨Master, a submenu appears listing the three masters (Slide, Handout, and Notes). Choose Slide Master to call up the Slide Master.

2. **Behold the Slide Master in all its splendor.**

   Figure 12-1 shows a typical Slide Master. You can see the placeholders for the slide title and body text in addition to other background objects. Note also that the Slide Master includes placeholders for three objects that appear at the bottom of each slide: the Date Area, Footer Area, and Number Area. These special areas are used when you choose View➪Header and Footer and are described later in this chapter, under the heading "Using Headers and Footers."

A thumbnail of all the Slide and Title Masters in your presentation is shown on the left side of the screen. In most cases, you'll see just two thumbnails here: one for the Slide Master and one for the Title Master. If your presentation has more than one Slide Master, you'll see additional thumbnails.

If the title slide was selected when you called up Slide Master View, you'll see the Title Master instead of the Slide Master. Do not fear! Just press the Page Up key to summon the Slide Master.

**3. Make any formatting changes that you want.**

Select the text to which you want to apply a new style and make your formatting changes. If you want all the slide titles to be in italics, for example, select the title text and press Ctrl+I or click the Italic button on the Formatting toolbar.

If you're not sure how to change text formats, consult Chapter 9.

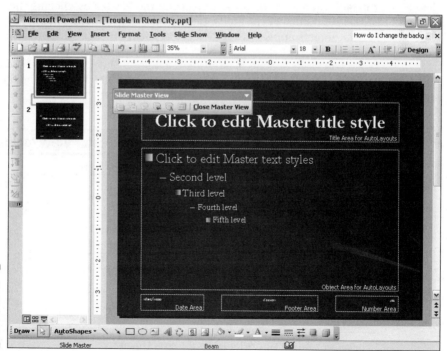

**Figure 12-1:**
Slide
Master
View.

**4. Click the Close Master View button on the Slide Master View toolbar to return to Normal View.**

Alternatively, you can just click the Normal View button. Either way, you'll be whisked back to your slides. The effect of any changes you made to the Slide Master should be apparent immediately.

PowerPoint applies character formats such as bold, italics, font size, and font to entire paragraphs when you work in Slide Master View. You don't have to select the entire paragraph before you apply a format; simply click anywhere in the paragraph.

Notice that the body object contains paragraphs for five outline levels formatted with different point sizes, indentations, and bullet styles. If you want to change the way an outline level is formatted, this is the place to do so.

You can type all you want in the title or object area placeholders, but the text that you type doesn't appear on the slides. The text that appears in these placeholders is provided only so that you can see the effect of the formatting changes you apply. (To insert text that appears on each slide, see the next section, "Adding recurring text.")

You can edit any of the other objects on the Master by clicking them. Unlike the title and object area placeholders, any text that you type in other Slide Master objects appears exactly as you type it on each slide.

When you work in Slide Master View, a helpful Slide Master View toolbar appears. Table 12-1 summarizes the functions of its buttons. You'll learn what many of these buttons do as you read this chapter.

| Table 12-1 | Buttons on the Slide Master View toolbar |
|---|---|
| *Button* | *What It Does* |
|  | Inserts a new Slide Master |
|  | Inserts a new Title Master |
|  | Deletes the selected master |
|  | Preserves the selected master |
|  | Renames the selected master |

| Button | What It Does |
|---|---|
| | Displays the Master Layout dialog box |
| Close Master View | Returns to Normal View |

# Adding recurring text

To add recurring text to each slide, follow this procedure:

1. **Call up the Slide Master if it's not displayed already.**

   You can choose View➪Master➪Slide Master, or you can Shift+click the Slide View button.

2. **Click the Text Box button on the Drawing toolbar.**

   This step highlights the Text Box button. The mouse cursor turns into an upside-down cross.

3. **Click where you want to add text.**

   PowerPoint places a text object at that location.

4. **Type the text that you want to appear on each slide.**

   For example: **Call 1-800-555-NERD today! Don't delay! Operators are standing by!**

5. **Format the text however you want.**

   For example, if you want bold, press Ctrl+B.

6. **Click the Normal View button to return to your presentation.**

   Now's the time to gloat over your work. Lasso some coworkers and show 'em how proud you are.

You can add other types of objects to the Slide Master, too. You can add clip art, pictures, or even a video or sound clip. Anything that you can add to an individual slide can be added to the Slide Master.

After you place an object on the Slide Master, you can grab it with the mouse and move it around or resize it in any way you want. The object appears in the same location and size on each slide.

To delete an object from the Slide Master, click it and press the Delete key. To delete a text object, you must first click the object and then click again on the object frame. Then press Delete.

If you can't highlight the object no matter how many times you click it, you have probably returned to Slide View. Shift+click the Slide View button or choose View➪Master➪Slide Master again to call up the Slide Master.

## Changing the Master color scheme

You can use the Slide Master to change the color scheme used for all slides in a presentation. To do that, follow these steps:

1. **Choose View➪Master➪Slide Master or Shift+click the Normal View button at the bottom left of the PowerPoint window to summon the Slide Master.**

2. **Choose the Format➪Slide Design to call up the Slide Design task pane. Then click Color Schemes and apply the color scheme that you want to use.**

   Treat yourself to a bag of Cheetos if it works the first time. If it doesn't work, have a bag of Cheetos anyway. Then rub all that orange gunk that sticks to your fingers on the computer screen. That will turn your Slide Master orange, at least temporarily.

PowerPoint color schemes are hefty enough that I have devoted an entire chapter to them. Go back to Chapter 11 if you forgot how they work.

If you don't have a color printer, don't waste your time messing with the color scheme unless you're going to be giving your presentation on-screen or with a projector. Mauve, teal, azure, and cerulean all look like gray when they're printed on a non-color laser printer.

Professionals who are colorblind in no more than one eye chose the PowerPoint color schemes. Stick to these schemes to avoid embarrassing color combinations! (I wish that my sock drawer came with a similar color-scheme feature.)

If you want to adjust the shading that's applied to the background slide color, choose Format➪Background. Chapter 11 walks you through this feature.

# Changing the Title Master

PowerPoint keeps a separate Master layout for title slides. That way, you can give your title slides a different layout than the other slides in your presentation. In Slide Master View, a thumbnail of the Title Master appears beneath the Slide Master thumbnail on the left side of the screen. Click the Title Master's thumbnail and the Title Master appears.

Figure 12-2 shows a Title Master. As you can see, it contains the same layout elements as the Slide Master, except that the "Object Area for AutoLayouts" is replaced with "Subtitle Area for AutoLayouts."

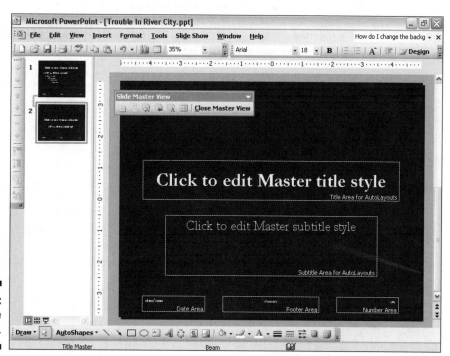

**Figure 12-2:**
A Title
Master.

# Adjusting the Handout and Notes Masters

Like the Slide Master, the Handout and Notes Masters contain formatting information that's automatically applied to your presentation. This section tells you how you can modify these Masters.

## Changing the Handout Master

Follow these simple steps to change the Handout Master:

1. **Choose View⇨Master⇨Handout Master or hold down the Shift key and click the Slide Sorter View button.**

   The Handout Master rears its ugly head, as shown in Figure 12-3.

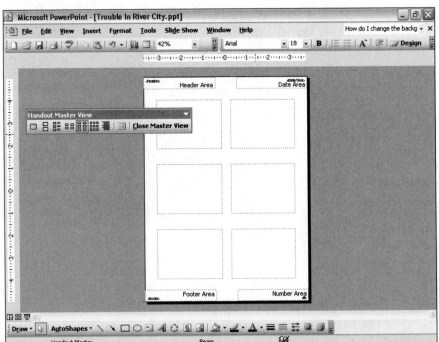

**Figure 12-3:**
The
Handout
Master.

**2. Mess around with it.**

The Handout Master shows the arrangement of handouts for slides printed two, three, four, six and nine per page, plus the arrangement for printing outlines. You can switch among these different handout layouts by clicking the buttons on the floating Handout Master toolbar. Unfortunately, you can't move, resize, or delete the slide and outline placeholders that appear in the Handout Master. You *can,* however, add or change elements that you want to appear on each handout page, such as your name and phone number, a page number, and maybe a good lawyer joke.

**3. Click Close Master View in the Handout Master View toolbar.**

You are returned to Normal View.

**4. Print a handout to see if your changes worked.**

Handout Master elements are invisible until you print them, so you should print at least one handout page to check your work.

When you print handout pages, the slides are formatted according to the Slide Master. You can't change the appearance of the slides from the Handout Master.

# Changing the Notes Master

Notes pages consist of a reduced image of the slide, plus notes that you type to go along with the slide. For more information about creating and using notes pages, refer to Chapter 5.

When printed, notes pages are formatted according to the Notes Master. To change the Notes Master, follow these steps:

**1. Choose View⇨Master⇨Notes Master.**

The Notes Master comes to life, as shown in Figure 12-4.

**2. Indulge yourself.**

The Notes Master contains two main placeholders — one for your notes text and the other for the slide. You can move or change the size of either of these objects, and you can change the format of the text in the notes placeholder. You also can add or change elements that you want to appear on each handout page. Also notice the convenient placement of the header, footer, date, and page number blocks.

**3. Click Close Master View in the Notes Master View toolbar.**

You are returned to Normal View.

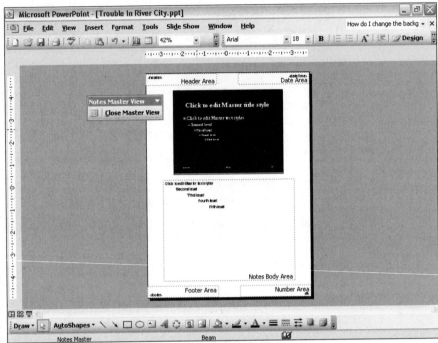

Figure 12-4:
The Notes
Master.

**4. Print your notes to see if your changes worked.**

If you prefer, choose File➪Print Preview to check out your notes pages without actually committing them to paper.

At the least, add page numbers to your speaker notes. That way, if you drop a stack of notes pages without page numbers, you'll be able to quickly sort them back into order.

If public speaking gives you severe stomach cramps, add the text "Just picture them naked" to the Notes Master. It works every time for me.

# Using Masters

You don't have to do anything special to apply the formats from a master to your slide; all slides automatically pick up the master format unless you specify otherwise. So this section really should be titled "Not Using Masters" because it talks about how to *not* use the formats provided by masters.

## *Overriding the master text style*

To override the text style specified by a Slide or Title Master, simply format the text however you want while you're working in Normal View. The formatting changes you make apply only to the selected text. The Slide and Title Masters are not affected.

The only way to change one of the masters is to do it directly by switching to the appropriate Master View. Thus, any formatting changes you make while in Slide View affect only that slide.

If you change the layout or formatting of text elements on a slide (for example, if you move the title placeholder or change the title font) and then decide that you liked it better the way it was, you can quickly reapply the text style from the Slide Master. Choose Format⇨Slide Layout to bring up the Slide Layout task pane. Then click the arrow to the right of the master you want to reapply and choose Reapply Layout from the menu that appears.

## *Hiding background objects*

Slide and Title Masters enable you to add background objects that appear on every slide in your presentation. You can, however, hide the background objects for selected slides. You can also change the background color or effect used for an individual slide. These steps show you how:

1. **Display the slide that you want to show with a plain background.**

2. **Choose Format⇨Background.**

   The Background dialog box appears, as shown in Figure 12-5. For notes, use Format⇨Notes Background. (The Notes Background dialog box looks much like the Background dialog box; the only difference is their titles.)

**Figure 12-5:**
The
Background
dialog box.

3. **Check the Omit Background Graphics from Master check box.**

Check this box if you want to hide the master's background objects.

4. **Change the Background Fill if you want.**

You can change to a different background color, or you can add an effect such as a pattern fill or a texture. These details are covered in Chapter 11.

5. **Click the Apply button or press Enter.**

If you checked the Omit Background Graphics from Master check box (Step 3), the background objects from the Slide Master vanish from the active slide. If you changed the background color or effect, you see that change, too.

To omit background graphics from all slides in the presentation, click Apply All instead of Apply in Step 5. (Or better yet, remove the unwanted object from the Slide Master!)

Hiding background objects or changing the background color or effect applies only to the current slide. Other slides are unaffected.

If you want to remove some but not all the background objects from a single slide, try this trick:

1. **Follow the preceding Steps 1 through 5 to hide background objects for the slide.**

2. **Call up the Slide Master (View⇨Master⇨Slide Master).**

3. **Hold down the Shift key and click each object that you want to appear.**

4. **Press Ctrl+C to copy these objects to the Clipboard.**

5. **Return to Slide View.**

6. **Press Ctrl+V to paste the objects from the Clipboard.**

7. **Choose Draw⇨Order⇨Send to Back if the background objects obscure other slide objects or text.**

The Draw menu is found on the Drawing toolbar.

# Using Headers and Footers

Headers and footers provide a convenient way to place repeating text at the top or bottom of each slide, handout, or notes page. You can add the time and date, slide number or page number, or any other information that you want to appear on each slide or page, such as your name or the title of your presentation.

The PowerPoint Slide and Title Masters include three placeholders for such information:

- ✔ The *date area* can be used to display a date and time.
- ✔ The *number area* can be used to display the slide number.
- ✔ The *footer area* can be used to display any text that you want to see on each slide.

In addition, Handout and Notes Masters include a fourth placeholder, the *header area,* which provides an additional area for text that you want to see on each page.

Although the date, number, and footer areas normally appear at the bottom of the slide in the Slide and Title Masters, you can move them to the top by switching to Slide or Title Master View and then dragging the placeholders to the top of the slide.

## Adding a date, number, or footer to slides

To add a date, a slide number, or a footer to your slides, follow these steps:

1. **Choose View⇨Header and Footer.**

   The Header and Footer dialog box appears, as shown in Figure 12-6. (If necessary, click the Slide tab so that you see the slide footer options as shown in the figure.)

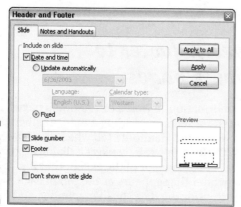

**Figure 12-6:**
The Header and Footer dialog box.

2. **To display the date, check the Date and Time check box. Then select the date format that you want in the list box beneath the Update Automatically option button.**

Alternatively, you can select the Fixed radio button, then type any text that you want in the Fixed text box. The text that you type appears in the Date area of the Slide or Title Master.

If you're the sort of bloke who begins a presentation with "G'day mates!" then you may want to change the Language and Calendar Type settings.

3. **To display slide numbers, check the Slide Number check box.**

4. **To display a footer on each slide, check the Footer check box and then type the text that you want to appear on each slide in the Footer text box.**

   For example, you may type your name, your company name, a subliminal message, or the name of your presentation.

5. **If you want the date, number, and footer to appear on every slide except for the title slide, check the Don't Show on Title Slide check box.**

6. **Click Apply to All.**

If you're going to be giving a presentation on a certain date in the future (for example, at a sales conference or a trade show), type the date that you'll be giving the presentation directly into the Fixed text box. You can use the same technique to postdate presentations that you never really gave but need to supply to your legal counsel to back up your alibi.

If you want to change the footer areas for just one slide, click Apply instead of Apply to All. This option comes in handy for those occasional slides that contain a graphic or a block of text that crowd up against the footer areas. You can easily suppress the footer information for that slide to make room for the large graphic or text.

## Adding a header or footer to Notes or Handouts pages

To add header and footer information to Notes or Handouts pages, follow the steps described in the preceding section, "Adding a date, number, or footer to slides," except click the Notes and Handouts tab when the Header and Footer dialog box appears. Clicking this tab displays a dialog box that's similar to the Header and Footer dialog box for Slide, except that it gives you an additional option to add a header that appears at the top of each page. After you indicate how you want to print the date, header, number, and footer areas, click the Apply to All button.

## Editing the header and footer placeholders directly

If you want, you can edit the text that appears in the header and footer placeholders directly. First, display the appropriate master — Slide, Title, Handouts, or Notes. Then click on the date, number, footer, or header placeholder and start typing.

You may notice that the placeholders include special codes for the options that you indicated in the Header and Footer dialog box. For example, the Date placeholder may contain the text *<date,time>* if you indicated that the date should be displayed. You can type text before or after these codes, but you should leave the codes themselves alone.

# Yes, You Can Serve Two Masters

In spite of the Biblical edict, Microsoft has endowed PowerPoint with the ability to have more than one Slide and Title Master. This feature lets you set up two or more Slide and Title Masters, and then choose which master to use for each slide in your presentation.

Before I show you how to use this feature, I want to make sure you understand the relationship between Slide Masters and Title Masters. Every presentation has at least one Slide Master. Each Slide Master in a presentation may have a corresponding Title Master, but this is not required.

Suppose that you create a new presentation that starts out with one Slide Master and one Title Master. Then, as you work with the presentation, you add two additional Slide Masters to create new slide designs. Now, the presentation has three Slide Masters but still only one Title Master.

If you want to add an additional Title Master, the new Title Master must be paired with an existing Slide Master that doesn't already have a Title Master. So, you can add a new Title Master to either of the two Slide Masters you created.

The following sections explain how to use the multiple masters feature.

## Creating a new Slide Master

To add a new master to a presentation, follow these steps:

1. **Choose View➪Master➪Slide Master to switch to Slide Master View.**

   Or if you prefer, hold down the Shift key and click the Normal View button near the lower-left corner of the screen.

2. **Click the Insert New Slide Master button in the floating Slide Master View toolbar.**

   A new Slide Master appears, as shown in Figure 12-7. Notice that a thumbnail for the new Slide Master has been added to the list of thumbnails on the left side of the screen, and that the new Slide Master uses PowerPoint's default settings (white background, black text, and so forth).

   If you don't like the floating Slide Master toolbar, you can right-click anywhere in the thumbnail area and choose New Slide Master from the pop-up menu that appears.

3. **Modify the new Slide Master to your liking.**

   You can make any formatting changes you want: Change the background color and text styles, add additional background objects, and so on.

4. **Click Close Master View on the Slide Master View toolbar to return to Normal View.**

   You can now begin using the new master that you created. (See the "Applying masters" section later in this chapter for more information.)

Another way to create a new Slide Master is to duplicate one of your presentation's existing Slide Masters. When you do that, the new Slide Master inherits the formatting of the original one. This can save you a lot of work, especially if you want to create a new Slide Master that varies from an existing one in only a minor way, such as having a different background color.

To duplicate a Slide Master, click the master that you want to duplicate in the thumbnails on the left of the screen, and then press Ctrl+D or choose Edit➪ Duplicate.

To delete a Slide Master, click the master that you want to delete and click the Delete Master button in the Slide Master View toolbar, choose Edit➪Delete Master, or press the Delete key.

## Creating a new Title Master

You can add a new Title Master to any Slide Master that doesn't yet have a Title Master paired with it. To add a Title Master, first select an available Slide Master by clicking its thumbnail on the left of the screen, and then choose Insert➪New Title Master. A new Title Master appears, as shown in Figure 12-8.

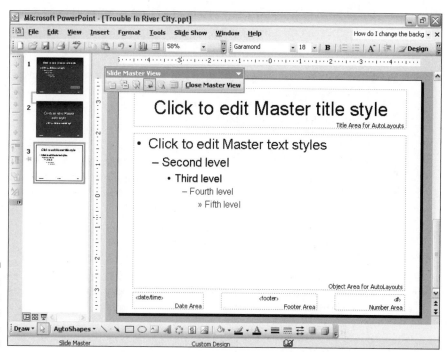

**Figure 12-7:**
Creating a
new Slide
Master.

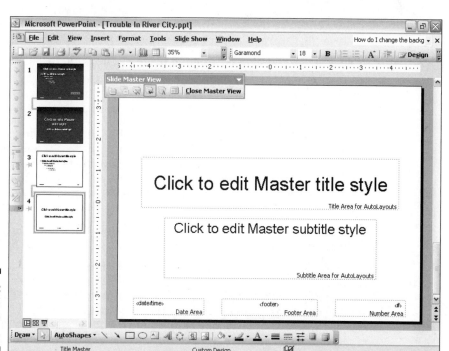

**Figure 12-8:**
Creating a
new Title
Master.

In Figure 12-8, you can see that the Title Master and Slide Master thumbnails are connected by a line, which indicates that these Slide and Title Masters are paired.

When you create a Title Master, the Title Master inherits any formatting from its Slide Master. However, once created, the Title Master and Slide Master are formatted independently. Thus, you can change the format of the Slide Master without affecting its Title Master, and vice versa.

To delete a Title Master, click the master that you want to delete and click the Delete Master button in the Slide Master View toolbar, choose Edit➪Delete Master, or press the Delete key. If you delete a Slide Master that is paired with a Title Master, the Title Master is deleted as well.

## Applying masters

If you have created multiple masters for a presentation, you can select which master to use for each slide in your presentation. To apply a master to one or more slides, follow these steps:

1. **Select the slide or slides to which you want to apply the alternate Slide Master.**

   The easiest way to do this is to click the slide that you want in the thumbnails on the left of the screen. To select more than one slide, hold down the Ctrl key and click each slide that you want to select.

2. **Choose Format➪Slide Design to bring up the Slide Design task pane.**

   Figure 12-9 shows the Slide Design task pane, with two slides selected in the thumbnail list.

   The Slide Design task pane shows a thumbnail list of Slide Masters and Design Templates that you can apply to your slides. The first section of this list, labeled "Used in This Presentation," shows a thumbnail of each Slide Master in the presentation. The other sections list the Design Templates that you've used recently and all of the Design Templates that are available to PowerPoint. (For more information about Design Templates, see Chapter 13.)

3. **Click the arrow next to the Slide Master that you want to apply to the slides you've selected, and then choose Apply to Selected Slides.**

   The Slide Master is applied to the selected slides.

Do not simply click the Slide Master that you want to use in the Slide Design task pane or you may be surprised by the results. If you select two or more slides and then click a Slide Master, the Slide Master is applied to the slides you selected. However, if you select only one slide and click a Slide Master, the Slide Master is applied to *all* the slides in the presentation — not just the one you selected! Worse yet, chances are good that PowerPoint will also delete the Slide Master that was applied to the other slides in the presentation. (This depends on whether the master has the Preserve setting, which you can find out about in the next section, "Preserving your Masters.")

To avoid this, I always click the arrow next to the Slide Master so I can select the Apply to Selected Slides command from the menu.

If you accidentally apply a Slide Master to all slides in your presentation and PowerPoint deletes the original Slide Master, just press Ctrl+Z or choose Edit⇨Undo to restore sanity to your presentation.

## Preserving your Masters

PowerPoint has a bad habit of deleting Slide Masters when they are no longer used in your presentation. For example, if you create a new Slide Master and then apply it to all the slides in your presentation, PowerPoint assumes that you no longer need the original Slide Master. So the original is deleted. Poof! Your presentation is now one pickle short of a full jar.

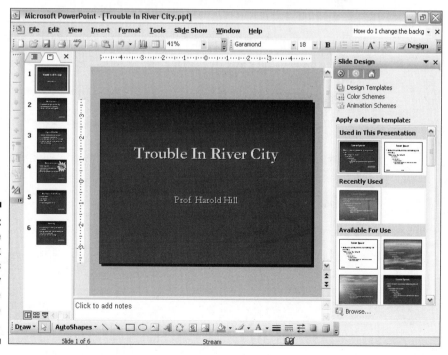

**Figure 12-9:**
The Slide Design task pane lets you apply Slide Masters to your slides.

You can prevent this from happening by using the Preserve Master option for your Slide Masters. Any new Slide Masters that you create automatically get the Preserve Master option, so they won't be deleted. However, the Slide and Title Masters that your presentations start off with don't have the Preserve Master option, so you may want to set it yourself.

To preserve a master, switch to Slide Master view, click the thumbnail for the master that you want to preserve, and then click the Preserve Master button in the Slide Master View toolbar. A little pushpin icon appears next to the master's thumbnail to show that the master will be preserved.

Don't click the Preserve Master button indiscriminately! If you click it for a master that already has the Preserve Master setting, Preserve Master is removed for that master. Then the master is subject to premature deletion.

# Restoring Lost Placeholders

If you've played around with your masters too much, you may inadvertently delete a layout placeholder that you wish you could get back. For example, suppose that you delete the footer placeholder from your Title Master and now you want it back. No problem! Just follow these steps:

1. **Choose View⇨Master⇨Slide Master to go to Slide Master View.**

   You can also shift-click the Normal View button near the bottom left of the screen.

2. **Call up the master with the missing placeholder.**

3. **Choose Format⇨Master Layout or click the Master Layout button in the Slide Master View toolbar.**

   This calls up the Master Layout dialog box, shown in Figure 12-10.

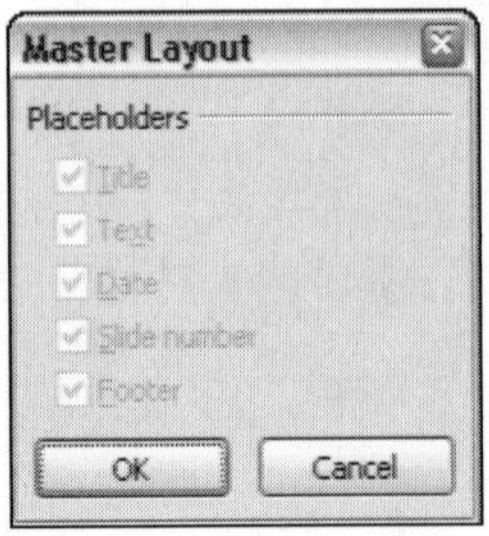

**Figure 12-10:**
The Master
Layout
dialog box.

| Master Layout |
| --- |
| Placeholders |
| ☑ Title |
| ☑ Text |
| ☑ Date |
| ☑ Slide number |
| ☑ Footer |
| OK    Cancel |

The Master Layout dialog box is one of the strangest dialog boxes you'll encounter. If you summon it for a master that still has all its placeholders, all the check boxes on the Master Layout dialog box will be grayed out. So all you can do is look at the controls, grunt, scratch your head, and click OK to dismiss the seemingly useless dialog box. However, if you *have* deleted one or more placeholders, the check boxes for the missing placeholders will be available.

4. **Click the check boxes for the placeholders that you want to restore.**

5. **Click OK.**

The missing placeholders reappear.

# Chapter 13

# All About Templates

*I*f you had to create every presentation from scratch, starting with a blank slide and a plain Slide Master with basic black text on a basic white background, you would probably put PowerPoint back in its box and use it as a bookend. Creating a presentation is easy, but creating one that looks good is a different story. Making a good-looking presentation is tough, even for the artistically inclined. For right-brain, nonartistic types like me, it's next to impossible.

Thank heavens for templates. A *template* is simply a PowerPoint presentation file with predefined Slide and Title Masters. When you create a presentation, PowerPoint 2003 gives you the option of stealing Masters from an existing template. Any PowerPoint presentation can serve as a template, including presentations that you create yourself. However, PowerPoint comes with more than 40 templates designed by professional artists who understand color combinations and balance and all that other artsy stuff. Have a croissant and celebrate.

Because the templates that come with PowerPoint look good, any presentation that you create by using one of them looks good, too. It's as simple as that. The template also supplies the color scheme for your presentation. You can override it, of course, but you do so at your own risk. The color police are everywhere, you know. You don't want to be taken in for Felony Color Clash.

Templates use the special file extension `.pot`, but you can also use ordinary PowerPoint presentation files (PPT) as templates. You can, therefore, use any of your own presentations as a template. If you make extensive changes to a presentation's Masters, you can use that presentation as a template for other presentations that you create. Or, you can save the presentation as a template by using the `.pot` file extension.

Some templates contain just Slide and Title Masters. Because these templates affect the design of your presentations but don't offer any content of their own, they are called *Design templates*. Other templates have, in addition to Slide and Title Masters, actual slides with sample content. These templates are known as *Content templates* and are used primarily by the AutoContent Wizard (which I cover in Chapter 1).

Because a template is a presentation, you can open it and change it if you want.

# Creating a Presentation Based on a Template

To create a new presentation based on a template, choose File⇨New to summon the New Presentation task pane, and then click From Design Template in the New section. The Slide Design task pane appears, as shown in Figure 13-1. Click the template that you want to use and a new presentation will be created using it.

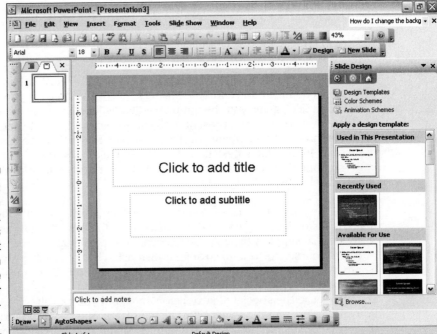

**Figure 13-1:** The Slide Design task pane lets you select a Design template for your presentation.

The most recent templates that you used are listed directly in the Recently Used Templates section of the New Presentation task pane. If the template that you want to use is listed, you can click it instead of clicking From Design Template. Then you won't have to deal with the Slide Design task pane.

Another way to create a new presentation by using a template is to click the On My Computer link found near the bottom of the Other Templates section of the New Presentation task pane. This brings up the dialog box shown in Figure 13-2, which lets you choose the template that you want to use. Notice the tabs across the top of this dialog box. Click these tabs to bring up several different categories of templates that you can use. When you have selected the template that you want to use, click OK.

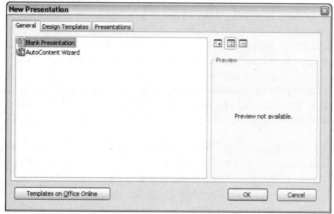

**Figure 13-2:**
The New Presentation dialog box.

The New Presentation task pane also has links that let you look for templates on your own Web sites or on Microsoft's Templates home page.

# Switching Templates

You're halfway through creating a new presentation when you realize that you can't stand the look of the slides. Oops — you picked the wrong template when you started the new presentation! Don't panic. PowerPoint enables you to assign a new presentation template at any time. These steps show you how:

1. **Choose Format⇨Slide Design or click the Design button in the Formatting toolbar.**

   The Slide Design task pane appears (refer to Figure 13-1).

2. **Rummage around for a template you like better.**

   Scroll down the list to the Available for Use section, where you can find the Design templates that come with PowerPoint.

3. **Point the mouse at the template thumbnail that you want to use, and then click the arrow that appears next to the thumbnail and choose the Apply to All Slides command.**

   The Slide and Title Masters in the template you chose are applied to your presentation.

You may still want to make minor adjustments to the Slide and Title Masters to make the slides look just right. Refer to Chapter 12 for the necessary instructions.

When you apply a new template, PowerPoint copies the Masters and the color scheme into your presentation. As a result, any changes you made to the presentation's Masters or color scheme are lost. If you added background objects to the Slide Master, you have to add them again.

You don't have to worry about the new template undoing any formatting changes that you've made to individual slides. PowerPoint remembers these deviations from the Master format when it applies a new template.

Another way to bring up the Slide Design taskbar is to double-click the name of the template in the status bar at the bottom of the PowerPoint window.

# Creating a New Template

If none of the templates that come with PowerPoint appeals to you, you can easily create your own. All you have to do is create a presentation with the Masters and the color scheme set up just the way you want and then save it as a template. Here are a few points to remember about templates:

 ✔ If you want to make minor modifications to one of the supplied templates, open the template by choosing File➪Open and then immediately save it under a new name by choosing File➪Save As. Then change the Masters and the color scheme. Don't forget to save the file again when you're finished!

 ✔ You can also create your own presentation templates, complete with skeleton slides. Just create the template as a normal presentation and add however many slides that you want to include.

 ✔ When you are ready to save your template, use the Save As Type command. Set your type to Design template, with the .pot extension.

# Creating a New Default Template

When you create a new presentation by clicking the New button, or by choosing Blank Presentation from the New Presentation task pane, PowerPoint creates a blank presentation using default black text on a white background. What you probably don't realize is that even blank presentations can use a template — a template named Blank.pot is automatically applied to new blank presentations.

If you want to create your own default template, all you have to do is save your template file by using the filename Blank.pot. Then whenever you create a blank presentation, the Masters and the color scheme are copied from your new default template rather than from the bland default template that comes with PowerPoint.

To revert to the plain black-on-white blank template, just delete the Blank.pot file. If PowerPoint can't find the Blank.pot template, it uses the default black-on-white layout.

These steps show you how to create a new default template:

1. **Create a new presentation by clicking the New button or choosing Blank Presentation from the New Presentation task pane.**

2. **Choose View➪Master➪Slide Master to switch to Slide Master View.**

3. **Make any changes that you want to the Slide and Title Masters.**

   For example, change the background color and the text fonts and colors.

4. **Click the Save button.**

5. **Change the Save As Type control to Design template, with the .pot extension.**

   When you do this, the Save in control automatically changes to the folder where your templates are stored.

6. **Type Blank in the File Name field.**

7. **Click Save.**

# Part III
# PowerPoint Gone Wild

The 5th Wave          By Rich Tennant

DAD ADDS MULTIMEDIA SOUND AND GRAPHICS TO THE TRADITIONAL CAMPFIRE GHOST STORY.

# In this part . . .

The chapters in this part will show you in graphic detail how to create unashamedly wild PowerPoint presentations with embellishments such as drawings, graphs, charts, movies, custom animations, and more! You can even make your presentations belch on command.

Not that any of this is easy. That's why I devote an entire part to wrestling with these ornaments.

# Chapter 14

# Drawing on Your Slides

*C*him-chiminey, chim-chiminey, chim-chim cheroo, I draws what I likes and I likes what I drew. . . .

Art time! Everybody get your crayons and glue and don an old paint shirt. You're going to cut out some simple shapes and paste them on your PowerPoint slides so that people either think that you are a wonderful artist or scoff at you for not using clip art.

This chapter covers the drawing features of PowerPoint 2003. One of the best things about PowerPoint is the cool drawing tools. Once upon a time, PowerPoint had but rudimentary drawing tools — the equivalent of a box of crayons — but PowerPoint now has powerful drawing tools that are sufficient for all but the most sophisticated aspiring artists among us.

# Some General Drawing Tips

Before getting into the specifics of using each PowerPoint drawing tool, this section describes a handful of general tips for drawing pictures.

## Zoom in

When you work with the PowerPoint drawing tools, you may want to increase the zoom factor so that you can draw more accurately. I often work at 200, 300, or even 400 percent when I'm drawing. To change the zoom factor, click the down arrow next to the Zoom Control button (near the right side of the Standard toolbar) and choose a zoom factor from the list. Or you can click the zoom factor, type a new zoom percentage, and press Enter.

Before you change the zoom factor to edit an object, choose the object that you want to edit. This way, PowerPoint zooms in on that area of the slide. If you don't choose an object before you zoom in, you may need to scroll around to find the right location.

Also, get rid of the task pane when you're drawing in order to make more room on the screen for the slide. To create even more room, close the Slides/Outline pane on the left side of the window by clicking the Close button at the top right corner of the pane. To get the pane back, choose View➪Normal (Restore Panes).

## Display the ruler

If you want to be precise about lining up objects on the slide, make sure that the ruler is on. If you can't see the ruler on-screen, choose View➪Ruler to display it. Figure 14-1 shows how PowerPoint looks when the ruler is activated.

When you work with drawing objects, PowerPoint formats the ruler so that zero is at the middle of the slide. When you edit a text object, the ruler changes to a text ruler that measures from the margins and indicates tab positions.

## Stick to the color scheme

You can assign individual colors to each object that you draw, but the purpose of the PowerPoint color schemes (described in Chapter 11) is to talk you out of doing that. If possible, let solid objects default to the color scheme's fill color. The beauty of doing this is that if you change the color scheme later on, the fill color for objects changes to reflect the new fill color. After you change the fill color, however, the object ignores any change to the slide's color scheme.

If you must assign a separate color to an object, choose one of the eight colors that are part of the color scheme. (If you decide to arbitrarily choose one of PowerPoint's 64 million colors for an object, a good lawyer may be able to get you off by using the "irresistible urge" defense.)

## Save frequently

Drawing is tedious work. You don't want to spend two hours working on a particularly important drawing only to lose it all just because a comet strikes your building or an errant Scud lands in your backyard. You can prevent catastrophic loss from incidents such as these by pressing Ctrl+S or by frequently clicking the Save button with your mouse as you work. And always wear protective eyewear.

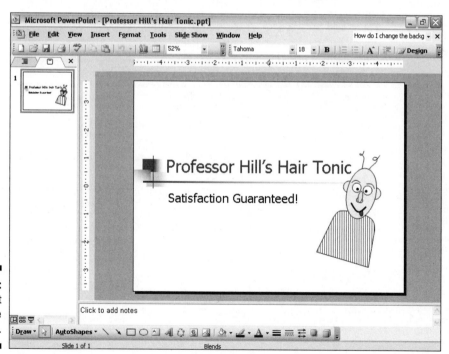

**Figure 14-1:**
PowerPoint
with the
rulers on.

## Don't forget Ctrl+Z

In my opinion, Ctrl+Z — the ubiquitous Undo command — is the most important key in any Windows program, and PowerPoint is no exception. Always remember that you're never more than one keystroke away from erasing a boo-boo. If you do something silly — like forgetting to group a complex picture before trying to move it — you can always press Ctrl+Z to undo your last action. Ctrl+Z is my favorite and most frequently used PowerPoint key combination. (For left-handed mouse users, Alt+Backspace does the same thing.) And for those not ready to climb shrieking on a chair at the first sign of a mouse, try the handy Undo button on the Formatting toolbar or choose Edit⇨Undo.

# Working with the Drawing Toolbar

PowerPoint provides a whole row of drawing tools, located on the Drawing toolbar. If the Drawing toolbar has disappeared, you can make it appear again by choosing View⇨Toolbars and checking the Drawing check box.

Table 14-1 shows you what each drawing tool does.

**Table 14-1 Buttons on the Drawing Toolbar**

| *Drawing Tool* | *What It's Called* | *What It Does* |
|---|---|---|
|  | Draw menu | Displays a menu of drawing commands. |
|  | Select Objects button | Not really a drawing tool, but rather the generic mouse pointer used to choose objects. |
|  | AutoShapes button | Pops up the AutoShapes menu, which contains a bevy of shapes that you can draw, including fancy lines, arrows, crosses, flowchart symbols, stars, and more! |
|  | Line button | Draws a line. |
|  | Arrow button | Draws an arrow. |

| Drawing Tool | What It's Called | What It Does |
|---|---|---|
| | Rectangle button | Draws a rectangle. To make a perfect square, hold down the Shift key while you draw. |
| | Oval button | Draws circles and ovals. To create a perfect circle, hold down the Shift key while you draw. |
| | Text box button | Adds a text object. |
| | Insert WordArt button | Summons forth WordArt, which lets you create all sorts of fancy text effects. |
| | Insert Diagram | Inserts a diagram or organization chart. |
| | Insert Clip Art button | Summons the Clip Gallery dialog box. |
| | Insert Picture | Inserts a picture. |
| | Fill Color button | Sets the color used to fill solid objects, such as circles and ellipses, as well as AutoShapes. |
| | Line Color button | Sets the color used to draw lines, including lines around rectangles, ellipses, and AutoShapes. |
| | Font Color button | Sets the color used for text. |
| | Line Style button | Sets the style used for lines. |
| | Dash Style button | Creates dashed lines. |

*(continued)*

**Table 14-1** *(continued)*

| Drawing Tool | What It's Called | What It Does |
|---|---|---|
| | Arrow Style button | Creates lines with arrowheads. |
| | Shadow Style button | Creates shadows. |
| | 3-D Style button | Creates 3-D effects. |

The good folks at Microsoft couldn't decide whether the Drawing toolbar should contain buttons or menus, so they threw in some of both. The Draw and AutoShapes buttons are actually menus that behave just like menus on a normal menu bar: Click them to reveal a menu of choices or use the Alt key shortcuts to activate them (Alt+R activates the Draw menu, and Alt+U activates the AutoShapes menu).

# Drawing Simple Objects

To draw an object on a slide, click the button that represents the object that you want to draw and then use the mouse to draw the object on the slide. Well, it's not always as simple as that. You find detailed instructions for drawing with the more important tools in the following sections. Before I get to that, though, I want to give you some pointers to keep in mind:

- **Choosing a location:** Before you draw an object, move to the slide on which you want to draw the object. If you want the object to appear on every slide in the presentation, display the Slide Master by choosing View➪Master➪Slide Master or by Shift+clicking the Normal View button on the status bar.

- **Adding text to an object:** PowerPoint has two types of objects: shapes — such as circles, rectangles, and crosses — and lines/arcs. PowerPoint enables you to add text to any shape object, but you can't add text to a line or arc object.

✔ **Fix a mistake:** You can delete the object that you just drew by pressing the Delete key; then try drawing the object again. Or you can change its size or stretch it by clicking it and dragging its love handles.

Table 14-2 summarizes some handy shortcuts that you can use while drawing.

| Table 14-2 | Drawing Shortcuts |
|---|---|
| *Shortcut* | *What It Does* |
| Shift | Hold down the Shift key to force lines to be horizontal or vertical, to force arcs and ellipses to be true circles, to force rectangles to be squares, or to draw other regular shapes. |
| Ctrl | Hold down the Ctrl key to draw objects from the center rather than from end to end. |
| Ctrl+Shift | Hold down these two keys to draw from the center and to enforce squareness or circleness. |
| Double-click | Double-click any drawing button on the Drawing tool bar if you want to draw several objects of the same type. |

The last shortcut in Table 14-2 needs a bit of explanation. If you click a drawing tool button once (such as the rectangle or ellipse button), the mouse cursor reverts to an arrow after you draw an object. To draw another object, you must click a drawing tool button again. If you know in advance that you want to draw more than one object of the same type, double-click the drawing tool button. Then you can keep drawing objects of the selected type. To stop drawing, click the Selection tool button (the arrow at the top of the Drawing toolbar).

## Drawing straight lines

You use the Line button to draw straight lines on your slides. Here's the procedure:

1. **Click the Line button.**

2. **Point to where you want the line to start.**

3. **Click and drag the mouse cursor to where you want the line to end.**

4. **Release the mouse button when you reach your destination.**

You can choose Format⇨Colors and Lines to change the line color and other features (thickness, dashes, and arrowheads) for a line or arc object. Or you can click the Line Style button or Line Color button on the Drawing toolbar (refer to Table 14-1) to change these attributes.

After you've drawn a line, you can adjust it by clicking it and then dragging the handles that appear on each end of the line.

Remember that you can force a line to be perfectly horizontal or vertical by holding down the Shift key while you draw. If you hold the Shift key and drag diagonally while you draw the line, the line will be constrained to perfect 45-degree angles.

## Drawing rectangles, squares, ovals, and circles

To draw a rectangle, follow these steps:

1. **Click the Rectangle button.**
2. **Point to where you want one corner of the rectangle to be positioned.**
3. **Click the mouse button and drag to where you want the opposite corner of the rectangle to be positioned.**
4. **Release the mouse button.**

The steps for drawing an oval are the same as the steps for drawing a rectangle except that you click the Oval button rather than the Rectangle button. To draw a square or perfectly round circle, select the Oval button or the Rectangle button, but hold down the Shift key while you draw.

You can choose the Format⇨Colors and Lines to change the fill color or the line style for a rectangle or oval object. You also can use the Line Style button or the Fill Color button on the Drawing toolbar.

To apply a shadow, use the Shadow button. See the section "Applying a Shadow" later in this chapter for more information.

You can adjust the size or shape of a rectangle or circle by clicking it and dragging any of its love handles.

## Using AutoShapes

Rectangles and circles aren't the only two shapes that PowerPoint can draw automatically. When you click the AutoShapes button on the Drawing toolbar, a whole menu of AutoShapes appears. These AutoShapes make it easy to draw common shapes such as pentagons, stars, and flowchart symbols.

The AutoShapes menu organizes AutoShapes into the following categories:

✔ **Lines:** Straight lines, curved lines, lines with arrowheads, scribbly lines, and free-form shapes that can become polygons if you want. The free-form AutoShape is useful enough to merit its own section, "Drawing a Polygon or Free-form Shape," which immediately follows this section.

✔ **Connectors:** Lines with various shapes and arrowheads with connecting dots on the ends.

✔ **Basic Shapes:** Squares, rectangles, triangles, crosses, happy faces, lightning bolts, and more.

✔ **Block Arrows:** Fat arrows pointing in various directions.

✔ **Flowchart:** Various flowcharting symbols.

✔ **Stars and Banner:** Shapes that add sparkle to your presentations.

✔ **Callouts:** Text boxes and speech bubbles like those used in comic strips.

✔ **Action Buttons:** Buttons that you can add to your slides and click during a slide show to go directly to another slide or to run a macro.

✔ **More AutoShapes:** In fact, 73 more. Some of these work great for your Web page presentation, including one that looks like a Christmas tree.

The following steps explain how to draw an AutoShape:

1. **Click the AutoShapes button on the Drawing toolbar.**

   The AutoShapes menu appears.

2. **Choose the AutoShape category that you want.**

   A toolbar of AutoShapes appears. Figure 14-2 shows all the toolbars that you can access from the AutoShapes menu. Look this figure over to see what kind of AutoShapes are available. (Of course, when you actually use PowerPoint, only one of these toolbars is visible at a time.)

3. **Click the AutoShape that you want to draw.**

4. **Click the slide where you want the shape to appear and then drag the shape to the desired size.**

   Hold down the Shift key while drawing the AutoShape to create an undistorted shape.

   When you release the mouse button, the AutoShape object takes on the current fill color and line style.

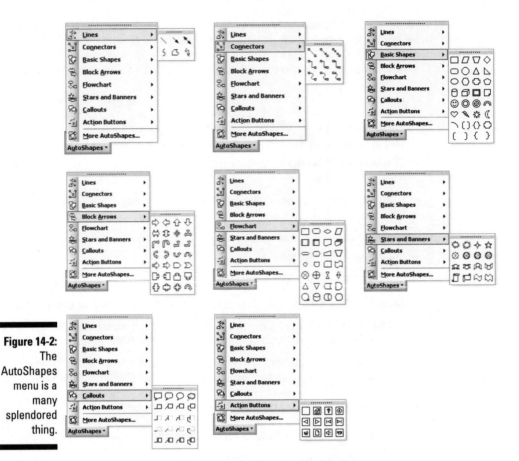

**Figure 14-2:**
The
AutoShapes
menu is a
many
splendored
thing.

**5. Start typing if you want the shape to contain text.**

After you've typed your text, you can use PowerPoint's formatting features to change its typeface, size, color, and so on. For more information, refer to Chapter 9.

Some AutoShapes — especially the stars and banners — cry out for text. Figure 14-3 shows how you can use a star shape to add a jazzy burst to a slide.

You can change an object's AutoShape at any time by selecting the object and then choosing Draw➪Change AutoShape.

Many AutoShape buttons have an extra handle shaped like a yellow diamond that enables you to adjust some aspect of the object's shape. For example, the block arrows have a handle that enables you to increase or decrease the size of the arrowhead. The location of these handles varies depending on the shape you're working with. Figure 14-4 shows how you can use these extra handles to vary the shapes produced by six different AutoShapes. For each of the six shapes, the first object shows how the AutoShape is initially drawn; the other two objects drawn with each AutoShape show how you can change the shape by dragging the extra handle.

**Figure 14-3:**
Use a star shape to make your presentation look like a late-night infomercial.

**Figure 14-4:**
You can create interesting variations by grabbing the extra handles on these Auto-Shapes.

# Drawing a Polygon or Free-form Shape

Mr. Arnold, my seventh-grade math teacher, taught me that a *polygon* is a shape that has many sides and has nothing to do with having more than one spouse (one is certainly enough for most of us). Triangles, squares, and rectangles are polygons, but so are hexagons and pentagons, as are any unusual shapes whose sides all consist of straight lines. Politicians are continually inventing new polygons when they revise the boundaries of congressional districts.

One of the most useful AutoShapes is the Freeform tool. It's designed to create polygons, with a twist: Not all the sides have to be straight lines. The Freeform AutoShape tool lets you build a shape whose sides are a mixture of straight lines and free-form curves. Figure 14-5 shows three examples of shapes that I created with the Freeform AutoShape tool.

Follow these steps to create a polygon or free-form shape:

1. **Click the AutoShapes button and then choose Lines.**

    The Lines toolbar appears.

2. **Click the Freeform button.**

3. **Click where you want to position the first corner of the object.**

4. **Click where you want to position the second corner of the object.**

5. **Keep clicking wherever you want to position a corner.**

6. **To draw a free-form side on the shape, hold down the mouse button when you click a corner, and then draw the free-form shape with the mouse. When you get to the end of the free-form side, release the mouse button.**

    You can then click again to add more corners. Shape 3 in Figure 14-5 has one free-form side.

7. **To finish the shape, click near the first corner — the one that you created in Step 3.**

    You don't have to be exact: If you click anywhere near the first corner that you put down, PowerPoint assumes that the shape is finished.

You're finished! The object assumes the line and fill color from the slide's color scheme.

You can reshape a polygon or free-form shape by double-clicking it and then dragging any of the love handles that appear on the corners.

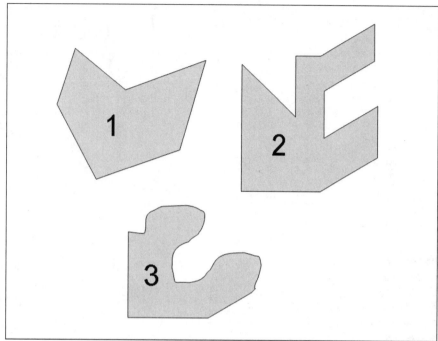

**Figure 14-5:**
Three
free-form
shapes.

If you hold down the Shift key while you draw a polygon, the sides are con-strained to 45-degree angles. Shape 2 in Figure 14-5 was drawn in this manner. How about a constitutional amendment requiring Congress to use the Shift key when it redraws congressional boundaries?

You also can use the Freeform AutoShape tool to draw a multisegmented line, called an *open shape*. To draw an open shape, you can follow the steps in this section, except that you skip Step 6. Instead, double-click or press the Esc key when the line is done.

# Drawing a Curved Line or Shape

Another useful AutoShape tool is the Curve button, which lets you draw curved lines or shapes. Figure 14-6 shows several examples of curved lines and shapes drawn with the Curve AutoShape tool.

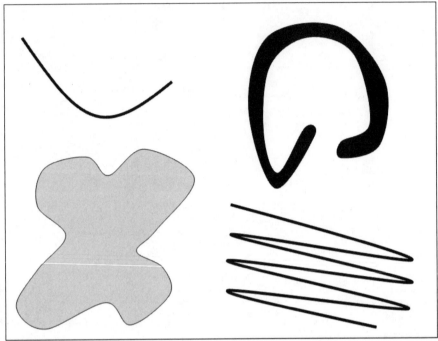

**Figure 14-6:**
Examples of
curved lines
and shapes.

Here is the procedure for drawing a curved line or shape:

1. **Click the AutoShapes button and then choose Lines.**

   The Lines toolbar appears.

2. **Click the Curve button.**

3. **Click where you want the curved line or shape to begin.**

4. **Click where you want the first turn in the curve to appear.**

   The straight line turns to a curved line, bent around the point where you clicked. As you move the mouse, the bend of the curve changes.

5. **Click to add additional turns to the curve.**

   Each time you click, a new bend is added to the line. Keep clicking until the line is as twisty as you want.

6. **To finish a line, double-click where you want the end of the curved line to appear. To create a closed shape, double-click over the starting point, where you clicked in Step 3.**

# Creating a Text Box

A text box is a special type of shape that is designed to place text on your slides. To create a text box, click the Text Box button; click where you want one corner of the text box to appear and drag to where you want the opposite corner, just like you're drawing a rectangle. When you release the mouse button, you can type text.

You can format the text that you type in the text box by highlighting the text and using the text formatting controls on the Formatting toolbar. For more information about formatting text, refer to Chapter 9.

You can format the text box itself by using the Fill Color, Line Color, and Line Style buttons, described in the next section. By default, text boxes have no fill or line color so the box itself is invisible on the slide — only the text is visible.

Most AutoShapes also function as text boxes. If you want to add text to an AutoShape, just click the shape and start typing. The text appears centered over the shape. (The only AutoShapes that don't accept text are lines and connectors.)

# Setting the Fill, Line, and Font Color

The three color controls that appear on the Drawing toolbar let you set the fill color (that is, the color used to fill a solid object), the line color, and the color of an object's text. These buttons behave a little strangely, so they merit a bit of explanation. Note that the current color for each button is displayed in a little horizontal stripe beneath the button's icon.

Each of the color buttons actually consists of two parts: a button and an arrow. Click the button to assign the current fill, line, or text color to the selected object. Click the arrow to apply any color that you want to the selected object.

When you click the arrow, a menu appears. For example, Figure 14-7 shows the Fill Color menu that appears when you click the arrow attached to the Fill Color button. As you can see, this menu includes a palette of colors that you can select. If you want to use a color that isn't visible on the menu, select More Fill Colors; this displays a dialog box that includes a color wheel from which you can select just about any color under the sun. Chapter 11 carefully explains this dialog box, so I won't review it here.

If you set the Fill Color, Line Color, or Font Color to Automatic, the fill color changes whenever you change the presentation's color scheme.

You can also apply a fill effect — such as gradient fill, a pattern, a texture, or a picture — to an object by choosing the Fill Effects command from the Fill Color menu. This pops up the Fill Effects dialog box, which Chapter 11 describes in detail.

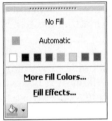

**Figure 14-7:**
The Fill
Color menu.

The Line Color and Font Color menus have similar commands. In addition, the Line Color menu includes a Patterned Lines command that lets you pick a pattern to apply to lines.

## *Setting the Line Style*

Three buttons in the Drawing toolbar let you change the style of line objects:

- ✔ **Line Style:** The thickness of the lines that outline the object.
- ✔ **Dash Style:** The dashing pattern used for the lines that outline the object. The default uses a solid line, but different patterns are available to create dashed lines.
- ✔ **Arrow Style:** Lines can have an arrowhead at either or both ends. Arrowheads are used mostly on line and arc objects.

To change any of these object attributes, simply select the object or objects that you want to change and then click the appropriate button to change the style. A menu of style options appears.

The Line Style menu includes a More Lines command that summons the dialog box shown in Figure 14-8. From this dialog box, you can control all aspects of a line's style: its color, width, dash pattern, and end style (various arrowheads can be applied). The Arrow Style command includes a More Arrows command that summons the same dialog box.

**Figure 14-8:**
Setting the line style.

# Applying a Shadow

To apply a shadow effect to an object, select the object and click the Shadow button. The Shadow menu shown in Figure 14-9 appears, offering several shadow styles. Click the shadow style that you want the object to assume.

If you select the Shadow Settings command from the Shadow menu, the Shadow Settings toolbar appears. The buttons on this toolbar allow you to nudge the shadow into exactly the right position and change the shadow color to create a custom shadow effect.

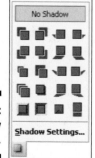

**Figure 14-9:**
The Shadow menu.

# Adding 3-D Effects

The 3-D button is one of the coolest buttons on the Drawing toolbar. This button lets you transform a dull and lifeless flat object into an exciting, breathtaking three-dimensional object. Figure 14-10 shows how you can use the 3-D button to transform several shapes into 3-D objects. In each case, the object on the left is a simple AutoShape, and the three objects to the right of the simple AutoShape are three-dimensional versions of the same shape.

To apply a 3-D effect to a shape, select the shape and click the 3-D button. The 3-D menu shown in Figure 14-11 appears. Click the effect that you want to apply. Or click No 3-D if you want to remove 3-D effects.

If you select 3-D Settings from the 3-D menu, the 3-D Toolbar appears. You can use the controls on this toolbar to tweak the 3-D settings of the object to obtain just the right effect. You can tilt the object in any direction, set its depth, and change the lighting and surface textures.

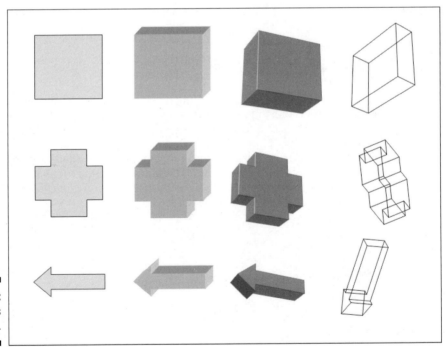

**Figure 14-10:**
3-D effects
are cool.

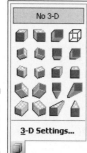

**Figure 14-11:**
The 3-D
menu.

# Flipping and Rotating Objects

To *flip* an object means to create a mirror image of it. To *rotate* an object means to turn it about its center. PowerPoint lets you flip objects horizontally or vertically, rotate objects in 90-degree increments, or freely rotate an object to any angle.

Rotation works for text boxes and AutoShape text. Thus, you can use rotation to create vertical text or text skewed to any angle you want. However, flipping an object doesn't affect the object's text.

## Flipping an object

PowerPoint enables you to flip an object vertically or horizontally to create a mirror image of the object. To flip an object, follow these steps:

1. **Choose the object that you want to flip.**

2. **Click the Draw button to reveal the Draw menu, choose Rotate or Flip, and then choose Flip Horizontal or Flip Vertical.**

## Rotating an object 90 degrees

You can rotate an object in 90-degree increments by following these steps:

1. **Choose the object that you want to rotate.**

2. **Click the Draw button to reveal the Draw menu, choose Rotate or Flip, and then choose Rotate Left or Rotate Right.**

3. **To rotate the object 180 degrees, click the appropriate Rotate button again.**

## *Using the rotate handle*

Remember how all the bad guys' hideouts were slanted in the old *Batman* TV show? The rotate handle lets you give your drawings that same kind of slant. With the rotate handle, you can rotate an object to any arbitrary angle just by dragging it with the mouse.

The rotate handle is the green handle that appears above the object, connected to the object by a line, as shown in Figure 14-12. You can rotate an object to any angle simply by dragging the rotate handle.

Rotate handles

**Figure 14-12:**
The rotate
handle lets
you rotate
an object
to any
arbitrary
angle.

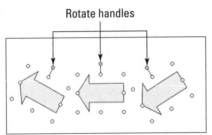

The following steps show you how to use the rotate handle:

1. **Click the object that you want to rotate.**

2. **Drag the rotate handle in the direction that you want to rotate the object.**

   As you drag, an outline of the object rotates around. When you get the object's outline to the angle you want, release the mouse button, and the object is redrawn at the new angle.

Another way to rotate an object is to select the object, click the Draw button, click Rotate or Flip, and then choose Free Rotate. Rotation handles then appear at all four corners of the object. You can rotate the object by dragging any of the four handles.

To restrict the rotation angle to 15-degree increments, hold the Shift key while dragging around the rotation handle.

When you hold down the Ctrl key while dragging a corner handle, the object rotates about the opposite corner handle rather than the center. This feature is very strange, but it's occasionally useful.

# Drawing a Complicated Picture

When you add more than one object to a slide, you may run into several problems. What happens when the objects overlap? How do you line up objects so that they don't look like they were thrown at the slide from a moving car? And how do you keep together objects that belong together?

This section shows you how to use PowerPoint features to handle over-lapped objects, and how to align and group objects.

## Changing layers

Whenever you have more than one object on a slide, the potential exists for objects to overlap one another. Like most drawing programs, PowerPoint handles this problem by layering objects like a stack of plates. The first object that you draw is at the bottom of the stack; the second object is on top of the first; the third is atop the second object; and so on. If two objects overlap, the one that's at the highest layer wins; objects below it are partially covered. (Note that PowerPoint's layers aren't nearly as powerful as layers in programs like Adobe Illustrator or Corel Draw!. All they really do is set the stacking order when objects are placed on top of one another.)

So far, so good — but what if you don't remember to draw the objects in the correct order? What if you draw a shape that you want to tuck behind a shape that you've already drawn, or what if you want to bring an existing shape to the top of the pecking order? No problem. PowerPoint enables you to change the stacking order by moving objects toward the front or back so that they overlap just the way you want.

The Draw menu on the Drawing toolbar provides four commands for changing the stacking order, all grouped under the Order command:

 ✔ **Draw⇨Order⇨Bring to Front:** Brings the chosen object to the top of the stack.

 ✔ **Draw⇨Order⇨Send to Back:** Sends the chosen object to the back of the stack.

 ✔ **Draw⇨Order⇨Bring Forward:** Brings the chosen object one step closer to the front of the stack.

 ✔ **Draw⇨Order⇨Send Backward:** Sends the object one rung down the ladder.

Layering problems are most obvious when objects have a fill color. If an object has no fill color, objects behind it are allowed to show through. In this case, the layering doesn't matter much.

To bring an object to the top of another, you may have to use the Bring Forward command several times. The reason is that even though the two objects appear to be adjacent, other objects may occupy the layers between them.

## Line 'em up

Nothing looks more amateurish than objects dropped randomly on a slide with no apparent concern for how they line up with each other. The Draw menu on the Drawing toolbar provides several alignment commands. To use them, first select the objects that you want to align. Then click the Draw button, click Align or Distribute, and then choose one of the following commands from the menu that appears:

- Align Left
- Align Center
- Align Right
- Align Top
- Align Middle
- Align Bottom

The first three commands align items horizontally; the last three align items vertically.

You can also distribute several items so that they are spaced evenly. Select the items that you want to distribute, click the Draw button, choose Align or Distribute, and then choose Distribute Horizontally or Distribute Vertically.

If you want objects to automatically adhere to an invisible grid when you draw them or move them about, click the Draw button, click Snap, and then choose To Grid. To turn the snap-to-grid feature off, choose Draw➪Snap➪To Grid again.

## Using the grids and guides

To help you create well-ordered slides, PowerPoint lets you display a grid of evenly spaced lines over the slide. These lines aren't actually a part of the slide, so your audience won't see them when you give your presentation. They exist simply to make the task of lining things up a bit easier.

In addition to the grid, PowerPoint also lets you use guides. The guides are two lines — one horizontal, the other vertical — that appear on-screen.

Although the gridlines are fixed in their location on your slides, you can move the guides around as you want. Any object that comes within a pixel's breath of one of these guidelines snaps to it. Like the grid, the guides don't show up when you give your presentation. They appear only when you're editing your slides. Guides are a great way to line up objects in a neat row.

To display the grid or guides, choose View⇨Grid and Guides (the Grid and Guides command is also available on the Draw menu). This command summons the Grid and Guides dialog box, shown in Figure 14-13. (You can also summon this dialog box by pressing Ctrl+G.)

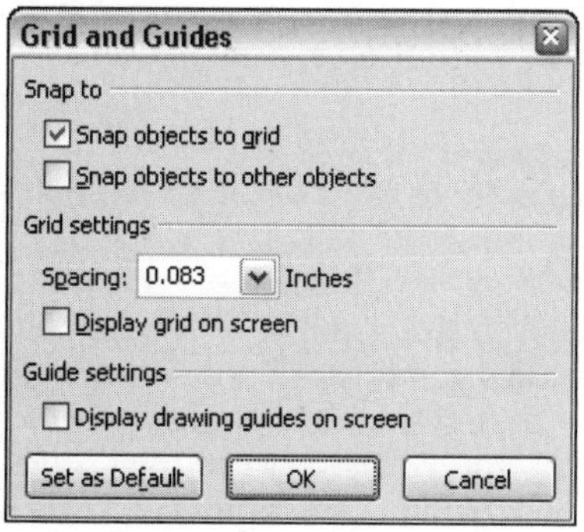

**Figure 14-13:**
The Grid
and Guides
dialog box.

**Grid and Guides**

Snap to
☑ Snap objects to grid
☐ Snap objects to other objects

Grid settings
Spacing: 0.083 ▾ Inches
☐ Display grid on screen

Guide settings
☐ Display drawing guides on screen

Set as Default    OK    Cancel

To activate the grid, check the Snap Objects to Grid check box, and then adjust the grid spacing to whatever setting you want. If you want to actually see the grid on the screen, check the Display Grid on Screen check box.

To fire up the guides, check the Display Drawing Guides on Screen setting. After the guides are visible, you can move them around the slide by clicking and dragging them with the mouse.

## Group therapy

A *group* is a collection of objects that PowerPoint treats as though it were one object. Using groups properly is one key to putting simple shapes together to make complex pictures without becoming so frustrated that you have to join a therapy group. ("Hello, my name is Doug, and PowerPoint drives me crazy.")

To create a group, follow these steps:

**1. Choose all objects that you want to include in the group.**

You can do this by holding down the Shift key and clicking each of the items, or by holding down the mouse button and dragging the resulting rectangle around all the items.

   **2. Click Draw in the Drawing toolbar and then select the Group command.**

To take a group apart so that PowerPoint treats the objects as individuals again, follow these steps:

   **1. Select the object group that you want to break up.**

   **2. Choose Draw⇨Ungroup.**

If you create a group and then ungroup it so that you can work on its elements individually, you can easily regroup the objects. These steps show you how:

   **1. Select at least one object that was in the original group.**

   **2. Choose Draw⇨Regroup.**

   PowerPoint remembers which objects were in the group and automatically includes them.

PowerPoint enables you to create groups of groups. This capability is useful for complex pictures because it enables you to work on one part of the picture, group it, and then work on the next part of the picture without worrying about accidentally disturbing the part that you've already grouped. After you have several such groups, select them and group them. You can create groups of groups of groups and so on, ad nauseam.

# Chapter 15

# Charts, Diagrams, and Other Embellishments

### In This Chapter

▶ Adding charts and graphs to PowerPoint

▶ Creating a diagram or an organization chart

▶ Embellishing your presentation with WordArt or a fancy table

*Y*ou'll hear nothing but yawns from the back row if your presentation consists of slide after slide of text and bulleted lists with an occasional bit of clip art thrown in for good measure. Mercifully, PowerPoint is well equipped to add all sorts of embellishments to your slides, including charts, diagrams, fancy-schmancy text, and so on. This chapter shows you how to use a hodgepodge of the most interesting of these embellishments.

## Creating a Chart

One of the best ways to prove a point is with numbers, and one of the best ways to present numbers is in a chart. With PowerPoint, adding a chart to your presentation is easy. And getting the chart to look the way you want is usually easy, too. It takes a little bit of pointing and clicking, but it works.

### Understanding charts

If you've never attempted to add a chart to a slide, the process can be a little confusing. A *chart* is simply a series of numbers rendered as a graph. You can supply the numbers yourself, or you can copy them from a separate file, such as an Excel spreadsheet. You can create all kinds of different charts, ranging from simple bar charts and pie charts to exotic doughnut charts and radar charts. Very cool, but a little confusing to the uninitiated.

The following list details some of the jargon that you have to contend with when you're working with charts:

- **Graph or chart:** Same thing. These terms are used interchangeably. A graph or chart is nothing more than a bunch of numbers turned into a picture. After all, a picture is worth a thousand numbers.

- **Microsoft Graph:** Charts (or graphs, if you prefer) are actually created by a separate program called Microsoft Graph. However, Microsoft Graph is so well integrated with PowerPoint that if I hadn't just told you, you probably wouldn't realize that it's a separate program from PowerPoint.

- **Chart type:** Microsoft Graph supports several chart types: bar charts, column charts, pie charts, line charts, scatter charts, area charts, radar charts, Dunkin' Donut charts, and others. Microsoft Graph can even create cone charts that look like something that fell off a Fembot in an Austin Powers movie. Different types of charts are better suited to displaying different types of data.

- **3-D chart:** Some chart types have a 3-D effect that gives them a jazzier look. Nothing special here — the effect is mostly cosmetic.

- **Datasheet:** Supplies the underlying data for a chart. After all, a chart is nothing more than a bunch of numbers made into a picture. The numbers come from the datasheet, which works like a simple spreadsheet program. So if you know how to use Excel or Lotus 1-2-3, finding out how to use the datasheet should take you about 30 seconds. The datasheet is part of the Graph object, but it doesn't appear on the slide. Instead, the datasheet appears only when you edit the Graph object.

- **Series:** A collection of related numbers. For example, a chart of quarterly sales by region may have a series for each region. Each series has four sales totals, one for each quarter. Each series is usually represented by a row on the datasheet, but you can change the datasheet so that each column represents a series. Most chart types can plot more than one series. Pie charts can chart only one series at a time, however.

- **Axes:** The lines on the edges of a chart. The *X-axis* is the line along the bottom of the chart; the *Y-axis* is the line along the left edge of the chart. The X-axis usually indicates categories. Actual data values are plotted along the Y-axis. Microsoft Graph automatically provides labels for the X- and Y-axes, but you can change them.

- **Legend:** A box used to identify the various series plotted on the chart. Microsoft Graph can create a legend automatically if you want one.

The Microsoft Graph that comes with PowerPoint is used for the charting functions in Excel. So if you know how to use Excel to create charts, you can pretty much skip the rest of this section: You already know everything you need to know.

When you create or edit a chart, Microsoft Graph comes to life. Rather than popping up in its own window, Microsoft Graph sort of takes over the PowerPoint window and replaces the PowerPoint menus and toolbars with its own. So don't panic if the room seems to spin and your toolbar changes. You're not having a seizure; this is normal.

Microsoft Graph has its own Help system. To see Help information for Microsoft Graph, first call up Microsoft Graph by inserting a chart or by double-clicking an existing chart. Then press F1, click the Help button, or use the Help menu to access Graph help directly.

## Adding a chart to your presentation

To add a chart to your presentation, you have two options:

- ✔ Create a new slide by using an AutoLayout that includes a chart object.
- ✔ Add a chart object to an existing slide.

Using an AutoLayout is the easier way to create a new slide because the AutoLayout positions other elements on the slide for you. If you add a chart to an existing slide, you probably have to adjust the size and position of existing objects in order to make room for the chart object.

### Adding a new slide

The following procedure shows how to insert a new slide that contains a chart:

1. **Move to the slide that you want the new slide to follow.**

2. **Choose Insert⇨New Slide to create a new slide and summon the Slide Layout task pane.**

3. **Click one of the slide layouts that includes a chart.**

   Several slide types include chart objects. Choose the one that you want and then click OK. PowerPoint adds a new slide of the chosen type. The chart object is simply a placeholder; you have to use Microsoft Graph to complete the chart.

   Some of the slide layouts include a *Content item*. If you choose this layout, the slide will have a placeholder for a Content item that has six little icons. These icons let you add a table, a chart, a clip art picture, a picture from a file, a diagram, or a media clip, depending on which icon you click.

4. **Double-click the chart object to conjure up Microsoft Graph.**

Or, if you chose a slide layout with a Content item, just single-click the Chart icon in the Content placeholder. Either way, PowerPoint awakens Microsoft Graph from its slumber, and the two programs spend a few moments exchanging news from home. Then Microsoft Graph takes over, creating a sample chart with make-believe data, as shown in Figure 15-1. Notice that your regular toolbar setup goes away to make room for the Graph toolbar buttons.

5. **Change the sample data to something more realistic.**

The *datasheet,* visible in Figure 15-1, supplies the data on which the chart is based. The datasheet is in a separate window and is not a part of the slide. The datasheet works just like a spreadsheet program. For more information about using it, see the section "Working with the Datasheet" later in this chapter.

6. **Return to the slide.**

Click anywhere on the slide outside the chart or the datasheet to leave Microsoft Graph and return to the slide. You can then see the chart with the new numbers, as shown in Figure 15-2.

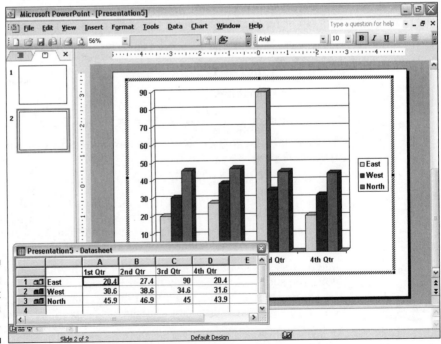

**Figure 15-1:** Microsoft Graph takes over.

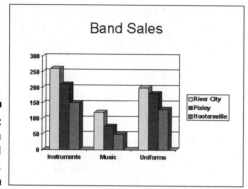

**Figure 15-2:**
A slide with
a finished
chart.

### Adding a chart to an existing slide

If you prefer, you can add a chart to an existing slide by following these steps:

1. **Move to the slide on which you want to place the chart.**

2. **Choose Insert⇨Chart.**

   Or click the Insert Chart button, located near the middle of the Standard toolbar.

3. **Type your data in the datasheet.**

   Replace the sample data with your numbers.

4. **Click outside the chart to return to the slide.**

5. **Rearrange everything.**

   The chart undoubtedly falls on top of something else already on the slide. You probably need to resize the chart by selecting it, and then dragging it by the love handles. You can move the chart like any other object: just click and drag it to a new location. You may also need to move, resize, or delete other objects to make room for the chart.

After you've added a chart to a slide, you can edit the contents or format of the chart by double-clicking the chart. To stop editing the chart so you can work on other parts of the slide, just click anywhere outside of the chart.

## Working with the datasheet

The datasheet contains the numbers plotted in your Microsoft Graph chart. The datasheet works like a simple spreadsheet program with values stored in cells that are arranged in rows and columns. Like a spreadsheet, each column is assigned a letter, and each row is assigned a number. You can identify each cell in the datasheet, therefore, by combining the column letter and row number, as in A1 or B17. (Bingo!)

Ordinarily, each series of numbers is represented by a row in the spreadsheet. You can change this orientation so that each series is represented by a column; to do so, click the By Column button on the toolbar or choose Data⇨Series in Columns. The Data menu is a function of Microsoft Graph and like the toolbar, it vanishes when your datasheet is complete.

The first row and column in the datasheet are used for headings and are not assigned a letter or number.

If you want to chart a large number of data values, you may want to increase the size of the datasheet window. Unfortunately, someone forgot to put the maximize button on the datasheet window, but you can still increase the size of the datasheet window by dragging any of its corners.

You can choose an entire column by clicking its column letter, or you can choose an entire row by clicking its row number. You also can choose the entire datasheet by clicking the blank box in the upper-left corner of the datasheet.

You can change the font used in the datasheet by choosing Format⇨Font. You also can change the numeric format by choosing Format⇨Number. Changing the font and number format for the datasheet affects not only the way the datasheet is displayed, but also the format of data value labels included in the chart.

Although the datasheet resembles a spreadsheet, you can't use formulas or functions in a datasheet. If you want to use formulas or functions to calculate the values to be plotted, use a spreadsheet program, such as Excel, to create the spreadsheet and then import it into Microsoft Graph. (Or create the chart in Excel rather than in PowerPoint. Then import the Excel chart into the PowerPoint presentation by choosing Insert⇨Object or copy the chart into PowerPoint by way of the Clipboard.)

To hide the datasheet, click the datasheet's close button; this action doesn't delete the datasheet, it just hides the datasheet. You can call it up again later by choosing View⇨DataSheet.

## Changing the chart type

Microsoft Graph enables you to create 14 basic types of charts. Each type conveys information with a different emphasis. Sales data plotted in a column chart may emphasize the relative performance of different regions, for example, and the same data plotted as a line chart may emphasize an increase or decrease in sales over time. The type of chart that's best for your data depends on the nature of the data and which aspects of it that you want to emphasize.

Fortunately, PowerPoint doesn't force you to decide the final chart type up front. You can easily change the chart type at any time without changing the chart data. These steps show you how:

1. **Double-click the chart to activate Microsoft Graph.**

2. **Choose Chart⇨Chart Type.**

   Microsoft Graph displays the Chart Type dialog box. From this dialog box, you can choose the chart type that you want to use. The chart types are arranged in two groups: standard on the Standard Types tab and custom on the Custom Types tab. (To show the custom types, click the Custom Types tab at the top of the dialog box.)

3. **Click the chart type that you want.**

4. **To use a variant of the chart type, click the chart subtype that you want to use.**

   For example, the Column chart type has seven subtypes that enable you to use flat columns or three-dimensional columns and to change how the columns are positioned relative to each other.

5. **Click OK and you're done.**

Another way to summon the Chart Types dialog box is to double-click the chart to edit it, right click the chart, and then choose Chart Type from the menu that appears. Make sure your arrow is on a series value when you double-click (one of those bars in the graph), or it won't work. The chart area is very sensitive to random clicking, so be careful and proceed with patience.

You can change the chart type another way by using the Chart Type button on the Microsoft Graph toolbar. When you click the down arrow next to the button, a palette of chart types appears. The Chart Type button provides an assortment of 18 popular types of charts. If you want to use a chart type that isn't listed under the button, choose Chart⇨Chart Type.

If you choose one of the 3-D chart types, you can adjust the angle from which you view the chart by choosing Chart⇨3-D View. Experiment with this one; it's kind of fun.

## Embellishing a chart

Microsoft Graph enables you to embellish a chart in many ways: You can add titles, labels, legends, and who knows what else. You add these embellishments by choosing Chart⇨Chart Options, which summons a Chart Options dialog box that has several tabs from which you can control the appearance of the chart.

To add a chart embellishment, choose Chart⇔Chart Options, click the tab that relates to the embellishment that you want to add, fiddle with the settings, and click OK. The following paragraphs describe each of the Chart Options tabs in turn:

- **Chart titles:** You can add two types of titles to your chart: a *chart title,* which describes the chart's contents, and *axis titles,* which explain the meaning of each chart axis. Most charts use two axes: the *category axis* (the X axis) and the *value axis* (the Y axis). Some 3-D chart types use a third axis called the *series axis.*

    In most cases, the slide title serves as a chart title for a chart included on a PowerPoint slide. If that's the case, you don't need to use a chart title.

- **Axes:** Sometimes an axe is what you'd like to use to fix your computer. But in this case, *axes* refer to the X- and Y-axis on which chart data is plotted. The *X-axis* is the horizontal axis of the chart, and the *Y-axis* is the vertical axis. For 3-D charts, a third axis — *Z* — is also used. The Axes tab of the Chart Options dialog box lets you show or hide the labels used for each chart axis.

- **Gridlines:** *Gridlines* are light lines drawn behind a chart to make it easier to judge the position of each dot, bar, or line plotted by the chart. You can turn gridlines on or off via the Gridlines tab.

- **Legends:** A *legend* explains the color scheme used in the chart. If you want a legend to appear in your chart, click the Legend tab of the Chart Options dialog box, indicate where you want the legend to be placed (Bottom, Corner, Top, Right, or Left), and then click OK.

    Microsoft Graph enables you to create a legend, but you're on your own if you need a myth or fable.

- **Data labels:** A *data label* is the text that's attached to each data point plotted on the chart. You can tell Microsoft Graph to use the actual data value for the label, or you can use the category heading for the label. The Data Labels tab controls this setting. For most slide types, data labels add unnecessary clutter without adding much useful information. Use labels only if you think that you must back up your chart with exact numbers.

- **Data table:** The *data table* is a table that shows the data used to create a chart. The Data Table tab holds the controls that let you add a data table to your chart.

# Creating and Inserting a Diagram

PowerPoint includes a nifty little feature called the Diagram Gallery, which lets you add several different types of useful diagrams to your slides. With the Diagram Gallery, you can create Organization Charts, Cycle Diagrams, Radial Diagrams, Pyramid Diagrams, Venn Diagrams, and Target Diagrams.

Of the six types of diagrams that you can create with the Diagram Gallery, all of them except the Organization Chart are variations on the same theme: They show simple relationships among the elements in a diagram. In fact, after you have created a diagram, you can easily change the diagram to a different type. Thus, if you start with a Radial Diagram but decide that a Pyramid Diagram would better make your point, you can change the diagram to a Pyramid Diagram. Organization Charts, however, show more complex relationships. So you can't change an Organization Chart to one of the other diagram types.

The easiest way to create a diagram is to insert a new slide by using a slide layout that has a placeholder for a diagram. Just follow these steps:

1. **Choose Insert➪New Slide or press Ctrl+M to insert a new slide.**

   A new slide is created and the Slide Layout task pane is summoned so that you can choose a layout for the slide.

2. **Choose the Title and Diagram or Organization Chart layout for the slide.**

   You'll have to scroll through the list of slide layouts to find the Title and Diagram or Organization Chart layout because it's located near the end of the list in the Other Layouts section.

3. **Double click the Diagram or Organization Chart placeholder.**

   This action summons the Diagram Gallery dialog box, shown in Figure 15-3.

**Figure 15-3:** The Diagram Gallery dialog box comes to life.

4. **Choose the diagram type that you want to create.**

   The Diagram Gallery lets you create six different types of diagrams. These diagram types are pictured and described in Table 15-1.

5. **Click OK.**

    The Chart is created. Figure 15-4 shows how an Organization Chart appears when you first create it. The other diagram types have a similar appearance.

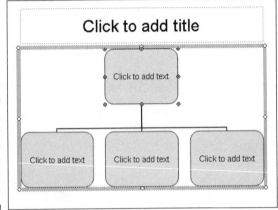

**Figure 15-4:**
An
Organization
chart ready
to be
organized.

6. **Modify the diagram however you see fit.**

    For more information on modifying diagrams, see the sections "Working with Organization Charts" and "Working with Other Diagrams" later in this chapter.

7. **You're done!**

    Well, you're never really done. You can keep tweaking your diagram until the end of time to get it perfect. But at some point, you have to say, "enough is enough" and call it finished.

If you want to add a diagram to an existing slide without using the Title and Diagram or Organization Chart slide layout, click the Insert Diagram or Organization Chart button in the Drawing toolbar (shown in the margin). This brings up the Diagram Gallery dialog box. Choose the type of diagram that you want to add, and then click OK. The diagram is added to the slide.

| Table 15-1 | Types of Diagrams You Can Create | |
|---|---|---|
| *Icon* | *Diagram Type* | *Description* |
| | Organization Chart | Used to show hierarchical relationships among elements. |

| Icon | Diagram Type | Description |
|------|-------------|-------------|
| | Cycle Diagram | Used to show a process that repeats a continuous cycle. |
| | Radial Diagram | Used to show how elements relate to a central element. |
| | Pyramid Diagram | Used to show how elements build upon one another to form a foundation. |
| | Venn Diagram | Used to show how different elements overlap one another. |
| | Target Diagram | Used to show elements that progress towards a goal. |

# Working with Organization Charts

Organization charts — you know, those box-and-line charts that show who reports to whom, where the buck stops, and who got the lateral arabesque — are an essential part of many presentations. You can draw organization charts by using the PowerPoint 2002 standard rectangle- and line-drawing tools, but that process is tedious at best. If Jones gets booted over to advertising, the task of redrawing the chart can take hours.

Mercifully, the new Diagram Gallery feature is adept at drawing organization charts. You can create diagrams that show bosses, subordinates, coworkers, and assistants. You can easily rearrange the chain of command and add new boxes or delete boxes. Figure 15-5 shows a finished organization chart.

Keep in mind that organization charts are useful for more than showing employee relationships. You also can use them to show any kind of hierarchical structure. For example, back when I wrote computer programs for a living, I used organization charts to plan the structure of my computer programs. They're also great for recording family genealogies, although they don't have any way to indicate that Aunt Milly hasn't spoken to Aunt Beatrice in 30 years.

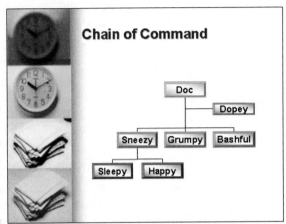

**Figure 15-5:**
A finished
organization
chart.

Previous versions of PowerPoint used a clumsy program called Microsoft
Organization Chart to handle organization charts. The new Diagram Gallery
Organization Chart feature is easier to use, though it isn't as adept at creating
complicated charts as the old program was.

## Adding text to boxes

To add text to an organization chart box, click the box and start typing. If
necessary, PowerPoint adjusts the size of the box to accommodate the text
you type.

You can use any of PowerPoint's text formatting features to format text in
your organization chart boxes. To keep the boxes small, avoid typing long
names or job titles. To create two or more lines of text in a box, just press
Enter whenever you want to start a new line.

Because of an annoying glitch in PowerPoint, the text in organization charts
sometimes becomes too small to read. If that happens, click the top shape in
the chart, and then click the Select button in the Organization Chart toolbar
and choose Branch. Then adjust the font size (using the Font Size control in
the Formatting toolbar) to adjust the text to a more readable size.

## Adding boxes to a chart

To add a new box to an organization chart, follow these steps:

1. **Click the box you want the new box to be below or next to.**

2. **Click the arrow next to the Insert Shape button in the Organization Chart toolbar, and then click one of the following buttons:**

   **Subordinate:** Inserts a new box beneath the selected box.

   **Coworker:** Inserts a new box at the same level as the selected box.

   **Assistant:** Inserts a new box beneath the selected box, but connected with a special elbow connector to indicate that the box is an assistant, and not a subordinate.

3. **Click the new box, and then type whatever text you want to appear in the box.**

4. **If necessary, drag the box to adjust its location.**

## Deleting chart boxes

To delete a box from an organization chart, click the box to select it and press Delete. PowerPoint automatically adjusts the chart to compensate for the lost box.

When you delete a box from an organization chart, you should observe a moment of somber silence — or throw a party. It all depends on whose name was on the box, I suppose.

## Moving a box

To move a box to a different position on the chart, drag the box with the mouse until it lands right on top of the box that you want it to be subordinate to. PowerPoint automatically rearranges the chart to accommodate the new arrangement. Dragging boxes can be a handy way to reorganize a chart that has gotten a little out of hand.

PowerPoint won't let you move a box that has subordinates unless you select all the subordinate boxes. You can do that easily by selecting the box you want to use, clicking the Select button in the Organization Chart toolbar, and clicking the Branch button. You can then move the entire branch.

## Changing the chart layout

PowerPoint lets you choose from one of four methods of arranging subordinates in an organization chart branch:

✔ **Standard:** Subordinate shapes are placed at the same level beneath the superior shape.

✔ **Both Hanging:** Subordinates are placed two per level beneath the superior with the connecting line between them.

✔ **Left Hanging:** Subordinates are stacked vertically beneath the superior, to the left of the connecting line.

✔ **Right Hanging:** Subordinates are stacked vertically beneath the superior, to the right of the connecting line.

Figure 15-6 shows an organization chart that uses all four of these layouts. The first layer of shapes beneath the top level uses the Standard layout. Beneath the first shape on this layer are two shapes with the Both Hanging layout. The other two shapes each have three subordinate shapes with the Left Hanging and Right Hanging layout.

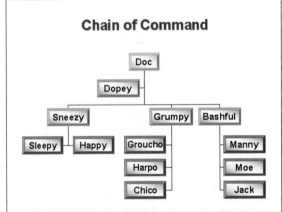

**Figure 15-6:** An organization chart that uses all four layout types.

To change the layout of a branch of your chart, first click the shape at the top of the branch. Then, click the Layout button in the Organization Chart toolbar and choose the layout type you want to use from the menu that appears.

## Changing the chart style

You can fiddle for hours with the formatting for the boxes, lines, and text of an organization chart. But if you want to quickly apply a good-looking format to your chart, click the Autoformat button in the Organization Chart toolbar. This summons the Organization Chart Style Gallery, shown in Figure 15-7. Select the style that you want to apply to your chart, and then click Apply.

**Figure 15-7:**
The
Organization
Chart Style
Gallery lets
you create
a good-
looking
chart
without
much fuss.

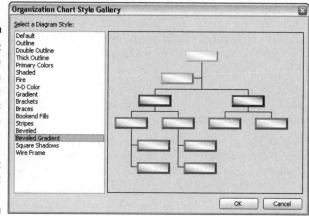

# *Working with Other Diagrams*

Cycle, Radial, Pyramid, Venn, and Target Diagrams are all useful in various situations to illustrate how different items relate to one another. For example, a Target Diagram can help your audience see how working through a series of steps or achieving a series of goals helps advance you toward your ultimate goal. A Pyramid Diagram helps your audience see how one task or idea provides a foundation for other tasks or ideas.

You use similar toolbar controls and menus to create and format all five of these chart types. In fact, you can even switch a chart from one type to another. So if you decide that a Venn Diagram would be better than a Pyramid Diagram, you can simply switch types.

If you don't believe me, look at the two diagrams in Figure 15-8. Both present the same information, one as a Pyramid Diagram, the other as a Target Diagram. To create these diagrams, I first created the Pyramid Diagram. Then, I chose Edit⇨Duplicate to duplicate the chart, and then changed the chart type to Target Diagram.

The following list describes the basics of working with Cycle, Radial, Pyramid, Venn, and Target diagrams:

✔ **Change the diagram type:** To change the diagram type, click the Change To button in the Diagram toolbar and choose the type of diagram you want to change to. (You can only change the diagram type if you use the AutoFormat feature to format the diagram. If AutoFormat is not turned on for the diagram, a dialog box will appear asking if you want to use AutoFormat.)

**Format the diagram:** Any formatting changes you make to the chart, such as changing the colors of individual shapes or changing text fonts or size is lost if you change the diagram type. As a result, you should settle on a diagram type before you make extensive modifications to the diagram's formatting.

✔ **Add text to a shape:** To add text to a shape, click the shape and type. You can use PowerPoint's text formatting features to change the font, size, color, and style of your text.

✔ **Add a shape to the diagram:** To add a shape to the diagram, click the Insert Shape button. PowerPoint adds a shape that is appropriate for your diagram type and automatically resizes and repositions the other shapes in the diagram to accommodate the new shape.

✔ **Delete a shape:** To delete a shape, click the shape to select it and press Delete.

**Figure 15-8:**
Two
diagrams
that present
the same
information
in different
ways.

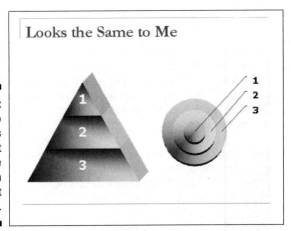

Looks the Same to Me

✔ **Reverse the order of shapes:** You can reverse the order of shapes in the diagram by clicking the Reverse Diagram button.

✔ **Change the order of shapes:** To change the order of shapes in the diagram, click the shape that you want to move, and then click the Move Shape Forward or Move Shape Backward button. (Each diagram type uses a different icon for these buttons, but they are always located next to the Reverse Diagram button.)

✔ **Apply a built-in format to the diagram:** To apply a built-in format to the diagram, click the AutoFormat button. This brings up the Diagram Style Gallery dialog box. Select the diagram style you want, and then click Apply.

✔ **Change the color or style of a shape:** To change the color or style of an individual shape, click the shape to change it, and then use buttons in the drawing toolbar to change the shape's fill or line color, line style, shadow style, or 3-D style. (If you've applied an AutoFormat to the diagram, you must first right-click the diagram and uncheck the Use AutoFormat command.)

✔ **Animate the elements of a diagram:** You can animate the individual elements of a diagram in clever ways. For more information, refer to Chapter 17.

# Creating Fancy Text with WordArt

WordArt is a nifty little feature that takes a snippet of ordinary text and transforms it into something that looks like you paid an ad agency an arm and a leg to design. And the best part — WordArt is free! Figure 15-9 is an example of what you can do with WordArt in about three minutes.

**Figure 15-9:** You, too, can create fancy text effects like this by using WordArt.

You're in luck if you already know how to use WordArt in Word. WordArt is the same in PowerPoint and Word.

Follow these steps to transform mundane text into something worth looking at:

1. **Choose Insert➪Picture➪WordArt.**

   The WordArt Gallery appears, as shown in Figure 15-10.

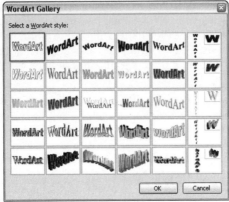

**Figure 15-10:**
The
WordArt
Gallery
offers a
choice of
WordArt
styles.

2. **Click the WordArt style that most closely resembles the WordArt that you want to create and then click OK.**

The Edit WordArt Text dialog box appears, as shown in Figure 15-11.

**Figure 15-11:**
The Edit
WordArt
Text dialog
box.

3. **Type the text that you want to use for your WordArt in the Edit WordArt Text dialog box and then click OK.**

The WordArt object appears along with the WordArt toolbar.

4. **Fool around with other WordArt controls.**

The various controls available on the WordArt toolbar are identified in Figure 15-12. Experiment as much as you want until you get the text to look just right.

5. **Click anywhere outside the WordArt frame to return to the slide.**

# Flowcharts, Anyone?

One type of diagram that people often want to create with PowerPoint is a flowchart. Although the Diagram Gallery doesn't have an option for creating flowcharts, you can easily create flowcharts by using PowerPoint's AutoShapes. For example, take a look at the nearby flowchart, which I created with just a few minutes work.

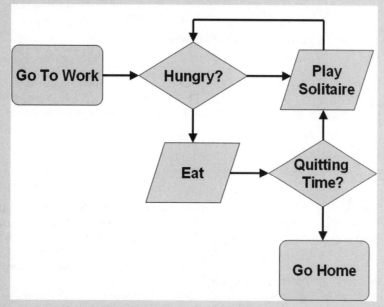

To create a flowchart like this, follow these basic steps:

1. **Draw each flowchart shape by clicking AutoShapes in the Drawing toolbar, and then choosing the shape you want to use from the Flowchart menu.**

2. **Type text into each flowchart shape by clicking the shape and typing.**

   If necessary, adjust the text font and size.

3. **Connect the flowchart shapes by using the Connectors AutoShapes.**

   First choose the type of connector that you want to use by clicking AutoShapes in the Drawing toolbar, and then choose the connector from the Connectors menu. Click the first shape you want the connector to attach to, and then click the second shape. Notice that as you move the mouse around when you have selected a connector AutoShape, connection handles will appear on objects when you have moved within range. Slide the mouse over to one of these connection handles and click to snap the connector to the object.

4. **Now adjust the alignment of your shapes.**

   Here's where the flowcharting AutoShapes really shine: The connectors stay attached to the shapes even when you move the shapes around! Pretty slick, eh?

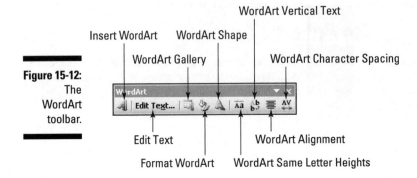

WordArt Vertical Text

Insert WordArt    WordArt Shape

WordArt Gallery      WordArt Character Spacing

Edit Text      WordArt Alignment

Format WordArt      WordArt Same Letter Heights

**Figure 15-12:**
The
WordArt
toolbar.

Don't forget that, in the eyes of PowerPoint, a WordArt object is not text. You can't edit it just by clicking it and typing. Instead, you have to double-click it to conjure up WordArt and then edit the text from within WordArt.

# Using Tables

Tables are a great way to present lots of information in an orderly fashion. For example, if you want to create a slide that shows how many people like or hate various computer presentation programs, a table is the way to go. Or if you're considering purchasing some new computer equipment and want to list the prices for five different computer configurations from three different vendors, a table is the best way.

Basic tables are simple to create in PowerPoint. The easiest way to create a slide that contains a table is to use the Title and Table slide layout. Just follow these steps:

1. **Choose Insert⇨New Slide or press Ctrl+M.**

   A new slide is created, and the Slide Layout task pane appears.

2. **In the Slide Layout task pane, choose the Title and Table slide layout for the new slide.**

   You'll have to scroll down almost to the bottom of the list of slide lay-outs in the Slide Layout task pane to find the Title and Table layout. (It's hidden in the Other Layouts section.) Figure 15-13 shows how a slide with this layout initially appears.

3. **Double-click the Table placeholder in the new slide.**

   The Insert Table dialog box appears, as shown in Figure 15-14.

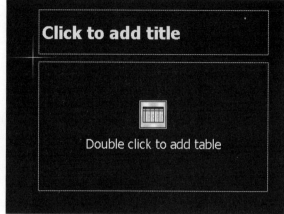

**Figure 15-13:**
A slide that
uses the
Title and
Table layout.

4. **Set the number of rows and columns you want for the table, then click OK.**

   The table appears, as shown in Figure 15-15. Near the table is a floating Tables and Borders toolbar that contains buttons you can use to adjust the table's layout and formatting.

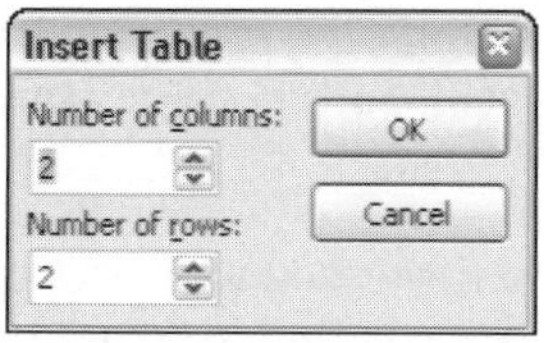

**Figure 15-14:**
The Insert
Table dialog
box.

5. **Type information into the table's cells.**

   You can click any cell in the table and start typing. Or you can move from cell to cell by pressing the tab key or the arrow keys.

6. **Play with the formatting if you want.**

   You may want to change the format of the text in each cell. Or you may want to use the buttons in the floating Tables and Borders toolbar to adjust the borders around each table cell.

7. **Stop and smell the roses.**

   When you're done, you're done. Admire your work.

Figure 15-16 shows an example of a finished table. For this table, I used the Tables and Borders toolbar to erase all the table's borders, and I adjusted the height and width of the rows and columns to fit the text.

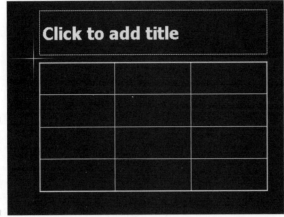

**Figure 15-15:**
An empty
table,
waiting for
data.

If you want to add a table to an existing slide, you have two choices:

- ✔ **Choose Insert➪Table.** This summons the Insert Table dialog box (refer to Figure 15-14). Indicate the number of rows and columns you want, and then click OK.

- ✔ **Click the Insert Table button in the Standard toolbar.** This displays a grid-like menu that enables you to select up to four rows and five columns for the table. Simply drag the mouse over this menu to select the number of rows and columns you want, and then click to add the table to the slide.

The Tables and Borders toolbar appears whenever you work in a table. The controls in this toolbar let you adjust the cells that make up the table or play with the border lines. Wear a helmet if you decide to go exploring in this toolbar.

### Three Popular Programs

|  | Love It | Hate It |
|---|---|---|
| PowerPoint | 93% | 7% |
| Binford Razzle-Dazzle | 48% | 52% |
| Ronko Slide-O-Matic | 35% | 65% |

**Figure 15-16:**
A finished
table.

# Chapter 16

# Lights! Camera! Action! (Adding Sound and Video)

*O*ne of the cool things about PowerPoint is that it lets you create slides that contain not only text and pictures but also sounds and even movies. You can add sound effects such as screeching brakes or breaking glass to liven up dull presentations. You can even add your own applause, making your presentation like a TV sitcom or game show. You can also add a musical background to your presentation.

Additionally, you can insert a film clip from *The African Queen* or a picture of the space shuttle launching if you think that will help keep people awake. This chapter shows you how to add those special effects.

This chapter is short because you can't do as much with sound and video in PowerPoint as you can with, say, a professional multimedia-authoring program such as Macromedia Director. Still, PowerPoint allows you to paste sound and video elements into your slide show, thus giving you the power to craft some impressive high-tech presentations.

## Getting Ready to Add Sound to a Slide

A sterile *beep* used to be the only sound you could get from your computer. Nowadays, you can make your computer talk almost as well as the computers in the *Star Trek* movies, or you can give your computer a sophomoric sense of audible distaste. At last, the computer can be as obnoxious as the user!

As with all good things, there's a catch. Your computer must be equipped with a *sound card* to play these types of sounds. Chances are good that if you bought your computer after 1997, it already has a sound card. If you can't hear sounds from your computer, it's probably because the speakers aren't connected or the volume is turned down.

If you have an older computer that doesn't have sound capability, you can buy and install a sound card for under $50. However, any computer that is old enough to not have a sound card probably isn't capable of running PowerPoint 2003, at least not very well. Maybe it's about time you fork out the dough for a new computer.

# Investigating Sound Files

Computer sounds are stored in *sound files,* which come in two basic varieties:

- **Wave files:** Wave files contain digitized recordings of real sounds. These sounds can be sound effects, such as cars screeching, guns firing, or drums rolling; music; or even quotes from movies or your favorite TV shows. (Imagine Darth Vadar saying to your audience, "I find your lack of faith disturbing.")

  Wave files come in several formats:

  - **WAV:** The basic format for wave files is the standard Windows WAV format. Both Windows and PowerPoint come with a collection of WAV files that provide simple sound effects such as swooshes, blips, applause, and drum rolls.

    **MP3 and WMA:** For longer sound clips, such as complete songs, the popular formats to use include MP3, a compressed format that is popular for sounds obtained from the Internet, and WMA, a newer audio format developed by Microsoft for newer versions of Windows. You can tell the format of a sound file by the filename's extension (.mp3 or .wma).

- **MIDI files:** MIDI files contain music stored in a form that the sound card's synthesizer can play. Windows comes with several MIDI files, and you can download many more from the Internet. MIDI files have the file extension .mid.

To insert a sound into a PowerPoint presentation, all you have to do is paste one of these sound files into a slide. Then when you run the presentation in Slide Show View, you can have the sounds play automatically during slide transitions, or you can play them manually by clicking the Sound button.

## MP3 and the Internet

MP3 files are a compressed form of wave files that allow entire songs to be squeezed into a reasonable amount of disk space. For example, the Steppenwolf song, "Wild Thing," weighs in at just under 2.5MB in an MP3 file. The same file in WAV format requires a whopping 26MB — more than ten times the space.

Napster, the online file exchange system that let users swap MP3 files, popularized the MP3 format. Of course, this file swapping bothered the music industry, which sued because they said users were illegally trading copyrighted music without paying for it, which of course they were and we (oops, I mean they) all knew it.

Napster is now defunct, but a number of other Internet sources have risen to take its place. You can legally download music from sources such as mp3.com, and you can still find plenty of online sources to trade music under the table.

Another popular way to obtain MP3 files is to rip them from a music CD. You can find software to do that by using a search engine (such as www.google.com) for "CD rip."

Keep in mind, however, that the legality of using copyrighted music in your PowerPoint presentations is questionable. So if you use hot MP3 files you got from the Internet or ripped from a CD, don't blame me if one day you wake up and find your house surrounded by federal agents and CNN news crews, who refer to you as a "dangerous copyright abuser" and your house as a "compound." They'll probably even interview your ninth-grade English teacher, who will tell the nation that all you could talk about when you were a troubled teen was stealing Aerosmith music from the Internet and using it in illegal PowerPoint presentations.

You're more likely to use wave files than MIDI files in a PowerPoint presentation. MIDI files are great for playing music, but the wave files enable you to add truly obnoxious sounds to a presentation.

Fortunately, we have no national shortage of sound files. PowerPoint comes with a handful of useful sound files, including drum rolls, breaking glass, gunshots, and typewriter sounds. Windows comes with some useful sounds, too. If you have access to the Web, you have a virtually unlimited supply of sounds at your disposal. Pop into any of the popular search engines (such as www.yahoo.com or www.google.com) and perform a general search, such as "WAV file collection," or a specific search, such as "Star Trek sounds."

Also, Windows includes a sound recorder in its Accessories folder that enables you to experiment with your own sounds — if you dare. Move your computer into the living room some weekend, plug a microphone into the microphone jack on the back of your computer, and rent the following movies:

- ✔ *Star Wars* ("I find your lack of faith disturbing." and "Apology accepted.")
- ✔ *The Princess Bride* ("As you wish." and "He's been mostly dead all day.")

✔ Any of the Saturday Night Live *Best Of* tapes ("Live from New York!")

✔ Monty Python's *Holy Grail* ("It's just a flesh wound.")

✔ *2001: A Space Odyssey* ("I'm sorry Dave." and "Daisy, Daisy, Give me your answer do . . .")

Have a ball, but remember not to violate any copyright laws with what you use. The copyright cops may be watching!

Sound files consume large amounts of disk space. Even just a few seconds of sound can take 100K or more. It may not seem like much space, but it adds up.

# *Inserting a Sound Object*

In this section, I explain how to insert a sound object onto a slide. You can configure the sound object to play automatically whenever you display the slide, or you can set it up so that it will play only when you click the sound object's icon. This is not to say that if you want the sound to play automatically, and the sound is a WAV file, it's easier to add it to the slide transition (as described in Chapter 17) than to add it as a separate object. It you want to control when the sound plays, or if the sound file is in a format other than WAV, follow these steps:

1. **Move to the slide to which you want to add the sound.**

2. **Choose Insert➪Movies and Sounds➪Sound from File.**

   The Insert Sound dialog box appears, as shown in Figure 16-1.

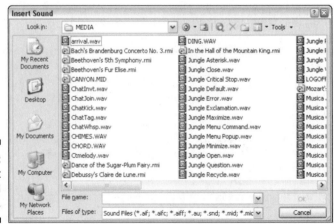

**Figure 16-1:**
The Insert
Sound
dialog box.

3. **Select the sound file that you want to insert.**

   You may have to rummage about your hard drive to find the folder that contains your sound files.

4. **Click OK.**

   A dialog box appears, asking if you want the sound to play automatically when you display the sound, or play only when you click the sound's icon.

5. **Select Automatically or When Clicked.**

   Either way, the sound clip is added to your slide and represented by a little speaker icon.

You can also insert one of the many sounds that come with PowerPoint's Media Gallery or that are available online on the Microsoft Web site. To do so, choose Insert⇨Movies and Sounds⇨Sound From Clip Organizer. This summons the Clip Art task pane (see Figure 16-2), which features a list of sound files that are available for your use. Scroll through the list to find the sound you want, and then double-click the sound to add it to your file. (To hear a preview of the sound before you insert it, right-click the sound and choose the Preview/Properties command.)

Here are a few other random thoughts on adding sounds to your slides:

✔ To play a sound while working in Normal View, double-click the sound icon. However, to play the sound during a slide show, only one click is needed.

✔ If the sound file is smaller than 100KB, PowerPoint copies the sound file into your presentation file. However, if the sound file is larger than 100KB, PowerPoint just adds a link to the sound file so that your presentation won't become bloated with large sound files. If you use large sound files and then copy your presentation to another computer, be sure to copy the large sound files as well. (You can change the 100KB threshold by choosing Tools⇨Options to summon the Options dialog box and then changing the Link Sounds with File Size Greater Than setting under the General tab.)

✔ Remember that you can also play WAV files as a part of the slide transition. For more information, see Chapter 17.

✔ If you change your mind and decide you don't want any sounds, you can easily remove them. To remove a sound, click it and press the Delete key.

✔ You can also use sounds to embellish slide transitions and animations. This embellishing is covered in Chapter 19.

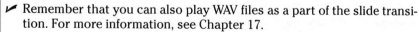

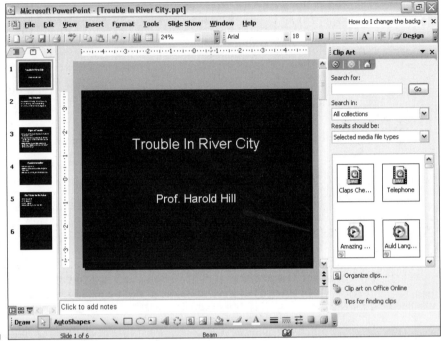

**Figure 16-2:**
Inserting a
sound from
the Media
Gallery.

✔ You can indicate whether you want PowerPoint to display audio controls
on the slide while the sound is playing by right-clicking the sound icon
and choosing the Edit➪Sound Object command. This brings up the Sound
Options dialog box, which is shown in Figure 16-3. In the Show Controls
drop-down list, you can choose whether you want PowerPoint to display
full controls, minimum controls (just Play and Volume), or no controls.

**Figure 16-3:**
Setting the
sound
options.

# Playing a Sound Over Several Slides

Sometimes, you have a sound file that you want to have played while you display several slides. You may even have a sound that you want to loop endlessly until your presentation ends. Unfortunately, PowerPoint has a nasty habit of stopping a sound when you move on to the next slide. However, you can alter this behavior by following these steps:

1. **Right-click the sound icon, and then choose Custom Animation from the menu that appears.**

    Yes, this is actually a Custom Animation feature and I don't cover Custom Animation until Chapter 17, but this particular aspect of Custom Animation is more closely related to playing sound files, so here it is.

    When you choose Custom Animation, the Custom Animation task pane appears to the right of the slide, as shown in Figure 16-4.

2. **Click the down arrow next to the sound item, and then choose Effect Options from the menu that appears.**

    This action summons the Play Sound dialog box, shown in Figure 16-5.

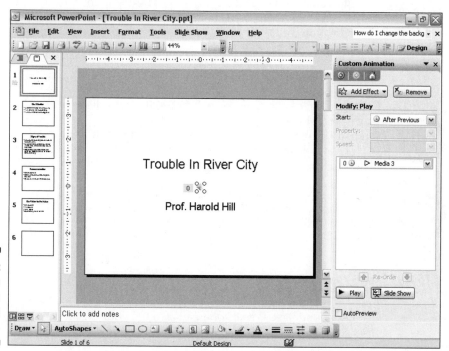

**Figure 16-4:**
The Custom
Animation
task pane
for a sound.

**Figure 16-5:**
The Play
Sound
dialog box.

3. **Click the After option button (in the Stop Playing section), and then set the number of slides you want the sound to play for.**

When you count the slides, start counting with the slide the sound is on. For example, suppose you have a presentation with 10 slides, and you insert a sound on slide 3 and you want the sound to play while slides 3, 4, 5, and 6 are displayed and to stop when slide 7 is displayed. In this case, you would set the number of slides to 4.

4. **Click OK.**

That's it!

If the sound file is not long enough to last through all the slides you want it to play over, right-click the sound icon, call up the Play Sound dialog box (pictured in Figure 16-5), click the Timing tab, and set the Repeat option to the number of times you want the sound to repeat. If you aren't sure, set the number of repeats to 9999. That way, the sound will repeat almost indefinitely.

Nothing stops you from including more than one sound on a slide if you want. For example, you can add background music and a sound effect such as applause or the sound of a train wreck.

# Playing a Track from a CD

Besides sound files, PowerPoint can also tell your CD player to play tracks from a regular audio CD. To use this feature, follow these steps:

1. **Get a CD that has music you want to play during your presentation, and make note of the track you want to play.**

   You won't be able to see the names of the tracks in PowerPoint, so you need to know which track number you want.

2. **Insert the CD in your computer's CD drive.**

3. **Choose Insert⇨Movies and Sounds⇨Play CD Audio Track.**

   This brings up the dialog box shown in Figure 16-6.

**Figure 16-6:**
The Insert
CD Audio
dialog box.

4. **Select the starting and ending track numbers.**

   To play just one track, set both the starting and ending track numbers to the track you want to play. Set these options to different numbers to play more than one track.

5. **Set the other sound options however you want.**

   You can adjust the sound's volume, specify whether you want an icon to appear on the slide, and tell PowerPoint whether you want the sound icon to appear while the sound is playing.

6. **Click OK.**

   A dialog box appears, asking if you want the sound to play automatically when the slide is displayed.

7. **Click Yes or No.**

   That's all there is to it! Now the CD will play when you show the presentation.

Don't forget you have to have the CD in your computer's CD drive when you show the presentation!

# Recording a Narration

PowerPoint includes a nifty feature that lets you record your own voice to use as a narration for the slide show. As you record your narration, PowerPoint stores the narration you record for each file separately so that when you play back your presentation with the narration, the slides are automatically synchronized with the narrations you recorded. PowerPoint can also store timings for each slide so that when you replay the presentation, PowerPoint automatically advances each slide along with the narration.

To record a narration, go to the first slide of your presentation, and then follow these steps:

1. **Choose Slide Show➪Record Narration.**

   The Record Narration dialog box, shown in Figure 16-7, appears. Notice that this dialog box helpfully informs you how much disk space you have available on your computer and calculates the maximum length of the narration that you can record, based on the amount of free disk space. In this example, I have 8,480MB of free disk space, enough to record 13,442 minutes of narration . . . about 224 hours.

**Figure 16-7:**
The Record
Narration
dialog box
lets you
record a
narration for
your slide
show.

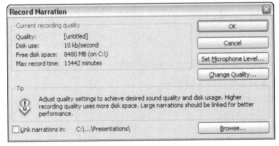

2. **Set the microphone level.**

   To do so, click the Set Microphone Level button. This brings up the Microphone Check dialog box, shown in Figure 16-8. Talk into the microphone, reading the text displayed in the dialog box. As you speak, PowerPoint adjusts your microphone sensitivity to an acceptable range. When you're finished, click OK.

   The Microphone Check dialog box doesn't really care what you say, just so long as you talk.

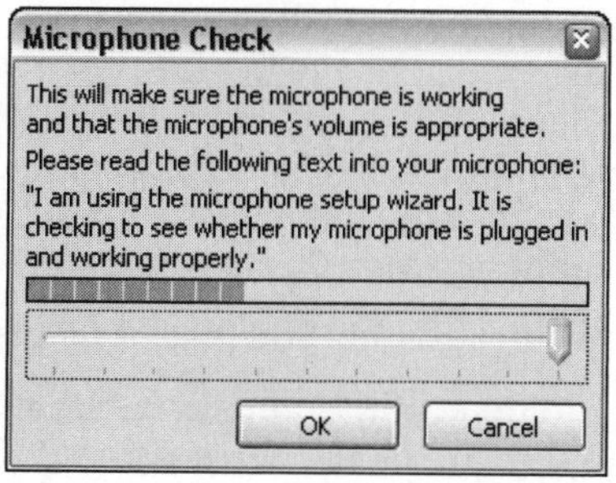

**Figure 16-8:**
Setting the
microphone
level.

**3. Click OK to begin the slide show.**

The first slide of your presentation is displayed.

**4. Speak your narration into the microphone. Press Enter each time you want to advance to a new slide.**

Or, if you have set up builds or other animations, press Enter to advance through the builds and animations.

When you reach the end of the slide show, PowerPoint displays the dialog box shown in Figure 16-9.

**Figure 16-9:**
The
narration is
recorded.
Do you want
to save
the slide
timings?

**5. Click Save if you want PowerPoint to automatically advance your slides in sequence with your narration. To advance slides manually, click Don't Save.**

You're taken to PowerPoint's Slide Sorter View, where the timing for each slide is displayed along with the slides.

**6. Press F5 or click the Slide Show button to begin the slide show so you can see if your narration works.**

The slide show begins. You should hear your narration through your computer's speakers, and the slides should advance automatically along with the narration if you clicked Save in Step 5.

Here are some additional things to keep in mind about narrations:

✔ As you record the narration, leave a little gap between each slide. PowerPoint records the narration for each slide as a separate sound file, and then attaches the sound to the slide. Unfortunately, you'll get cut off if you talk right through the slide transitions.

✔ The narration cancels out any other sounds you placed on the slides.

✔ If you want to show the presentation without the narration, choose Slide Show⇨Set Up Show, and then check the Show Without Narration check box.

✔ You can record or rerecord a narration for just one slide by calling up that slide in Normal View, and then choosing Slide Show⇨Record Narration. PowerPoint asks if you want to begin recording at the current slide or the first slide: Click the Current Slide button. When you're finished recording the slide's narration, press Esc to stop the show.

✔ To delete a narration, click the speaker icon in the corner of the slide and hit the Delete key. To delete the narration for an entire presentation, delete the speaker icon from every slide.

# Working with Video

Welcome to the MTV era of computing. If your computer has the chutzpah, you can add small video clips to your presentations and play them at will. I'm not sure why you would want to, but hey, who needs a reason?

Adding a movie motion clip to a slide is similar to adding a sound clip. A crucial difference exists, however, between motion clips and sound bites: Video is meant to be *seen* (and sometimes *heard*). An inserted motion clip should be given ample space on your slide.

If you think sound files are big, wait till you see how big motion clips are. Ha! The whole multimedia revolution is really a conspiracy started by hard drive manufacturers.

The following steps show you how to add a video clip to a slide:

**1. Find a good movie.**

The hardest part about using video in a PowerPoint presentation is finding a video file that's worth showing. Many good sources offer video clips. PowerPoint comes with movies in the Media Gallery, and Microsoft has additional movies that you can download from the online Media Gallery. You can also find a wide variety of video clips available for download on the Web.

**2. Move to the slide on which you want to insert the movie.**

Hopefully, you left a big blank space on the slide to put the movie in. If not, rearrange the existing slide objects to make room for the movie.

**3. Choose Insert⇨Movies and Sounds⇨Movie from File.**

The Insert Movie dialog box appears.

**4. Select the movie that you want to insert.**

You may need to scroll the list to find the movie you're looking for or navigate your way to a different folder.

**5. Click OK.**

PowerPoint asks if you want to play the movie automatically when the slide comes up or wait for you to click the movie before playing it. (If you select a simple type of movie called an animated GIF, this step is skipped.)

**6. Click Yes to play the movie automatically or No to start the movie manually.**

The movie is inserted on the slide, as shown in Figure 16-10.

**Figure 16-10:** A movie inserted on a slide.

**7. Resize the movie if you want and drag it to a new location on the slide.**

When you resize the movie, try to do it using one of the corner handles. If you drag one of the side handles, you'll distort the image.

To play the movie while you're working on the presentation in Normal View, double-click the movie. During a Slide Show, a single click will do the trick, unless you set the movie to play automatically. In that case, the movie will run as soon as you display the slide.

You can also insert a movie by choosing Insert⇨Movies and Sounds⇨Movie From Clip Organizer. This calls up the Clip Art task pane to display movies that you can access from the Clip Organizer. If you find a movie you're interested in, click the arrow next to the movie and choose Preview/Properties. This calls up the dialog box shown in Figure 16-11, from which you can preview the movie. If you like it, close the Preview/Properties dialog box, and then click the movie in the Clip Art task pane to insert it onto the slide.

**Figure 16-11:** The Preview/ Properties dialog box.

# Chapter 17

# Animation: It Ain't Disney, But It Sure Is Fun

. . . . . . . . . . . . . . . . . . . . . . . . . . . . . . . . . . . . . . . . . . . . . . . . . . . . . . . . . . . . .

### In This Chapter

▶ Using slide transitions

▶ Applying animation schemes

▶ Working with the Custom Animation task pane

▶ Animating text

▶ Setting animation timings

. . . . . . . . . . . . . . . . . . . . . . . . . . . . . . . . . . . . . . . . . . . . . . . . . . . . . . . . . . . . .

*I*f you plan to run your presentation on your computer's screen or on a computer projector, you can use or abuse a bagful of exciting on-screen PowerPoint animations. Your audience probably won't be fooled into thinking that you hired Disney to create your slides, but they'll be impressed all the same. Using animations is just one more example of how PowerPoint can make even the dullest content look spectacular.

This chapter begins with slide transitions, which are not technically animations because they don't involve movement of individual items on a slide. However, slide transitions are usually used in concert with animations to create presentations that are as much fun to watch as they are informative.

## Using Slide Transitions

A *transition* is how PowerPoint gets from one slide to the next during an on-screen slide show. The normal way to segue from slide to slide is simply to cut to the new slide — effective, yes, but also boring. PowerPoint enables you to assign any of more than 50 different special effects to each slide transition. For example, you can have the next slide scoot over the top of the current slide from any direction, or you can have the current slide scoot off the screen in any direction to reveal the next slide. You can have slides fade out, dissolve into each other, open up like Venetian blinds, or spin in like spokes on a wheel.

To use a slide transition, follow these steps:

**1. Move to the slide to which you want to apply the transition.**

If you want to apply the animation scheme to all your slides, you can skip this step because it won't matter which slide you start from.

If you want to apply different transitions to different slides, you may prefer to work in Slide Sorter View (click the Slide Sorter View button near the bottom left corner of the screen), which allows you to see more slides at once. Slide Sorter View also has a few added bells and whistles for working with transitions, which I'll explain in a bit. If you're going to use the same transition for all your slides, though, there's no benefit from switching to Slide Sorter View.

**2. Choose the Slide Show⇨Slide Transition.**

The Slide Transition task pane appears, as shown in Figure 17-1. (Figure 17-1 shows PowerPoint in Slide Sorter View, but the Slide Transition task pane looks the same in Normal View.)

**3. Click the slide transition that you want to use.**

PowerPoint previews the transition by animating the current slide. If you want to see the preview again, just click the transition again.

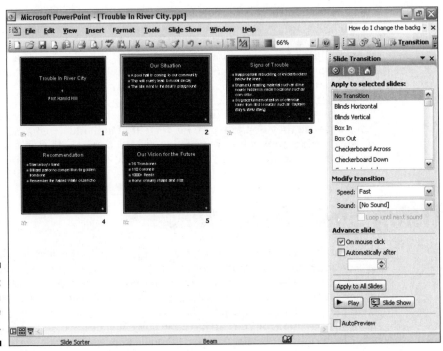

**Figure 17-1:** Setting a slide transition.

4. **Adjust the transition speed if you want.**

   You can choose from Slow, Medium, and Fast. Choose the setting that looks best on your computer.

5. **If you really want to be obnoxious, add a sound.**

   The Sound drop-down box lists a collection of standard transition sounds, such as applause, a cash register, and the standard "whoosh." You can also choose Other Sound to use your own .wav file.

6. **If you want the slide to advance automatically, check the Automatically check box and set the number of seconds.**

   If you leave this box unchecked, PowerPoint waits for you to click the mouse or press a key to advance to the next slide.

7. **If you want to apply the animation to the entire presentation, click Apply to All Slides.**

   This applies the animation to all the slides in the presentation.

Here are some additional points to keep in mind when using slide transitions:

- ✔ **Consider computer speed:** Transition effects look better on faster computers, which have more raw processing horsepower to implement the fancy pixel dexterity required to produce good-looking transitions. If your computer is a bit slow, change the speed setting to Fast so the transition won't drag.

- ✔ **Select sets of transitions:** Some of the transition effects come in matched sets that apply the same effect from different directions. You can create a cohesive set of transitions by alternating among these related effects from slide to slide. For example, set up the first slide using Wipe Right, the second slide using Wipe Left, the third with Wipe Down, and so on.

- ✔ **Use random transitions:** PowerPoint has a Random Transition option that picks a different transition effect randomly for each slide. Although you may be tempted by indecision to use this option, I recommend against it. Your presentation will be more cohesive if you pick a transition effect and stick to it. Using a different transition for every slide can be tacky.

- ✔ **Choose effective transitions:** If the next slide has the same color scheme as the current slide, even the most bizarre transition effects, such as "Wheel Clockwise, 8 Spokes" or "Wedge" looks pretty tame. To maximize the impact of the transitions, use slides with contrasting color schemes.

- ✔ **Preview transitions:** When you work in Slide Sorter View, you can click the little star icon beneath each slide to preview the transition for that slide. Also, the automatic slide timing is shown beneath the slide if you set the slide to advance automatically.

# Using Animation Schemes

The easiest way to use slide transitions is to use the predefined animation schemes that come with PowerPoint. An *animation scheme* is simply a predefined slide transition and a collection of animation effects applied to slide objects. One of the most basic animation schemes is called Appear, which sets up the body paragraphs so that they appear out of thin air one at a time. More complex animation schemes cause text to fly in, do back flips and somersaults, and spin around until it gets dizzy.

I suggest you take a few minutes someday to work your way through all the animation schemes to see how each one works. You can get a good idea about how each animation effect looks by using the previews in the Animation Scheme task pane. To really see how the animation schemes work, however, you should set up a simple presentation with four or five slides with several paragraphs on each slide and a couple of drawing objects here and there. Then, one at a time, apply each animation effect and run the slide show.

To apply an animation scheme to your slides, follow these steps:

1. **Move to the slide to which you want to apply the animation scheme.**

   If you want to apply the animation scheme to all your slides, you can skip this step because it won't matter which slide you start from.

2. **Choose Slide Show⇨Animation Schemes.**

   The Animation Schemes section of the Slide Design task pane appears, as shown in Figure 17-2.

3. **Click the animation scheme you want to use.**

   PowerPoint gives you a preview of what the animation looks like by animating the current slide. If you want to see the preview again, just click the animation scheme again.

The animation schemes are organized into three categories: Subtle, Moderate, and Exciting. At the very beginning of the list of animation schemes, you'll find the five schemes you've most recently used. In addition, you'll find a category called "No Animation" with just one entry, "No Animation," (duh) which removes all animation from the slide.

Clicking the animation scheme doesn't just preview the animation on the current slide, but actually assigns that scheme to the current slide. If you choose to retain the animation you had before, just press Ctrl+Z or choose Edit⇨Undo.

4. **If you want to apply the animation to the entire presentation, click Apply to All Slides.**

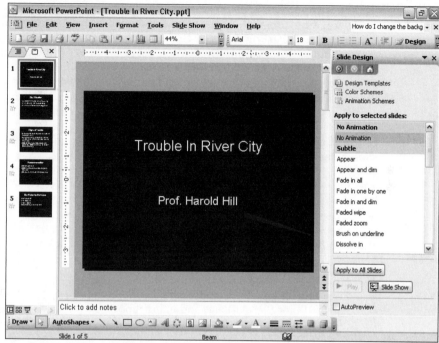

**Figure 17-2:**
Setting up
animation
effects
using
animation
schemes.

5. **Preview the entire show to make sure the animation works.**

You can start the slide show by clicking the Slide Show button in the Animation Scheme task pane, or by choosing Slide Show➪View Show or pressing F5.

# Custom Animation

Custom animation is the nitty-gritty of PowerPoint animation. Although you can create satisfactory animations using the predefined animation schemes, you can really dazzle your audience by using custom animation features. If you want, you can have objects moving all around your slides; some of them automatically, some of them when you click the mouse, two or more at a time, and with sound effects. Wow!

## Understanding custom animation

Before I get into the details of setting up custom animation, you need to understand some basic concepts. Don't worry — this won't get too technical. But this is stuff you need to know.

For starters, you can apply custom animations to any object on a slide, whether it's a text placeholder, a drawing object such as an AutoShape or a text box, or a clip art picture. For text objects, you can specify that the animation should be applied to the text object as a whole or to individual paragraphs within the object. You can also specify whether the effect should go all at once, word by word, or letter by letter. And you can indicate whether the effect should happen automatically or whether PowerPoint should wait for you to click the mouse or press Enter to initiate the animation.

Custom animation lets you create four basic types of animation effects for slide objects:

- ✔ **Entrance effect:** This is how an object enters the slide. If you don't specify an entrance effect, the object starts out in whatever position you have placed it on the slide. If you want to be more creative, though, you can have objects appear using any of 52 different effects, such as Appear, Blinds, Fade, Descend, Boomerang, Bounce, Sling, and many others.

- ✔ **Emphasis effect:** This effect lets you draw attention to an object that is already on the slide. PowerPoint offers 31 different emphasis effects, including Change Fill Color, Change Font Size, Grow/Shrink, Spin, Teeter, Flicker, Color Blend, Blast, and many more.

- ✔ **Exit effect:** This is how an object leaves the slide. Most objects don't have exit effects, but if you want an object to leave, you can apply one of 52 different effects which are similar to the entrance effects: Disappear, Blinds, Peek Out, Ease Out, Spiral Out, and so on.

- ✔ **Motion path:** Motion paths are the most interesting types of custom animation. A motion path lets you create a track along which the object travels when animated. PowerPoint provides you with 64 predefined motion paths, such as circles, stars, teardrops, spirals, springs, and so on. If that's not enough, you can draw your own custom path to make an object travel anywhere on the slide you want it to go.

    If the motion path begins off the slide and ends somewhere on the slide, then the motion path effect is similar to an entrance effect. If the path begins on the slide but ends off the slide, then the motion path effect is like an exit effect. And if the path begins and ends on the slide, it is similar to an emphasis effect. You can also create a path that both begins and ends off the slide. In that case, when the animation starts, the object appears, travels along its path, and then zips off the slide.

You can create more than one animation for a given object. For example, you can give an object an entrance effect, an emphasis effect, and an exit effect. That lets you bring the object onto the screen, draw attention to it, then have it leave. If you want, you can have several emphasis or motion path effects for a single object. You can also have more than one entrance and exit effect, but in most cases, one will do.

Each effect that you apply has one or more property settings you can tweak to customize the effect. All the effects have a speed setting that lets you set the speed for the animation. Some effects have an additional property setting that lets you control the range of an object's movement (for example, the Spin effect has an Amount setting that governs how far the object spins).

## Adding an effect

To animate an object on a slide, follow these steps:

1. **In Normal View, call up the slide that contains the object you want to animate and click the object to select it.**

2. **Choose Slide Show⇨Custom Animation.**

   The Custom Animation task pane appears, as shown in Figure 17-3. In this example, I want to animate a smiley face AutoShape.

3. **Click the Add Effect button, and then select the type of effect you want to create from the menu that appears.**

   The menu lists the four types of effects: Entrance, Emphasis, Exit, and Motion Path. In this example, I choose Entrance so that I can create an entrance effect. A menu listing the effects appears.

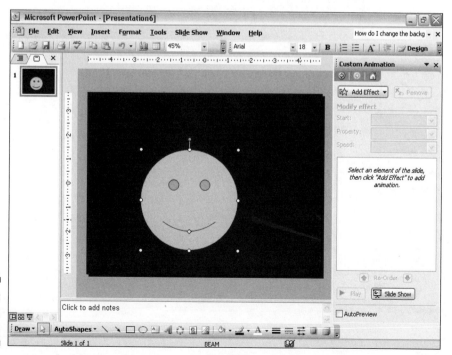

**Figure 17-3:**
Animating
an object.

4. **Choose the specific effect that you want to apply. If the effect that you want isn't on the menu, choose More Effects.**

   An Add Effect dialog box listing all the effects for the type you chose appears. For example, Figure 17-4 shows the Add Entrance Effect dialog box that appears if you choose Add Effect➪Entrance➪More Effects.

   The most commonly used effects for each type are listed right on the effect type menu. If the effect that you want to use appears on the menu, you can select it without calling up the Add Effect dialog box.

5. **Choose the effect that you want, and then click OK.**

   The entrance effect you selected is added to the Custom Animation List task pane, as shown in Figure 17-5. The effect's number (in this case, 1) also appears on the slide next to the object the effect applies to. (Fear not; this number appears on the slide in Normal View only, and only when the Custom Animation task pane is active. Your audience won't see the number when you show your presentation.)

6. **Adjust the property settings for the animation if you want.**

   In Figure 17-5, the effect has two property settings: Direction and Speed. The Direction setting indicates which direction the smiley face should fly in from, and the Speed setting indicates how fast it should move.

**Figure 17-4:**
The Add Entrance Effect dialog box lists all the possible entrance effects.

**Figure 17-5:**
The Custom
Animation
task pane
lists the
animations
you have
created.

7. **To preview the animation, click the Play button at the bottom of the Custom Animation task pane.**

    Or, if you prefer, just run the slide show to see how the animation looks. If nothing happens, try clicking the mouse to get the animation started.

If you add more than one effect to a slide, the effects are initiated one at a time by mouse clicks, in the order you create them. You can drag effects up or down in the custom animation list to change the order of the effects. For more information about changing the order or setting up automatic effects, see the section "Timing your animations" later in this chapter.

Notice in Figure 17-5 that the Add Effect button has changed to Change Effect because the Smiley Face Entrance effect is selected in the custom animation list. If you want to change the effect — for example, use the Magnify entrance effect instead of the Fly In effect — click the Change Effect button and choose a new effect.

You can further tweak an effect by clicking the down arrow that appears next to the effect in the custom animation list, and then choosing Effect Options. This brings up a dialog box similar to the one shown in Figure 17-6. This dialog box has settings that let you add a sound to the animation, change the color of the object after the animation completes, and specify how text is to be animated (all at once, one word at a time, or one letter at a time). Depending on the type of effect, additional controls may appear in this dialog box.

**Figure 17-6:**
The settings dialog box for an animation effect.

## Animating text

The most common reason for animating text is to draw attention to your text one paragraph at a time as you show your presentation. One way to do this is to create an entrance effect for the text placeholder; then adjust the effect settings so that the entrance effect is applied one paragraph at a time. When you do that, your slide initially appears empty except for the title. Click the mouse once and the first paragraph appears. Talk about that paragraph for a while, and then click the mouse again to bring up the second paragraph. You can keep talking and clicking until all the paragraphs have appeared. Then, when you click again, PowerPoint calls up the next slide.

Another approach is to use an emphasis effect instead of an entrance effect. This allows all the paragraphs to be displayed on the slide initially. When you click the mouse, the emphasis effect is applied to the first paragraph — it changes colors, increases in size, spins, whatever. Each time you click, the emphasis effect is applied to the next paragraph in sequence.

Either way, you must first add the effect for the text placeholder, and then call up the Effect Settings dialog box by clicking the down arrow next to the effect in the custom animation list and choosing Effect Settings. This summons the settings dialog box for the text object. Click the Text Animation tab to see the animation settings shown in Figure 17-7.

The Group Text setting is the one that controls how paragraphs appear when you click the mouse during the show, based on the paragraph's outline level.

If you have only one outline level on the slide, grouping By 1st Level Paragraphs will do. If you have two or more levels, leaving grouping text By 1st Level Paragraphs causes each paragraph to be animated along with any paragraphs that are subordinate to it. If you'd rather animate the second-level paragraphs separately, group your text By 2nd Level Paragraphs instead.

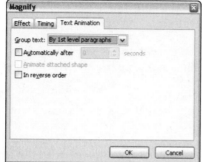

**Figure 17-7:**
Animating
text.

The other controls on this tab let you animate each paragraph automatically after a certain time interval or display the paragraphs in reverse order. (David Letterman, if you're reading this, you can use this feature when you present your Top Ten lists.)

## *Timing your animations*

Most animations are initiated by mouse clicks. However, you can set up several animations to activate automatically — in sequence or all at the same time. To do so, you must use PowerPoint's animation timing features.

The first trick to controlling animation timing is to get the effects listed in the custom animation list in the correct order. Effects are added to the list in the order you create them. If you plan carefully, you may be able to create the effects in the same order that you want to animate them. More likely, you'll need to change the order of the effects. Fortunately, you can do that easily enough by dragging the effects up or down in the custom animation list.

After you get the effects in the right order, choose an option from the Start drop-down list that's near the top of the Custom Animation task pane to set the start option for each effect. This control has three options:

✔ **On Click:** Starts the effect when you click the mouse or press Enter.

✔ **With Previous:** Starts the effect when the effect immediately above it starts. Use this option to animate two or more objects simultaneously.

✔ **After Previous:** Starts the effect as soon as the preceding effect finishes.

Starting with the first effect in the list, click each effect to select it, and then choose the Start option for the effect. If all the effects except the first are set to With Previous or After Previous, the entire slide's animations run automatically once you start the first effect by clicking the mouse.

For example, Figure 17-8 shows a slide with three polygons drawn to resemble pieces of a puzzle. You can animate this puzzle so that the three pieces come together at the same time.

Follow these steps to set up an animated puzzle like the one shown in Figure 17-8:

1. **Add a Fly In entrance effect for the top-left piece with the following settings:**

   • **Start:** On Click

   • **Direction:** From Top-Left

   • **Speed:** Medium

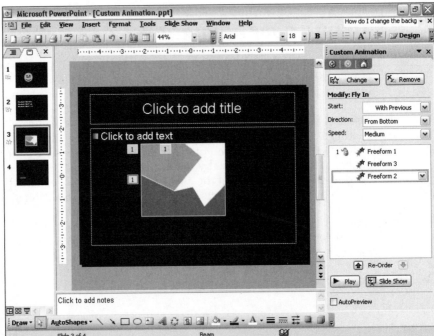

**Figure 17-8:** An animated puzzle.

2. **Add a Fly In entrance effect for the top-right piece with the following settings:**

    • **Start:** With Previous

    • **Direction:** From Top-Right

    • **Speed:** Medium

3. **Add a Fly In entrance effect for the bottom piece with the following settings:**

    • **Start:** With Previous

    • **Direction:** From Bottom

    • **Speed:** Medium

For even more control over an effect's timings, click the down arrow to the right of the effect and choose Timing. A dialog box similar to the one in Figure 17-9 appears. Here's the lowdown on the timing controls:

✔ **Start:** The same as the Start control in the Custom Animation task pane.

✔ **Delay:** Lets you delay the start of the animation by a specified number of seconds.

✔ **Speed:** The same as the Speed control in the Custom Animation task pane.

✔ **Repeat:** Lets you repeat the effect so the object is animated several times in succession.

✔ **Rewind when done playing:** Certain effects leave the object in a different condition than the object was when you started. For example, the object may change color or size or move to a new position on the slide. If you check the Rewind When Done Playing option, the object is restored to its original condition when the animation finishes.

**Figure 17-9:**
Setting the
timing
controls.

# Making Text Jiggle

One of my favorite cute little animations is to make text, especially a short heading, jiggle. Not a lot, just a little. The effect works best if the text has a funny typeface, such as Cosmic or Jokerman. By using a very small motion path and setting the timing options to repeat until the end of the slide, you can make the text jiggle just a little bit the entire time the slide is on-screen:

1. **Type the text that you want to jiggle and use the Font drop-down list to choose an appropriately silly typeface.**

2. **Zoom in to 400%.**

   You want to zoom way in so you can draw a very small motion path.

3. **Choose Slide Show⇨Custom Animation to call up the Custom Animation task pane.**

4. **Click Add Effect, then choose Motion Paths⇨Draw Custom Path⇨Scribble.**

   The mouse pointer changes to a little pencil.

5. **Draw a tightly knit scribble pattern right in the center of the text.**

   Just wiggle the pencil pointer back and forth and up and down in an area of just a few pixels. Go back and forth quite a few times to make the jiggle effect appear to be random.

6. **Zoom back out to normal size.**

7. **In the Custom Animation task pane, click the arrow next to the animation you just created, and then choose Timing.**

   This brings up the dialog box that lets you set the timing options.

8. **Change the speed to Very Fast and the Repeat drop-down to Until End of Slide, and then click OK.**

9. **Run the slide show to check the effect.**

You may have to try this several times before you get an effect you like. Don't be afraid to experiment!

# Chapter 18

# Working with Hyperlinks and Action Buttons

*I*magine that you, a community-minded businessperson, are giving a presentation on how a marching band can cure your town's budding juvenile delinquency problem, knowing full well that the local school board is hounding you, demanding to see your credentials. You have a slide in the presentation that lists your qualifications, but you don't know when you'll need to present it. At any moment, you might hear those fateful words, "Just a minute, Professor . . . we need to see your credentials!"

Is there a way to set up the presentation so that, with a single click of the mouse, you can get to that slide from any other slide? And, once there, maybe with another click of the mouse, go out to the Internet to the home page of the Gary Conservatory of Music? Of course there is! You need to use a hyperlink or an action button, and this chapter explains how to use them.

## Using Hyperlinks

In PowerPoint, a *hyperlink* is simply a bit of text or a graphic image that you can click when viewing a slide to summon another slide, another presentation, or perhaps some other type of document, such as a Word document or an Excel spreadsheet. The hyperlink may also lead to a page on the World Wide Web.

For example, suppose that you have a slide that contains a chart of sales trends. You can place a hyperlink on the slide that, if clicked during a slide show, summons another slide presenting the same data in the form of a table. That slide can in turn contain a hyperlink that, when clicked, summons an

Excel spreadsheet that contains the detailed data on which the chart is based.

Another common use for hyperlinks is to create a table of contents for your presentation. You can create a slide — usually the first or second slide in the presentation — that contains links to other slides in the presentation. The table of contents slide may include a link to every slide in the presentation, but more likely, it contains links to selected slides. For example, if a presentation contains several sections of slides, the table of contents slide may contain links to the first slide in each section.

Hyperlinks are not limited to slides in the current presentation. Hyperlinks can lead to other presentations. When you use this kind of hyperlink, a person viewing the slide show clicks the hyperlink, and PowerPoint automatically loads the indicated presentation. The hyperlink can lead to the first slide in the presentation, or it can lead to a specific slide within the presentation.

A common use for this type of hyperlink is to create a menu of presentations that can be viewed. For example, suppose that you have created the following four presentations:

- ✔ The Detrimental Effects of Pool
- ✔ Case Studies in Communities Destroyed by Pool Halls
- ✔ Marching Bands through the Ages
- ✔ Understanding the Think System

You can easily create a slide listing all four presentations and containing hyperlinks to them. The person viewing the slide show simply clicks on a hyperlink, and off he or she goes to the appropriate presentation.

Here are a few additional thoughts to ponder concerning hyperlinks:

- ✔ **Hyperlinks aren't limited to PowerPoint presentations.** In PowerPoint, you can create a hyperlink that leads to other types of Microsoft Office documents, such as Word documents or Excel spreadsheets. When the person viewing the slide show clicks one of these hyperlinks, PowerPoint automatically runs Word or Excel to open the document or spreadsheet.

- ✔ **A hyperlink can also lead to a page on the World Wide Web.** When the user clicks the hyperlink, PowerPoint runs Internet Explorer to connect to the Internet and displays the Web page.

  For more information about browsing the World Wide Web, see my book *Internet Explorer 6 For Windows For Dummies,* published by Wiley Publishing, Inc.

✔ **Hyperlinks work only when the presentation is shown in Slide Show View.** You can click on a hyperlink all you want while in Slide View, Outline View, or Slide Sorter View, and the only thing that happens is that your finger gets tired. Links are active only when viewing the slide show.

## *Creating a hyperlink to another slide*

Adding a hyperlink to a presentation is easy. Just follow these steps:

1. **Select the text or graphic object that you want to make into a hyperlink.**

   The most common type of hyperlink is based on a word or two of text in a slide's body text area.

2. **Choose Insert⇨Hyperlink.**

   Alternatively, click the Insert Hyperlink button found on the standard toolbar or use the keyboard shortcut Ctrl+K. One way or the other, the Insert Hyperlink dialog box, shown in Figure 18-1, is summoned.

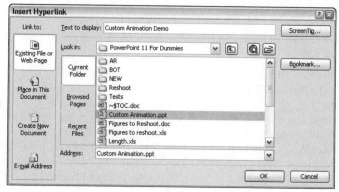

**Figure 18-1:**
The Insert Hyperlink dialog box.

3. **Click the Place in This Document icon in the list of four icons on the left side of the Insert Hyperlink dialog box.**

   The four icons are as follows:

   • **Existing File or Web Page:** This means you can link to another file in another application, or to a Web page on the Internet.

   • **Place in This Document:** This means you can link one part of your PowerPoint presentation to another part.

   • **Create New Document:** This is just what it says it is. You can, however, choose now or another time to edit the new document by clicking the appropriate button.

- **E-mail Address:** Use this to link to an e-mail address. This feature is useful in an intranet or Internet setting because this link allows the reader to write e-mail to the e-mail address that you link to.

If you click the Existing File or Web Page icon, you can then select your link from the following:

- **Current Folder:** Allows you to choose any page in the current folder.

- **Browsed Pages:** Allows you to choose any page that you have browsed using your Web browser recently.

- **Recent Files:** Enables you to view recently used files, which is a subdirectory in windows.

You can then make up your mind whether you want to browse for a file, a Web file, or a bookmark, or if you want to turn off the computer and go for coffee. Don't ask me which one I suggest. After you've found your desired item and clicked it, click OK. And you have lift off — er, I mean hyperlink.

Suppose that you want to just link something to something else in the same presentation. Click the Place in this Document icon, and the text box to the right displays the list of slides in your document. As you click each slide, you can see a slide preview.

4. **Click the slide that you want the hyperlink to lead to, and then click OK.**

   You return to Normal View. The Insert Hyperlink dialog box vanishes, and the hyperlink is created.

If you create the hyperlink on text, the text changes color and is underlined. Graphic objects such as AutoShapes, WordArt, or clip art pictures are not highlighted in any way to indicate that they are hyperlinks. However, the mouse pointer always changes to a hand pointer whenever it passes over a hyperlink, thus providing a visual clue that the user has found a hyperlink.

The color used to display hyperlinks is set by the color scheme. To change the color of the hyperlink, you edit the color scheme and change the Accent and Hyperlink color as well as the Accent and Followed Hyperlink color settings.

## Creating a hyperlink to another presentation

Creating a hyperlink that opens another presentation is much like the procedure described in the section "Creating a hyperlink to another slide," but with a couple important differences:

1. **Select the text or graphic object that you want to make into a hyperlink.**

2. **Choose Insert⇨Hyperlink or click the Insert Hyperlink button.**

   The Insert Hyperlink dialog box appears.

3. **Click Existing File or Web Page from the list of icons on the left side of the dialog box.**

4. **Click Current Folder.**

5. **Choose the file that you want to link to.**

   You may have to rummage about your hard drive to find the presentation.

6. **Click OK.**

The presentation that you link to doesn't have to be in the same folder or even on the same drive as the current presentation. In fact, you can link to a presentation that resides on a network file server, if you want.

You can also link to a specific slide within another presentation by clicking the Bookmark button. This brings up a dialog box listing the slides in the selected presentation. Choose the slide you want to link to; then click OK to return to the Insert Hyperlink dialog box.

If you want to create a hyperlink to an existing Web page, just type the address of the Web page in your outline or on your slide and a hyperlink automatically appears. You can select any page of a Web site as long as you know the URL for that specific page.

When you follow a link to another presentation, PowerPoint automatically opens the other presentation. This means that you now have both presentations open. After you're finished viewing the second presentation, close it to return to the original presentation.

To remove a hyperlink, right-click the hyperlink that you want to zap, and then choose Remove Hyperlink from the menu that appears. To change a hyperlink, right-click it and choose Edit Hyperlink.

# Using Action Buttons

An *action button* is a special type of AutoShape that places a button on the slide. When the user clicks the button during a slide show, PowerPoint takes whatever action you have designated for the button. The following sections describe how action buttons work and show you how to add them to your presentations.

## Button actions

When you create a button, you assign a shape for the button (you have 12 shapes to choose from; the shapes are described a bit later in this section) and an action to be taken when the user clicks the button or merely points the mouse pointer at it. The action for a button can be any of the following:

- ✔ **Activate a hyperlink:** This is the most common button action. It causes a different slide in the current presentation, a different presentation altogether, a non-PowerPoint document, or even an Internet Web page to appear.
- ✔ **Run a program:** For example, you can set up a button that runs Microsoft Word or Excel.
- ✔ **Run a macro:** PowerPoint lets you create *macros,* which are programs written in a powerful programming language called Visual Basic for Applications.
- ✔ **Play a sound:** This is just one way to add sound to a PowerPoint presentation. For more ways, refer to Chapter 16.

You can set up an action button as a hyperlink, so that when the user clicks the button, a different slide in the current presentation or a different presentation altogether is displayed. A well-planned arrangement of action buttons scattered throughout a presentation can make it easy for someone to view the presentation in any order he or she wants.

## Choosing button shapes

PowerPoint provides a selection of built-in shapes for action buttons. Table 18-1 lists the action button shapes that you can place in your presentation and indicates what type of action is associated with each type.

| Table 18-1 | Action Buttons | |
|---|---|---|
| **Button Image** | **Name** | **What Button Does** |
|  | Custom | No default action for this button type |
| | Home | Displays the first slide in the presentation |

| Button Image | Name | What Button Does |
|---|---|---|
| ? | Help | No default action for this button type |
| ⓘ | Information | No default action for this button type |
| ◀ | Back or Previous | Displays the previous slide in the presentation |
| ▶ | Forward or Next | Displays the next slide in the presentation |
| ◀\| | Beginning | Displays the first slide in the presentation |
| ▶\| | End | Displays the last slide in the presentation |
| ↺ | Return | Displays the most recently viewed slide |
| 📄 | Document | No default action for this button type |
| 🔊 | Sound | No default action for this button type |
| 🎥 | Movie | No default action for this button type |

# Creating a button

To add a button to a slide, follow these steps:

1. **Move to the slide on which you want to place a button.**

2. **Click the AutoShapes button in the drawing toolbar and then click Action Buttons.**

The Action Buttons toolbox appears.

**3. Click the button for the action button shape that you want to create.**

**4. Draw the button on the slide.**

Start by pointing to the spot where you want the upper-left corner of the button to appear. Then press and hold the left mouse button and drag the mouse to where you want the lower-right corner of the button to appear.

When you release the mouse button, the Action Settings dialog box appears, as shown in Figure 18-2.

**Figure 18-2:**
The Action
Settings
dialog box.

**5. If you want, change the action settings for the action button.**

In most cases, the default setting for the action button that you chose is appropriate for what you want the button to do. For example, the action setting for a Forward or Next Button is Hyperlink to Next Slide. If you want the slide to hyperlink to some other location, change the Hyperlink to setting.

**6. Click OK.**

The Action Settings dialog box vanishes, and the button is created.

Here are some additional thoughts concerning action buttons:

✔ **Change the look of a button:** Like many other AutoShapes, the action button shapes have an adjustment handle — a little diamond-shaped handle that floats nearby. You can drag the adjustment handle to change the apparent depth of the button image.

✔ **Move a button:** To move a button, just click it to select it. Then drag the button with the mouse to a new location.

✔ **Change the action setting for a button:** You can change the action setting for a button by right-clicking the button and choosing the Action Settings command.

✔ **Apply a fill color to a button:** Action buttons, by default, assume the fill color from the slide's color scheme. You can apply any fill color that you want to the button, just like you can to any other drawing object. Refer to Chapter 14 for details.

## Creating a navigation toolbar

Grouping action buttons into a navigation toolbar makes a slide show easy to navigate. You can add a set of navigation buttons to the bottom of your Slide Master. Figure 18-3 shows a slide with navigation buttons in the lower-right corner. These buttons make getting around the show a snap. For this example, I use Beginning, Backward or Previous, Forward or Next, and Ending buttons, but you can include any buttons you want.

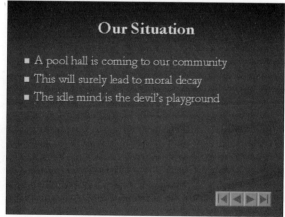

**Figure 18-3:** A slide with navigation buttons.

To create a navigation toolbar that appears on every slide, follow these steps:

1. **Switch to Slide Master View.**

   Choose View➪Master➪Slide Master. Or, if you like shortcuts, hold down the Shift key and press the Normal View button at the lower-left corner of the PowerPoint window.

**2. Create the action buttons that you want to include.**

Follow the procedure described earlier in the section "Creating a button" to create each button. Make sure that all the buttons are the same size and line them up to create a tight cluster of buttons.

You can easily duplicate a button by holding down the Ctrl key while you drag the button to a new location. This technique makes it easy to create several similar buttons such as navigation buttons.

**3. Return to Slide View.**

Click the Slide View button or choose View⇨Slide.

The buttons that you created appear on every slide in your presentation.

# Chapter 19

# Creating a Video Presentation with Microsoft Producer

*P*owerPoint is great for preparing presentations to give in person. But what about giving presentations when you can't be there? With digital video cameras practically being given away in cereal boxes these days, just about anyone can record a video of themselves giving a presentation. Wouldn't it be great if you could easily combine the slides from a PowerPoint presentation with a video of you presenting it? Then, anyone can watch the presentation later, when you can't be there. Microsoft Producer lets you do just that.

## Introducing Microsoft Producer

Microsoft Producer is an add-on product to PowerPoint that lets you combine slides from existing PowerPoint presentations with media files (audio or video) to create presentations that you can view using a Web browser. You can view the resulting presentation on your own computer, over a network, or even over the Internet. The audience watching the presentation doesn't even have to own PowerPoint. As long as they have a Web browser and a current version of Microsoft's Media Player, they can view the presentation.

Figure 19-1 shows a typical Producer presentation being viewed in Internet Explorer. This presentation uses one of Producer's built-in templates, which places the video portion of the presentation at the top left of the page, a table of contents below the video, and the presentation's slides on the right.

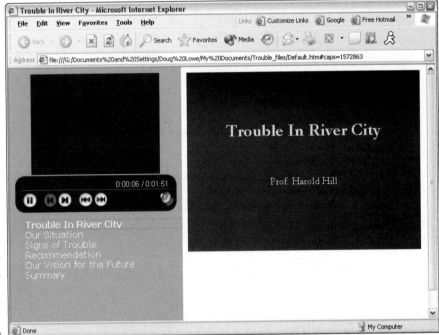

**Figure 19-1:**
A Microsoft
Producer
presen-
tation.

Although Microsoft Producer doesn't come with PowerPoint, you can download it free of charge from Microsoft's Web site. Just point your browser to `www.microsoft.com/office/powerpoint/producer`. If that doesn't work (Microsoft has an annoying habit of reorganizing its Web site once in awhile), go to a search service such as Google (`www.google.com`) and search for Microsoft Producer. After you find the page, follow the links to download the software and install it on your computer. Producer is a large download — about 23MB, so it may take a couple of hours to download if you don't have a high-speed Internet connection.

Although Producer can be used for more sophisticated video editing tasks than simply playing a video alongside PowerPoint slides, this is a PowerPoint book, not a Microsoft Producer book. So in this chapter, I'll just show you how to create a simple presentation that combines PowerPoint slides with video. After you learn how to do that, you can experiment on your own with Producer's additional features.

# Creating a Producer Presentation

Before you fire up Producer to create a video presentation, you need to first create the files that will comprise the presentation. First, create the

PowerPoint presentation with the slides that will be shown alongside the video. Then, create the video itself. To do that, you'll need to write a script, and then get hold of a digital video camera and record it. If possible, save the file in the same folder as the PowerPoint presentation. That way, you won't have to hunt for it later. Producer works with several popular video file formats, including ASF, AVI, MPG, and WMA.

The easiest way to create a new Producer presentation, especially while you're learning how to use Producer, is to use the New Presentation Wizard. Producer offers to run the wizard when you first start Producer. If you want to run the wizard again later, you can start it by choosing File⇨New Presentation Wizard.

Follow these steps to create a new presentation using the Wizard:

1. **Start the wizard**.

   Choose File⇨New Presentation Wizard, or select Use the New Presentation Wizard from the dialog box that appears when you start Producer. Either way, the wizard comes to life as shown in Figure 19-2.

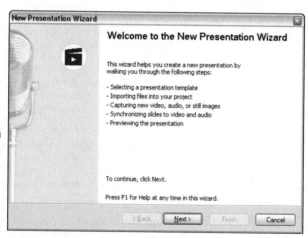

**Figure 19-2:**
The New Presentation Wizard.

2. **Click Next.**

   The wizard asks you to choose from one of its many presentation templates, as shown in Figure 19-3. Scroll through the list and look at the templates. They provide various combinations of sizes and layouts for the slides, video, and other elements that comprise a Producer presentation.

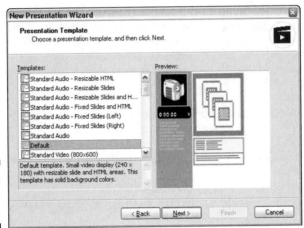

Figure 19-3:
Pick a
template.

3. **Pick the template that seems most suited to your presentation, and then click Next.**

   The wizard displays a selection of formatting options that let you choose fonts and colors. You can change these settings if you want to customize the appearance of your presentation.

4. **Change the font and colors for the presentation if you want, and then click Next.**

   You are now asked to provide descriptive information for the presentation, such as the title, author, and a brief description. The information that you provide here is displayed on the start page, before your presentation plays.

5. **Type the title, author, and introductory text for your presentation, and then click Next.**

   The wizard displays a page that lets you specify which PowerPoint presentation to use.

6. **Click the Browse button to summon the Browse dialog box, and then find your PowerPoint presentation. Click Open in the Browse dialog box to return to the wizard, and then click Next.**

   This action brings up the next page of the wizard, which looks remarkably like the previous page but lets you import audio or video media files rather than PowerPoint presentations.

7. **Click the Browse button to summon the Browse dialog box, and then find the video file that you want to include in the presentation. Click Open in the Browse dialog box to return to the wizard, and then click Next.**

   The next page asks if you want to synchronize the slides in the PowerPoint presentation with the video.

8. **Click Yes to synchronize the slides, and then click Next. When the final page of the wizard appears, click Finish to complete the wizard.**

   Producer grinds and whirs for a moment as it imports the files you specified in Steps 6 and 7 and builds the presentation. When it's all done, it clears its throat and displays the screen shown in Figure 19-4. This screen allows you to synchronize the slides with the video.

9. **Click the Play button (the big fat arrow beneath the video).**

   The video starts to play.

10. **Click Next Slide each time you want to advance to the next slide.**

    You have to pay attention during the video, which may be difficult because you're probably sick of the presentation by now. Each time you get to the point in the video where you want to advance to the next slide, click Next Slide. Producer keeps track of the time as you synchronize the slides so when you play the presentation back, each slide will advance at the right time.

11. **Click Finish when you're done.**

    Whew! You are now taken to the Producer screen, where you can continue to work on your presentation if you still have the energy.

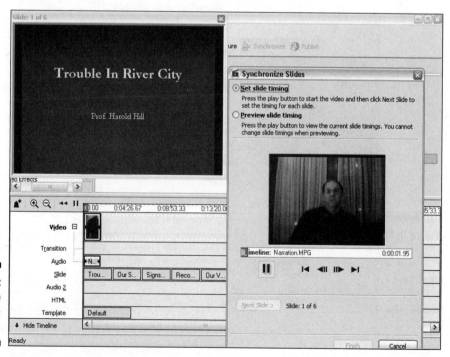

**Figure 19-4:** Get ready to synchronize!

# Editing a Presentation

After you have created a presentation in Producer, you can tweak its fine points in order to get the presentation just right. Figure 19-5 shows the Producer window. I won't go into all the details of working with presentations in Producer, but I want to point out some of the highlights to get you going:

✔ **The Timeline area:** At the bottom of the window is an area called the *Timeline*. The Timeline shows the various *tracks* that make up the presentation. In this case, four tracks are present. At the top is the video portion of a MPEG file that I imported in the New Presentation Wizard. It's linked to the audio portion of the MPEG file, which is shown as a separate track in the timeline. The PowerPoint slides comprise a third track, and the template used for those slides is the final track.

You can adjust the timing of items in the Timeline by selecting them, and then dragging their edges to make them longer or shorter. You can also rearrange items, such as individual slides in the Slides track, by dragging them to new locations.

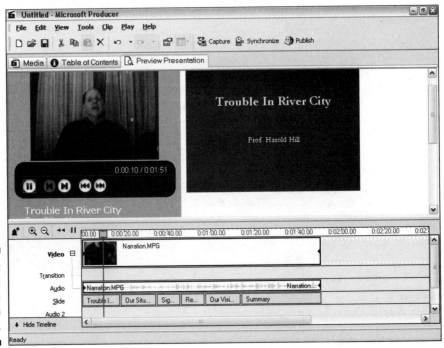

**Figure 19-5:**
Working
with a
presentation
in Producer.

✔ **The Media tab:** The middle section of the screen consists of three tabbed areas. This tab lists all of the files that have been imported into the presentation. You can use this area to add or remove files. If you import a file into the presentation by choosing File⇨Import, the file will appear in the Media tab. You can then drag the item onto the Timeline in order to incorporate it into the presentation.

✔ **The Table of Contents tab:** The Table of Contents tab lets you edit the entries in the presentation's table of contents, which is displayed when the presentation is run. Producer creates the table of contents based on the contents of the PowerPoint presentation. Use the Table of Contents tab if you want to change the entries that Producer creates.

✔ **The Preview Presentation tab:** The Preview Presentation tab lets you preview your presentation, as shown in Figure 19-5.

# Saving and Publishing a Presentation

In Producer, saving a presentation is different from publishing a presentation. You'll want to save a presentation often as you work on the presentation. You can save a presentation by clicking the Save button in the toolbar or by choosing File⇨Save. Saving the presentation creates a Microsoft Producer file that you can open later and work on some more.

To actually show your presentation, you must first publish it by choosing File⇨Publish. This creates the HTML files that actually comprise the final presentation. To publish a presentation, follow these steps:

1. **Choose File⇨Publish Presentation.**

   This summons the Publish Wizard, shown in Figure 19-6.

2. **Choose the location where you want the presentation to be published.**

   The Publish Wizard gives you three options:

   • **My Computer:** This option publishes the presentation to your own computer, either to your computer's hard drive or to a CD drive if you have a CD burner.

   • **My Network Places:** This option publishes the presentation to a network server. This option lets other people view your presentation over a network.

   • **Web Server:** This option publishes the presentation to a Web server.

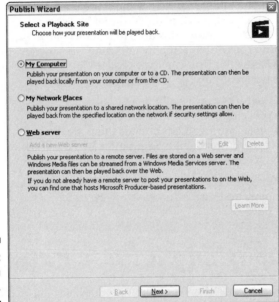

**Figure 19-6:**
The Publish
Wizard.

3. **Click Next.**

   You're taken to a page that lets you specify the location where you want the presentation to be published. The exact appearance of this page varies slightly depending on which option you specified in Step 2.

4. **Specify the location where you want the presentation published.**

   If you chose My Computer or My Network Places in Step 2, you can supply a filename for the presentation and browse your computer or network for the location where you want the presentation published. If you chose Web Server, you must supply the host address of the Web server you want to publish the presentation to, and you may be required to enter a username and password.

5. **Click Next.**

   A page displaying the presentation's title, the presenter's name, and a description of the presentation appears. The wizard displays the information that you supplied when you created the presentation, but you can use this page to change the information if you want.

6. **Click Next again.**

   Now the wizard displays a list of publishing profiles that are based on the user's connection speed. For users who will view the presentation from their own computer, either from the computer's hard drive or a CD, choose the first option: For Local Playback at 800 Kbps. The other options let you provide lower quality video for users with slower connections.

Note that you can choose more than one of these profiles. If you do, the user is given the option of picking which one to use based on the speed of his or her connection.

The faster connection speed profiles require more disk space. For example, if you set local playback to the local playback at 800 Kbps, the resulting file will be about three times larger than the file required for playback at 300 Kbps and about 6 times bigger than the file needed for 150 Kbps.

7. **Choose one or more profiles, then click Next.**

   The last page of the Publish Wizard appears. One more click is all you need. . . .

8. **Click Finish, and then take a nap.**

   Publishing a presentation is a time-consuming task. Even publishing a relatively short presentation to your local computer can take a few minutes. If you're publishing the presentation to a Web site, the process will take longer, depending on the speed of your Internet connection. The Publish Wizard displays progress bars to let you know how things are going. When it finishes, it asks if you want to view the published presentation.

9. **Click Yes to view the presentation or click No to skip it.**

   If you click Yes, a browser window opens so you can view the presentation. For more information, see the next section, "Viewing a Presentation."

# Viewing a Presentation

To view a presentation, just open the HTML file that you created with the Publish Wizard in your Web browser. If you published the file to the Internet, fire up Internet Explorer or your favorite browser and type the address of the published presentation in the Address bar. If you published the file to My Computer or My Network Places, open a My Computer or My Network Places window, locate the file, and double-click it.

The start page for a published presentation appears as shown in Figure 19-7. To play the presentation, just click the Play link.

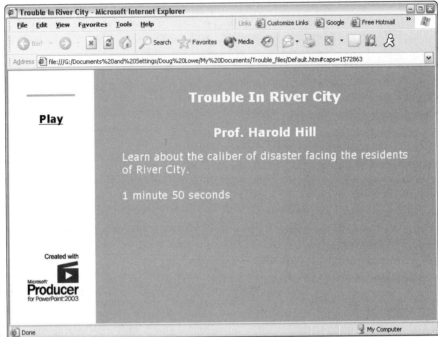

**Figure 19-7:**
Starting a
Presen-
tation.

# Part IV
# PowerPoint and the Net

## In this part . . .

You can't sneeze these days without someone blaming it on a computer virus you picked up from the Internet. Because the Microsoft programmers who work on PowerPoint sneeze a lot, it comes as no surprise that PowerPoint is rife with Internet features. You can save and retrieve presentations from the Internet, publish presentations to Web sites, and even collaborate on PowerPoint presentations with your Internet buddies. You can find all this and more in the next three chapters.

# Chapter 20

# Going Online with PowerPoint

*In This Chapter*

▶ Saving and retrieving presentations on a Web server

▶ Accessing FTP sites from PowerPoint

▶ Using the Web toolbar

▶ Broadcasting a presentation

*I*n the early, Bronze Age era of computing, the only way to the Internet was through special Internet programs such as e-mail programs and Web browsers. Now, however, you can access the Internet directly from the comfort of your favorite application programs, including PowerPoint. If you have access to a Web server, PowerPoint lets you save a presentation file directly to the server. And you can open a presentation directly from the Internet without leaving PowerPoint. Pretty cool, eh?

This entire chapter assumes that you have access to the Internet. If you don't have Internet access, you should first pick up a copy of my book, *Internet Explorer 6 For Windows For Dummies,* published by Wiley Publishing, Inc., which shows you how to get connected to the Internet, and as a bonus, shows you how to use Internet Explorer 6 to access the Internet.

## Saving a Presentation on a Web Server

Suppose that you create a PowerPoint presentation and decide to make it available to the general public via the Internet. You can do that by saving the presentation as an HTML file so that anyone with a Web browser can access the presentation. You'll learn how to do that in the next chapter. A simpler method is to save the .ppt file to a Web server. This way, anyone who has PowerPoint can open the presentation directly from the Web server and view the file from within PowerPoint.

Before you can save a PowerPoint presentation to a Web server, you need to obtain access to a Web server. You can do that by purchasing space on a Web server from a Web hosting company or by setting up your own Web server.

The details for doing that are a little beyond the scope of this book, but you can find out more in my book, *Internet Explorer 6 For Dummies*.

After you've gained access to a Web server, you'll need the address of the Web server. In addition, you'll need a user ID and password that grants you access to the server. You'll need to get those details from the person responsible for setting up the server.

After your Web server is set up, the next step is to set up a network place in your My Network Places folder. This will allow you to easily access the Web server when you want to save or retrieve presentations. To create a network place, choose My Network Places from the Start menu, and then click the Add a Network Place link that appears in the task pane. This launches a wizard that asks for the Web site address (such as `http://www.mywebsite.com`) and your user ID and password. When the wizard finishes, an icon for the Web server appears in your My Network Places folder.

When you've added a network place for your Web site, you can save a presentation to the site by opening the presentation and choosing File⇨Save As. In the Save As dialog box, click the My Network Places icon, double-click the icon for your Web server, and then click Save. The presentation is saved to your Web server.

# Opening a Presentation from a Web Server

To open a `.ppt` presentation that resides on a Web server in PowerPoint, choose File⇨Open. Note that although anyone can open a presentation you saved to a Web server, they must have a user ID and password for the server in order to save any changes they make to the presentation back to the server.

To open a presentation located on a Web server, you must know the complete address (called a *URL*) of the presentation that you want to open. This address usually consists of three parts: a server address, one or more directory names, and a filename for the presentation. The address must always begin with `http://` so that PowerPoint can distinguish the address from a normal filename. The other parts of the URL are separated by slashes.

For example, consider this address:

```
http://www.LoweWriter.com/trouble.ppt
```

Here, the host name is `www.LoweWriter.com` and the filename is `trouble.ppt`.

When you know the URL, all you have to do to open a presentation in PowerPoint is type its URL in the File Name field on the standard Open dialog box. Here's the complete procedure for opening a presentation at a Web site:

1. **Find out the complete URL of the presentation that you want to open.**

2. **Choose File⇨Open.**

   Alternatively, click the Open button or use the keyboard shortcut Ctrl+O. One way or the other, the Open dialog box appears.

3. **In the File Name field, type the URL of the presentation that you want to open.**

   For example, type `http://www.LoweWriter.com/trouble.ppt`.

4. **Click Open.**

   If you're not already connected to the Internet and you use a dialup connection, a Connect To dialog box appears so that you can make a connection.

5. **If prompted, enter the username and password for the site where the presentation resides.**

   Depending on how the Web site is set up, it may allow you to access the presentation without entering a username and password. If a username and password is required, you'll have to get the required information from the person who administers the site.

6. **Play a quick game of Solitaire.**

   Copying the file over the Internet to your computer takes a bit of time — perhaps even several minutes if the presentation is large and your connection is slow. When the transfer is finished, the presentation is displayed as normal.

If you have the Web toolbar displayed, you can enter the address in the Address box, press Enter, and voilà! The presentation is displayed. You can find more about the Web toolbar by reading the section "Using the Web Toolbar" later in this chapter.

PowerPoint doesn't care if the file identified by the URL is on a computer halfway around the globe, on a computer two floors up from you, or on your own computer. So long as the URL is valid, PowerPoint retrieves the presentation and displays it.

# Using an FTP Site

FTP, which stands for *File Transfer Protocol,* is one of the oldest parts of the Internet. FTP is designed to create Internet libraries in which files can be stored and retrieved by other Internet users.

FTP uses a directory structure that works much like Windows 95 or 98 folders. The main directory of an FTP site is called the *root*. Within the root are other directories, which may contain files, additional directories, or both. For example, a typical FTP server for a business may have directories such as Products (for storing files that contain product information), Company (for company information), Software (for software files that can be downloaded), and Docs (for documentation about the company's products).

Until Office 97, you had to use separate FTP software to retrieve files from an FTP site. Since Office 97 (and in PowerPoint 2003, of course), you can access FTP sites from the standard Open and Save As dialog boxes as if they were disk drives attached to your computer.

The following section — "Adding an FTP Site to Your Computer" — explains how you can set up an FTP site so that you can access it from within PowerPoint. The section after that — "Opening a presentation from an FTP site" — shows how to actually access an FTP site from PowerPoint.

# Adding an FTP Site to Your Computer

Before you can access files in an FTP site, you must add the address (URL) of the FTP site to your computer's list of FTP sites. To do that, follow these steps:

1. **In PowerPoint, choose File➪Open.**

   This command summons the Open dialog box.

2. **Click the down arrow for the Look In list box and then scroll down to select Add/Modify FTP Locations.**

   The dialog box shown in Figure 20-1 appears.

3. **Type the URL of the FTP site in the Name of FTP site field.**

   Be sure to include `ftp://` at the start of the URL. (You don't usually have to type `http://` to access Web sites, but you do have to type the `ftp://` to access an FTP site.)

4. **If this FTP site requires you to enter a username and password to gain access, click the User button and then type your username and password.**

   You have to get the username and password to use from the administrator of the FTP site you are accessing. (At many FTP sites, the username of "Anonymous" works, and the password is your e-mail address.)

5. **Click Add.**

   The new FTP site is added.

6. **Click OK.**

The Add/Modify FTP Locations dialog box vanishes, returning you to the Open dialog box.

**7. Click Cancel to return to PowerPoint.**

The FTP site is now added to the list of FTP sites that are available from within PowerPoint. To open a presentation from this site or another site you have previously added, follow the steps detailed in the next section.

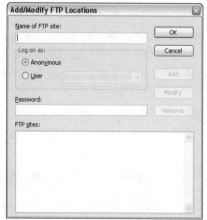

**Figure 20-1:**
Adding an
FTP site.

# Opening a presentation from an FTP site

To open a presentation from an FTP site, follow these steps:

**1. Choose File⇨Open.**

This summons the Open dialog box.

**2. Click the down arrow of the Look In list box and then scroll down to find and select the FTP site containing the presentation that you want to open.**

Your computer hesitates for a moment as it connects with the FTP site. Then the Open dialog box is displayed, listing the directories that appear at the FTP site's root.

**3. Select the file that you want to open.**

To open a directory, double-click the directory's icon. Click the icon of the file that you want to select.

**4. Click Open.**

Depending on the size of your presentation, you may have to wait for a few minutes for PowerPoint to download the presentation.

You're done!

## *Saving a presentation to an FTP site*

If you have access to an FTP site that lets you store your file (that is, if you have "write privileges" for the FTP site), you can also save a presentation directly to the FTP site from PowerPoint by choosing File⇨Save As. Here is the procedure:

1. **Choose File⇨Save As.**

   The familiar Save As dialog box appears.

2. **Click the down arrow for the Look In list box and then scroll down to find and select the FTP site on which you want to save the presentation.**

   Your computer connects to the FTP site (this may take a moment) and then displays the FTP site's root directory in the Save As dialog box.

3. **Navigate to the directory where you want to save the file.**

4. **Type a name for the file.**

5. **Click Save.**

   The file is copied to the FTP server. Depending on the size of the file, this may take a while. If the file has dozens of slides, each with large graphics, you may have enough time to catch a quick lunch while the file is copied to the FTP server.

# *Using the Web Toolbar*

PowerPoint sports a toolbar called the Web toolbar. The Web toolbar is designed to make it easier for you to view documents that contain hyperlinks or that were retrieved from the World Wide Web. Table 20-1 lists the function of each button and control on the Web toolbar.

To summon the Web toolbar, choose View⇨Toolbars⇨Web or click the Web toolbar button in the standard toolbar.

| Table 20-1 | Buttons on the Web Toolbar | |
|---|---|---|
| *Button* | *Name* | *What It Does* |
| ⇦ | Back | Goes to the previously displayed slide. |
| ⇨ | Forward | Returns to the slide you went back from. |

| Button | Name | What It Does |
|--------|------|--------------|
| ⊗ | Stop | Stops downloading the current page. |
| | Refresh Current Page | Reloads the current page. |
| | Start Page | Displays your designated start page. |
| | Search the WebPage | Displays your designated search page. |
| **Favorites ▾** | Favorites | Displays your favorites list, similar to clicking the Look In Favorites button in an Open or Save As dialog box. |
| **Go ▾** | Go | Displays a menu that includes the Back, Forward, Start, and Search commands that correspond to the Back, Forward, Start, and Search buttons. Also includes an Open Hyperlink command and commands to designate the current page as your start page or search page. |
| | Show only Web toolbar | Temporarily hides everything on the screen except the slide area and the Web toolbar. Click this button again to get the screen back to normal. |

If you find that you don't have all the buttons you want on your Web toolbar, remember the down arrow that leads you to the Add or Remove Buttons button. Go ahead and chant "Button, button, who's got the button?" while performing this task, and it works a lot better.

The Web toolbar is most useful when used in a slide show that is browsed by an individual rather than one that is printed out as slides or transparencies and shown with a projector. For example, suppose that you create a presentation that describes your company's employee benefits programs, and the presentation contains dozens of hyperlinks that bounce back and forth from slide to slide and perhaps even lead to other presentations. When individuals view this presentation, they'll want to activate the Web toolbar so they can use its controls to follow the presentation's hyperlinks and to go back to slides they've already viewed.

# Using Presentation Broadcast

Presentation Broadcast is a nifty PowerPoint add-on that lets you show a presentation over the Internet. Other Internet users can tune in to watch your presentation. This feature used to be built in to PowerPoint, but now it is an optional feature that you can download free of charge from Microsoft's Web site. The best part is that they don't even have to have PowerPoint to watch; any old Web browser will do. (Well, *really* old Web browsers won't work. Presentation Broadcasts are best viewed with Internet Explorer 5.1 or later.)

When you broadcast a presentation, the viewers can see the presentation's slides along with a table of contents that lets them click to move forward or backward through the presentation. In addition, viewers can hear your voice or see your picture if your computer has a microphone and a camera.

Here's what you need to broadcast a presentation:

- **A presentation:** Clearly you need to have presentation interesting enough to broadcast to someone who cares, and who can't just walk across the hall to watch the presentation on your computer. This may seem like an obvious point, but sometimes we get so wrapped up in technology that we forget the simple solutions. Presentation broadcast is too much fuss to use unless you really need it.

- **An Internet connection:** You should have high-speed Internet connection such as DSL, cable, or some such. Avoid using presentation broadcast with a dialup connection.

- **A microphone and video camera:** If you want to broadcast your voice or picture, you need a microphone and video camera.

- **A Web server:** You need a server computer that can host your broadcast unless only one or two people will view your presentation. If more than ten people will view your presentation, the server should run Windows Media Server software. (If you're sharing a presentation from your own computer, you must first save the presentation to a shared folder.)

# Chapter 21

# Creating Web Pages with PowerPoint

*In This Chapter*

▶ Understanding PowerPoint's Save As Web Page feature

▶ Playing with Web options

▶ Publishing a PowerPoint presentation to the Web

*P*owerPoint lets you save your presentations in HTML format so that they can be viewed using a Web browser such as Internet Explorer. By using this feature, you can distribute your presentations to users who don't have PowerPoint installed on their computers.

This chapter explores using PowerPoint as a tool for creating HTML pages. Keep in mind that PowerPoint was not designed to be a general-purpose Web page editor. It does an excellent job of converting PowerPoint formats to HTML so you can view them over the Internet using a Web browser. However, to create pages that aren't simply HTML versions of a presentation, you're better off using a Web page editor such as Microsoft FrontPage.

## About PowerPoint Web Pages

The Save As a Web Page feature converts PowerPoint presentations to HTML files that can be published on the World Wide Web and displayed by Web browsers such as Microsoft Internet Explorer and Netscape Navigator. When you choose File➪Save As a Web Page, you bring up a version of the Save As dialog box that gives you access to Web publishing features.

PowerPoint can save presentations in one of two Web formats:

✔ **Web Page format:** In Web Page format, PowerPoint creates a separate Web page for each slide in your presentation. All these Web pages, with the exception of the starting page, are stored in a folder created with the name of the presentation that you are converting. For example, if you save a presentation named `Trouble in River City.ppt` in Web Page format, PowerPoint creates a separate file for each page in the presentation in a folder named `Trouble in River City_files`. It also creates a file called `Trouble in River City.htm`.

✔ **Single File Web Page format:** When you choose Single File Web Page format, PowerPoint saves the entire presentation in a single file using a special format. This format is more compact than the Web Page format, but a presentation saved as a Single File Web Page can be viewed only by Internet Explorer version 5 or later. Users who use Netscape or another Web browser won't be able to view your presentation if you save it in Single File Web Page format.

# Setting the Web Options

Before you save a PowerPoint presentation as a Web page, you should spend a few moments with the Web Options dialog box, shown in Figure 21-1. This dialog box lets you set various options that affect how PowerPoint creates the Web pages for a presentation. To summon the Web Options dialog box, choose Tools⇨Options. Then, in the Options dialog box, click the General tab, and then click the Web Options button.

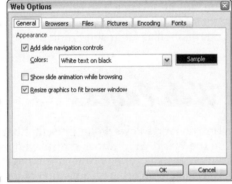

**Figure 21-1:**
The Web
Options
dialog box.

The Web Options dialog box has six different tabs, which are described in the following paragraphs.

The General tab contains three options that affect how the presentation will appear when the user views it in a browser:

- ✔ **Add Slide Navigation Controls:** This option displays a navigation area to the left of the slides, thus allowing the user to skip ahead to any slide that he or she wants to see. If you select this option, you can use the drop-down list to choose the font and background color for the navigation area.

- ✔ **Show Slide Animation While Browsing:** This option enables animation features such as slide transitions, paragraph builds, and other animations to operate when the user views the presentation in a browser.

- ✔ **Resize Graphics to Fit Browser Window:** This option adjusts the size of your slides to fit the user's browser window.

The Browsers tab lets you set the browsers that you want the presentation to be compatible with. For example, you can require that users must have Internet Explorer version 6, version 5 or later, or version 4 or later, and you can allow Netscape browsers. The higher browser versions enable more advanced PowerPoint features but limit the number of people who can view your presentation. Unless you are certain that everyone will have a certain browser version, your best bet is to stick with the default choice, Internet Explorer 4 or later. You can choose from a drop-down list of browsers, or you can pick the specific browser capabilities that you want the presentation to support.

The other tabs provide additional options you can set. If you're into setting options, feel free to explore these tabs. Otherwise, leave them be.

# Saving a Presentation as a Web Page

Before you attempt to save a presentation as a Web page, you should create a Network Place for the server to which you will save the files. (See Chapter 20 for more information on how to do this.) After you've set up a Network Place, you can save the presentation as a Web page by following these steps:

1. **Select File⇨Save as Web Page.**

   The Save As dialog box appears, as shown in Figure 21-2.

2. **Use the Save In drop-down list to select the location to which you want to save the presentation.**

   If you have not created a network place for your Web server, do so now. You'll find instructions for creating a network place in Chapter 20.

3. **If you want, change the page title by using the Change Title button.**

The Page Title field (above the File Name text box) indicates the text that will be displayed in the Title bar when your presentation is displayed in a Web browser. The page title defaults to the title of your presentation taken from the title slide. If you want, you can change the page title by clicking the Change Title button. This brings up a separate dialog box where you can type a new title. Click OK to return to the Save As dialog box.

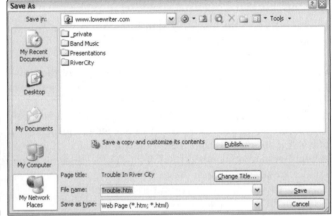

**Figure 21-2:**
The Save As
dialog box
for saving a
Web page.

4. **Use the Save As Type drop-down list to indicate the format that you want to save the presentation in.**

Select Single File Web Page or Web Page. For a description of the difference between these two formats, see the section "About PowerPoint Web Pages" earlier in this chapter.

5. **Click the Publish button.**

The Publish button is located near the center of the Save As dialog box. When you click it, the Publish as Web Page dialog box appears, as shown in Figure 21-3.

6. **Make your selections in the "Publish What?" section of the dialog box.**

Here, you decide if you are going to publish the whole presentation or just a number of slides from the presentation. You also get to choose whether to include your speaker notes. Make the appropriate selections, and you are ready to move on.

7. **Check the Open Published Web Page in Browser check box.**

This tells PowerPoint to start your Web browser so you can see the Web page after you complete the next step. You don't have to check this option, but it's a good idea.

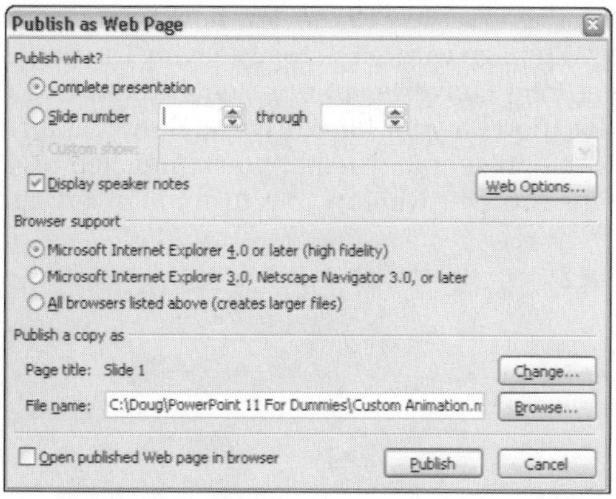

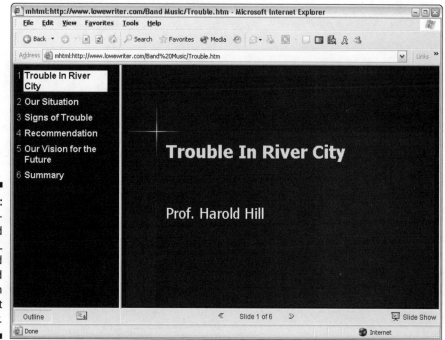

**Figure 21-3:**
The Publish
as Web
Page dialog
box.

8. **Click Publish.**

Your publication is saved as an HTML file. If you checked the Open
Published Web Page in Browser option in Step 7, your Web browser
magically starts up and displays your presentation in HTML format, as
shown in Figure 21-4.

**Figure 21-4:**
A presen-
tation saved
in HTML
format and
displayed
with
Internet
Explorer.

You can choose File⇨Web Page Preview to preview how a presentation will appear when saved as a Web page without actually saving the page. When you use this command, PowerPoint converts your presentation to Web format and saves it in a temporary location on your hard drive, and then launches a browser window to view the presentation. After you're finished previewing the presentation, just close the browser window to return to PowerPoint.

# Chapter 22

# Online Collaborations

*In This Chapter*

▶ Sending your presentation out for review

▶ Using SharePoint

*"W*orks well with others" is more than standard fare for rookie resumes. It's also one of the PowerPoint mantras. PowerPoint sports a number of collaboration features that simplify the task of working with others to create a presentation. These features work especially well if you and your collaborators are all connected to the Internet. This chapter shows you how to use those features.

## Using PowerPoint's Reviewing Features

The Reviewing feature allows you to e-mail a presentation to one or more of your buddies so they can make changes and add comments. Your reviewers can then return their marked-up copies of your presentation to you so that you can review their changes and comments one by one, accepting the good ones and rejecting the stupid ones. You can then combine all the changes into a final version of the presentation.

PowerPoint's Reviewing feature works best if everyone in the process uses Outlook as their e-mail program. Outlook automatically keeps track of presentations that you have sent out for review and offers to automatically combine them when the reviews come back. If you use another e-mail program (including Outlook Express), you must manually keep track of who has returned reviewed copies so you can combine them to create a final version.

# Sending a presentation to reviewers

When you're ready to put a presentation out for review, follow these steps:

1. **Open the presentation that you want to send out for review.**

   If the presentation is already open, choose File⇨Save to save any changes you've made since you opened it.

2. **Choose File⇨Send To⇨Mail Recipient (for Review).**

   PowerPoint summons Outlook (or whatever e-mail program you use) and creates a new message with the Subject line filled in ("Please review . . ."), the presentation attached to the message, and the message text set to "Please review the attached document."

3. **In the To field, add an e-mail address for each person to whom you want to send a review copy.**

   You can type the e-mail addresses directly into the To field, or you can click the To button to call up the Address Book. You can then use the Address Book to select your reviewers.

   If you want to send the presentation to more than one person, separate the e-mail addresses with semicolons.

4. **If you want, change the Subject field or message body.**

   You'll probably want to say something a little more cordial than the bland "Please review . . ." messages that PowerPoint creates automatically.

5. **Set any other Outlook options you want for the message.**

   You have a whole bevy of options to set for Outlook messages, such as high or low priority, signatures, stationery, read receipts, plain or HTML formatting, and more. But this isn't an Outlook book; I won't go into them here.

6. **Click the Send button.**

   Your message is whisked away, and will be delivered as soon as possible.

Another way to send a presentation to other users is to choose File⇨Send To⇨Mail Recipient (as Attachment). This command lets you send your presentation to e-mail recipients as a simple attachment without activating the Reviewing feature.

# Reviewing a presentation

If someone sends you a presentation for review, you can edit the presentation any way you want. PowerPoint keeps track of any changes you make to the presentation so your changes can be combined with changes made by other reviewers and then considered one by one.

In addition to making changes, you can also post comments to ask questions, make suggestions, or brag about your kids. To add a comment to a presentation, follow these steps:

1. **Call up the slide to which you want to add a comment.**

2. **Choose Insert⇨Comment or click the Insert Comment button.**

   A comment bubble appears on the slide. Your initials and a comment number appear in the small box next to the bubble.

3. **Type whatever you want in the comment bubble.**

   Offer some constructive criticism. Suggest an alternative approach. Or just comment on the weather. Figure 22-1 shows a completed comment.

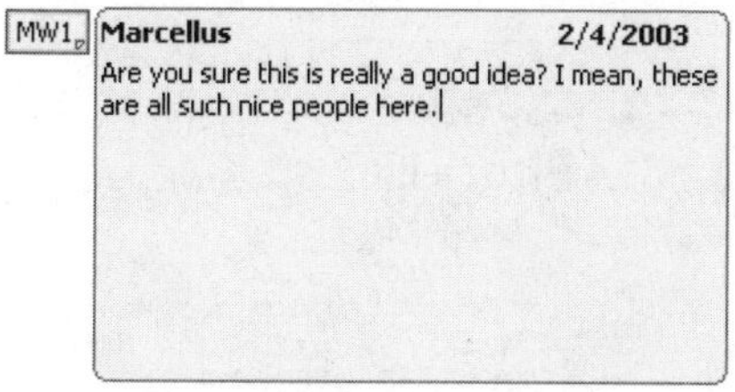

**Figure 22-1:**
Creating a
comment.

| MW1 | **Marcellus** | 2/4/2003 |

Are you sure this is really a good idea? I mean, these are all such nice people here.

4. **Click anywhere outside the comment bubble to make it disappear.**

   Only the comment tag (the little box with the reviewer's initials and comment number) remains.

5. **If you want, move the comment tag.**

   You can move the comment closer to the slide item on which you're commenting by dragging the comment tag around the slide.

To change a comment, double-click the comment tag, and then edit the text in the comment until you are satisfied.

To delete a comment, click the comment to select it, and then press the Delete key.

## Reading the reviews

When a reviewer returns a reviewed presentation to you via Outlook, you can open the reviewed presentation by double-clicking the presentation in the e-mail message. PowerPoint displays a dialog box informing you that you are opening a reviewed presentation and offering to combine the changes and comments from the review with the original presentation. Click Yes.

If you aren't using Outlook, PowerPoint doesn't automatically offer to combine reviewed presentations with the original. However, you can choose Tools⇨Compare and Merge Presentations to do so.

When you review changes made by other users, PowerPoint places a special change icon next to any object that was changed by a reviewer, as shown in Figure 22-2. As you can also see, a Revisions pane appears to the right of the slide.

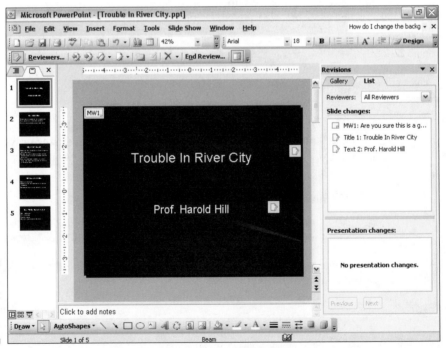

**Figure 22-2:**
PowerPoint highlights changes.

To see a change made by your reviewers, click the Change icon. The icon expands into a bubble listing the changes made to that item. To apply a change made by one of your reviewers, click the check box next to the change. If you don't like the effect of the change, click the check box again to uncheck it.

When you have reviewed all the changes in your presentation — checked the ones you like and unchecked the ones you don't like — click the End Review button in the Reviewing toolbar. This applies the changes you checked and discards the changes you unchecked. After you save the file, those changes become permanent.

# Using SharePoint Team Services

SharePoint Team Services, also known as STS, is a nifty feature that lets you set up an Web site where users can collaborate on documents. An STS site enables you do to the following:

- ✔ Save documents in shared libraries so everyone in your group can access the documents.
- ✔ Have online discussions in which you comment on each other's work, argue about politics, and otherwise confer, consult, and cajole.
- ✔ Track the progress of your project, post announcements, assign tasks, and even schedule meetings.
- ✔ Take surveys to gauge the opinions of your team members.
- ✔ Control who can access the site.

Setting up an STS Web site is a job for someone who's a bit of a computer guru and is well beyond the scope of this book. Whoever sets up your STS Web site will give you the information you need to access it. Specifically, you'll need to know three bits of information:

- ✔ The Internet address (URL) of the STS site, such as `http://rivercity.sts.conman.com`. I just made this name up as an example, so don't bother trying to go there.
- ✔ A username, such as `RCITY/Harold`.
- ✔ A password.

 To facilitate use of your STS site, you should open a My Network Places folder and create a new network place for the STS site. To do so, click Add a Network Place in the task pane of the My Network Places folder, and then answer the questions asked by the Add Network Place Wizard.

## Using a document library

One of the basic features of an STS site are the document libraries, which allow you to store documents that can be worked on by members of your group. You can choose File➪Save As and File➪Open to save or retrieve presentations in one of these libraries. Click the My Network Places icon in the Open or Save As dialog box, and then double-click the icon for the STS site. Then, double-click the library that you want to access. Figure 22-3 shows a shared document library in an Open dialog box.

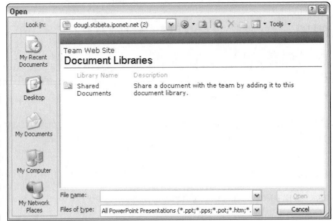

**Figure 22-3:**
Opening a presentation from a SharePoint Team Services site.

## Checking out

Like any good library, SharePoint document libraries let you check out a presentation so that others will know you're using them. After you're finished working with the presentation, you can check it back in. (Fortunately, the Check Out feature doesn't charge a fine for overdue items.)

To check out a presentation, open the presentation as usual. Then, choose File➪Check Out. While you have the presentation checked out, other users can access a read-only copy of the presentation. But they can't save changes to the presentation or see any changes that you make until you check the presentation back in.

To check in a presentation, choose File➪Check In. A dialog box appears in which you can type comments about the changes you made to the presentation. Then, PowerPoint saves the presentation. The presentation remains open in PowerPoint, but because it is no longer checked out, other users can open the presentation and make changes to it.

## Using the Shared Workspace task pane

The Shared Workspace task pane gives you direct access to many of the features of a SharePoint Team Services site. The Shared Workspace task pane is automatically displayed whenever you open a document from an STS site. You can also display it by choosing Tools⇨Shared Workspace.

The Shared Workspace task pane has six tabbed areas. The following paragraphs describe each of these tabs:

 ✔ **Status:** This tab displays information about the shared documents on which you're currently working.

 ✔ **Members:** This tab displays information about other members of the STS site. You can use this tab to find out who else is currently logged in to the site to send e-mail, schedule meetings, and perform other related tasks.

 ✔ **Tasks:** This tab is a handy to-do list. You can create new tasks for yourself or other members of your team, track pending tasks, and even send annoying e-mail reminders about uncompleted tasks.

 ✔ **Documents:** This tab provides quick access to the site's document folders.

 ✔ **Links:** This tab provides an area where you can create a list of useful links. For example, you can create links to Web sites that have information about topics that interest you.

 ✔ **Information:** This tab displays information about the presentation you're working on, such as who created it and when it was created.

## Visiting a SharePoint Team Services site

SharePoint Team Services sites have many features, such as discussion forums and announcements, that aren't available from within PowerPoint. To use these features, you can visit the SharePoint Team Services site from a Web browser such as Internet Explorer. Just type the address of the team site in the browser's address bar and type your user ID and password when prompted. Figure 22-4 shows a typical SharePoint Team Services site.

One of the best features of SharePoint is that it lets you customize the STS site in many ways. For starters, you can add your own announcements, add links to your important Web sites to the Links 22-section, and create additional document libraries. You can also click the Modify This Page link to call up a menu that lets you add or remove optional elements and change the appearance of the pages. And if you're gutsy, you can use Microsoft's Web page editor, FrontPage, to customize many other aspects of an STS site.

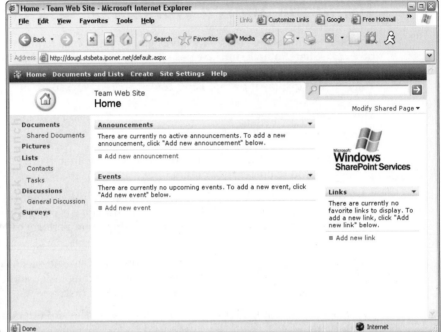

**Figure 22-4:**
A
SharePoint
Team
Services
site.

# Part V
# The Part of Tens

The 5th Wave                    By Rich Tennant

@RICHTENNANT

WELL, THERE'S YOUR DRAWING SCANNED INTO YOUR BOOK REPORT. I JUST CAN'T FIGURE OUT WHAT THAT GREY FUZZY THING IS ALONG THE EDGE.

## In this part . . .

PowerPoint is pretty good at slinging bullets, so I figured it would be fitting to end this book with a bevy of chapters that aren't much more than glorified bulleted lists. Each chapter in this part covers ten things (more or less) worth knowing about PowerPoint. Without further ado, here they are, direct from the home office in Fresno, California.

# Chapter 23

# Ten PowerPoint Commandments

• • • • • • • • • • • • • • • • • • • • • • • • • • • • • • • • • • • • • •

**A**nd the hapless Windows user said, "But who am I to make this presentation? For I am not eloquent, but I am slow of speech and of tongue, and my colors clasheth, and my charts runneth over." And Microsoft answered, "Fear not, for unto you this day is given a program, which shall be called PowerPoint, and it shall make for you slides, which shall bring forth titles and bullets and yea, even diagrams."

— Presentations 1:1

And so it came to pass that these ten PowerPoint commandments were passed down from generation to generation. Obey these commandments and it shall go well with you, with your flip chart, and with your overhead projector.

## 1. Thou Shalt Frequently Savest Thy Work

Every two or three minutes, press Ctrl+S. It takes only a second to save your file, and you never know when you'll be the victim of a rotating power outage (even if you don't live in California).

## 11. Thou Shalt Storeth Each Presentation In Its Proper Folder

Whenever you save a file, double-check the folder that you're saving it to. It's all too easy to save a presentation in the wrong folder and then spend hours searching for the file later. You'll wind up blaming the computer for losing your files.

# III. Thou Shalt Not Abuseth Thy Program's Formatting Features

Yes, PowerPoint lets you set every word in a different font, use 92 different colors on a single slide, and fill every last pixel of empty space with clip art. If you want your slides to look like ransom notes, go ahead. Otherwise, keep things simple.

# IV. Thou Shalt Not Stealeth Copyrighted Materials

Yup, Napster was cool while it lasted. But just as music is copyrighted, so are many of the pictures and clip art that you stumble across on the Internet. Don't use it if you don't have permission.

# V. Thou shalt abideth by thine color scheme, auto-layout, and template

Microsoft hired a crew of out-of-work artists to pick the colors for the color schemes, arrange things with the slide layouts, and create beautiful backgrounds for the Design templates. Humor them. They like it when you use their stuff.

# VI. Thou Shalt Not Abuse Thine Audience with an Endless Array of Cute Animations

PowerPoint animations are cute, and sometimes quite useful. But if you do a goofy animation on every slide, pretty soon your audience will just think you're strange.

## VII. Remember Thy Computer Gurus, to Keep Them Happy

If you have a friend or coworker who knows more about computers than you do, keep that person happy. Throw him or her an occasional Twinkie or a bag of Cheetos. Treat computer nerds as if they are human beings. After all, you want them to be your friends.

## VIII. Thou Shalt Backeth Up Thy Files Day by Day

Yes, every day. One of these days, you'll come to work only to discover a pile of rubble where your desk used to be. A federal agent will pick up what's left of your computer's keyboard and laugh. But if you back up every day, you won't lose more than a day's work.

## IX. Thou Shalt Fear No Evil, for Ctrl+Z Is Always with Thee

March ahead with boldness. Not sure what a button does? Click it! Click it twice if it makes you feel powerful! The worse that it can do is mess up your presentation. If that happens, you can press Ctrl+Z to set things back the way they should be.

If you really mess things up, just close the presentation without saving. Then, open the previously saved version. After all, you did obey the first commandment, didn't you?

## X. Thou Shalt Not Panic

You're the only one who knows you're nervous. You'll do just fine. Imagine the audience naked if that will help. (Unless, of course, you're making a presentation to a nudist club and they actually are naked, in which case try to imagine them with their clothes on.)

# Chapter 24

# Ten Tips for Creating Readable Slides

● ● ● ● ● ● ● ● ● ● ● ● ● ● ● ● ● ● ● ● ● ● ● ● ● ● ● ● ● ● ● ● ● ● ● ● ● ● ● ● ● ● ● ● ●

*T*his chapter gives you a few random tips and pointers that will help you produce readable slides.

## *Try Reading the Slide from the Back of the Room*

The number-one rule of creating readable slides is that everyone in the room must be able to read them. If you're not sure, there's one sure way to find out: Try it. Fire up the projector, call up the slide, walk to the back of the room, and see if you can read it. If you can't, you'll have to make an adjustment.

Remember that everyone's eyesight may not be as good as yours. If you have perfect vision, squint a little when you get to the back of the room to see how the slide may appear to someone whose vision isn't perfect.

## *No More than Five Bullets, Please*

Ever notice how David Letterman uses two slides to display his Top Ten lists? Dave's producers know that ten items is way too many for one screen. Five is just right. You may be able to slip in six now and again, but if you're up to seven or eight, try breaking the slide into two slides.

# Avoid Small Text

If you can't read a slide from the back of the room, it's probably because the text is too small. The rule of thumb is that 24-point type is the smallest you should use for text that you want people to read. A 12-point type may be perfectly readable in a Word document, but it's way too small for PowerPoint.

# Avoid Excessive Verbiage Lending to Excessively Lengthy Text That Is Not Only Redundant but Also Repetitive and Reiterative

See what I mean? Maybe the heading should have been, "Be Brief."

# Use Consistent Wording

One sign of an amateur presentation is wording in bullet lists that isn't grammatically consistent. Consider this list:

- ✔ Profits will be improved
- ✔ Expanding markets
- ✔ It will reduce the amount of overseas competition
- ✔ Production increase

Each sentence uses a different grammatical construction. The same points made with consistent wording have a more natural flow and make a more compelling case:

- ✔ Improved profits
- ✔ Expanded markets
- ✔ Reduced overseas competition
- ✔ Increased production

# Avoid Clashing Colors

The professionally chosen color schemes that come with PowerPoint are designed to create slides that are easy to read. If you venture away from them, be careful about choosing colors that are hard to read.

# Watch the Line Endings

Sometimes, PowerPoint will break a line at an awkward spot, which can make slides hard to read. For example, a bullet point may be one word too long to fit on a single line. When that happens, you may want to break the line elsewhere so the second line has more than one word. (Use Shift+Enter to create a line break that doesn't start a new paragraph.)

Alternatively, you may want to drag the right margin of the text placeholder to increase the margin width so that the line doesn't have to be broken at all.

Web addresses (URLs) are notoriously hard to squeeze onto a single line. If your presentation includes long URLs, pay special attention to how they fit.

# Keep the Background Simple

Don't splash a bunch of distracting clip art on the background unless it is essential. The purpose of the background is to provide a well-defined visual space for the slide's content. All too often, presenters put up slides that have text displayed on top of pictures of the mountains or city skylines, which makes the text almost impossible to read.

# Use Only Two Levels of Bullets

Sure, it's tempting to develop your subpoints into sub-subpoints and sub-sub-subpoints, but no one will be able to follow your logic. Don't make your slides more confusing than they need to be. If you need to make sub-sub-subpoints, you probably need a few more slides.

# Keep Charts and Diagrams Simple

PowerPoint can create elaborate graphs that even the best statisticians will marvel at. However, the most effective graphs are simple pie charts with three or four slices and simple column charts with three or four columns. Likewise, Pyramid, Venn, and other types of diagrams lose their impact when you add more than four or five elements. (See Chapter 15 for more on diagrams.)

If you remember only one rule when creating your presentations, remember this one: *Keep it simple, clean, and concise.*

# Chapter 25

# Ten Ways to Keep Your Audience Awake

· · · · · · · · · · · · · · · · · · · · · · · · · · · · · · · · · · · · · · · · · · · ·

*N*othing frightens a public speaker more than the prospect of the audience falling asleep during the speech. Here are some things you can do to prevent that from happening. (Yawn.)

## Don't Forget Your Purpose

Too many presentations ramble on and on with no clear sense of purpose. The temptation is to throw in every clever quotation and every interesting tidbit you can muster that is even remotely related to the topic of your presentation. The reason that this temptation is so big is that you most likely haven't identified what you hope to accomplish with your presentation. In other words, you haven't pinned down your *purpose*.

Don't confuse a presentation's title with its purpose. Suppose that you're asked to give a presentation to a prospective client on the advantages of your company's new, improved deluxe model ChronSimplastic Infindibulator. Your purpose in this presentation is not to convey information about the new Infindibulator, but to persuade your client to buy one of the $65 million beasties. The title of your presentation may be *Infindibulators for the Twenty-First Century* but the purpose is "convince these saps to buy one, or maybe two."

## Don't Become a Slave to Your Slides

PowerPoint makes such beautiful slides that the temptation is to let them be the show. That's a big mistake. *You* are the show — not the slides. The slides are merely visual aids, designed to make your presentation more effective, not to steal the show.

Your slides should supplement your talk, not repeat it. If you find yourself just reading your slides, you need to rethink what you put on the slides. The slides should summarize key points, not become the script for your speech.

# Don't Overwhelm Your Audience with Unnecessary Detail

On November 19, 1863, a crowd of 15,000 gathered in Gettysburg to hear Edward Everett, one of the greatest orators of the time. Mr. Everett spoke for two hours about the events that had transpired during the famous battle. When he finished, Abraham Lincoln rose to deliver a brief two-minute postscript that has become the most famous speech in American history.

If PowerPoint had been around in 1863, Everett probably would have spoken for four hours. PowerPoint practically begs you to talk too much. Once you start typing bullets, you can't stop. Pretty soon, you have 40 slides for a 20-minute presentation. That's about 35 more than you probably need. Try to shoot for one slide for every two to five minutes of your presentation.

# Don't Neglect Your Opening

As they say, you only get one opportunity to make a first impression. Don't waste it by telling a joke that has nothing to do with the topic, apologizing for your lack of preparation or nervousness, or listing your credentials. Don't pussyfoot around; get right to the point.

The best openings are those that capture the audience's attention with a provocative statement, a rhetorical question, or a compelling story. A joke is okay, but only if it sets the stage for the subject of your presentation.

# Be Relevant

The objective of any presentation is to lead your audience to say, "Me, too!" Unfortunately, many presentations leave the audience thinking, "So what?"

The key to being relevant is giving your audience what they need, and not what you think is interesting or important. The most persuasive presentations are those that present solutions to real problems rather than opinions about hypothetical problems.

# Don't Forget the Altar Call

What would a Billy Graham crusade be without the altar call? A wasted opportunity.

You've spent hours putting your presentation together. Don't forget to ask for the order. Invite your audience to respond and show them how. Make them an offer they can't refuse. Tell them your 800 number. Roll the pen across the table. Ask everyone to sing *Just As I Am*. Do whatever it takes.

# Practice, Practice, Practice

Back to good ol' Abe: Somehow a rumor got started that Abraham Lincoln hastily wrote the Gettysburg Address on the train, just before pulling into Gettysburg. In truth, Lincoln agonized for weeks over every word.

Practice, practice, practice. Work through the rough spots. Polish the opening and the altar call and all the awkward transitions in between. Practice in front of a mirror. Videotape yourself. Time yourself.

# Don't Panic

Don't worry! Be happy! Even the most gifted public speakers are scared silly every time they step up to the podium. Whether you're speaking to one person or 10,000, relax. In 20 minutes, it will all be over.

No matter how nervous you are, no one knows it except you. That is, unless you tell them. The number one rule of panic avoidance is to never apologize for your fears. Behind the podium, your knees may be knocking hard enough to bruise yourself. But no one else will notice. After you swab down your armpits and wipe the drool off your chin, people will say, "Weren't you nervous? You seemed so relaxed!"

# Expect the Unexpected

Plan on things to go wrong, because they will. The projector won't focus, the microphone won't listen, you'll drop your notes on the way to the podium. Who knows what else will happen?

Take things in stride, but be prepared for problems you can anticipate. Carry an extra set of notes in your pocket. Bring your own microphone if you have one. Have a backup projector ready if possible.

# Don't Be Boring

An audience can overlook almost anything, but one thing they'll never forgive you for is boring them. Above all, do not bore your audience.

This guideline doesn't mean you have to tell jokes, jump up and down, or talk fast. Jokes, excessive jumping, and rapid speech can be as boring as formatting disks. If you obey the other commandments — if you have a clear-cut purpose and stick to it, avoid unnecessary detail, and address real needs — you'll never be boring. Just be yourself and have fun. If you have fun, so will your audience.

# Chapter 26

# Ten Things That Often Go Wrong

· · · · · · · · · · · · · · · · · · · · · · · · · · · · · · · · · · · · · · · · · · · · · · · ·

*T*he actual number of things that can go wrong when working with PowerPoint is probably closer to 10,000, but these ten are among the things that go wrong most often.

## I Can't Find My File

You spent hours polishing that presentation and now you can't find the file. You know that you saved it, but it's not there! The problem is probably one of two things: Either you saved the file in a different folder, or you used a different name to save it than you intended. The solution? Use the search features of the Open command (choose File➪Open). Also, for a quick look, click the History icon in the upper-left corner of the Open dialog box. You'll see the history of your recently used files, displaying the contents of an appropriately titled folder: Recent. Or, if the missing presentation was one of the last ones you worked on, just look at the bottom of the File menu, where you'll find links to the last four presentations you worked on.

## I've Run Out of Disk Space

Nothing is more frustrating than creating a fancy PowerPoint presentation and then discovering that you're completely out of disk space. What to do? Start up a My Computer window and rummage through your hard drive, looking for files you don't need. Delete enough files to free up a few megabytes and then press Alt+Tab to move back to PowerPoint and save your file. I did this recently: I had to delete a bunch of music files that I had accumulated to make my own CDs. (It was either them or the Word document files for the first few chapters of this book. Not an easy decision.)

If your disk is full and you can't find more than a few files to delete, try double-clicking on the Recycle Bin icon and choosing File⇨Empty Recycle Bin. This often frees up additional disk space. If that doesn't work, click the Start menu, then choose Program Files⇨Accessories⇨System Tools⇨Disk Cleanup. The Disk Cleanup program scans your hard drive for unnecessary files and offers to remove them for you. It can often free up many megabytes of disk space.

If you often run out of disk space, consider adding a larger disk drive to your computer. Nowadays, you can buy a 20GB disk for less than $75, and you can get a 120GB disk drive for just twice that. If the thought of opening up your computer and installing a disk drive causes you to break out, you can also get external drives that plug into your computer's USB port.

## I've Run Out of Memory

Many people are still using computers with only 32MB of internal memory. Although you can run PowerPoint with as little as 32MB of memory, 64MB is a more reasonable minimum. 256MB is ideal. The additional memory helps your computer to not give up and crash from the overload of open applications. Memory is cheap! Why not make sure you have enough?

## PowerPoint Has Vanished!

You're working at your computer, minding your own business, when suddenly — whoosh! — PowerPoint disappears. What happened? Most likely, you clicked some area outside the PowerPoint window or you pressed Alt+Tab or Alt+Esc, which whisks you away to another program. To get PowerPoint back, press Alt+Tab. You may have to press Alt+Tab several times before PowerPoint comes back to life.

PowerPoint can also vanish into thin air if you use a screen-saver program. Try giving the mouse a nudge to see whether PowerPoint reappears.

## I Accidentally Deleted a File

Just learned how to delete files and couldn't stop yourself, eh? Relax. It happens to the best of us. Odds are that you can rescue the deleted file if you act fast enough. Double-click the Recycle Bin icon that sits on your desktop. There, you'll probably find the deleted file. Copy it back to the folder where it belongs.

# It Won't Let Me Edit That

No matter how hard you click the mouse, PowerPoint won't let you edit that doohickey on-screen. What gives? The doohickey is probably a part of the Slide Master. To edit it, choose View⇨Master⇨Slide Master. This step displays the Slide Master and enables you to edit it. However, the object you're trying to edit may be underneath another object. If so, move the other object aside temporarily. When you're done, drag the other object back into place.

# Something Seems to Be Missing

You just read the chapter about diagrams, but nothing happens when you try to insert a diagram. Or worse, PowerPoint locks up when you choose Insert⇨Diagram. Arghhhh!

It's possible that your PowerPoint installation has somehow become corrupted. Perhaps an important system file was accidentally deleted, or a problem has somehow managed to creep into the Windows Registry (the file that keeps track of settings for Windows as well as for programs you have installed on your computer).

Fear not! PowerPoint includes a feature called Detect and Repair that can correct such problems. Just fire up PowerPoint, choose Help⇨Detect and Repair, and follow the instructions that appear on-screen.

# What Happened to My Clip Art?

You just purchased and installed an expensive clip art collection that has 500 stunning images from the Neapolitan Museum of Art, but you can't find them in the Media Gallery. Where did they go? Nowhere. You just have to tell Media Gallery about them. Fire up the Gallery by clicking the Insert Picture button or by selecting Insert⇨Picture⇨Clip Art. Then click the Import Clips button. Now insert the filename of the images that you want to add in the File Name text box, click the appropriate clip import option, and click Import.

# One of the Toolbars (Or Toolbar Features) Is Missing

One of the most useful features of PowerPoint is that it lets you completely customize its menus and toolbars. Unfortunately, this feature has a downside:

it's all too easy to mess up a menu or toolbar, sometimes quite by accident and without even realizing it. Then all of a sudden, one day you reach for the Bold button and it's not there. Or maybe the whole Formatting toolbar seems to be missing.

What gives? Perhaps it's the new IntelliSense feature deciding which buttons on your toolbar you use 95 percent of the time. Luckily, menu choices are at the end of each menu, and down-arrow buttons on the toolbars enable you to see all the toolbar and menu commands so that you can select what is missing.

If your toolbar is missing altogether, you can't see all the choices available to you. Aside from the Standard and Formatting toolbars, you sometimes have to summon a toolbar if it somehow gets lost. It happens all the time, so don't feel bad. Just look in the mirror and say to yourself, "It's not my fault that the toolbar disappeared. It happens even to experts like that nice Mr. Lowe, who wrote a whole book about PowerPoint. I shouldn't blame myself. After all, I'm good enough, I'm smart enough, and, doggone it, people like me."

Then choose View⇨Toolbars, and then choose the toolbar you want to reactivate from the list of toolbars that appears.

You may also want to check out the Standard toolbar and select Tools⇨Customize⇨Options. By doing so, you have an opportunity to check a text box that combines the Standard and Formatting toolbar on one line! Some people have been known to go clinically insane when this text box was checked without their knowledge. Don't be caught unaware!

# The Projector Doesn't Work

An LCD projector may not be working for many reasons. Assuming that the computer and projector are both plugged in and turned on and you have used the correct video cable to connect your computer to the projector, here are two common problems you should check:

- ✔ Most projectors have two or more video input ports. The projector must be configured to use the input port to which your computer is connected. Look for a button on the projector to set the input source. The projector may use a menu to set the input source: In that case, use the button that calls up the menu, scroll through the choices to find the video input source, and then select the input port to which your computer is connected.

- ✔ If you're using a laptop, make sure that the external video port is activated. Most laptops have a function key on the keyboard to do this. Look for a key with an icon that represents a video monitor. You may have to hold down a function key (probably labeled "FN") while you press the monitor key.

# Chapter 27

# Ten Things That Didn't Fit Anywhere Else

*I* like things done decently and in order. However, try as I might, I can't always fit everything that's worth knowing about a subject into a rigid framework of chapters and parts. There always seems to be a few tidbits of information that just don't fit neatly into any of the chapters. Rather than just leave that stuff out, I decided to lump them all together in this chapter. Enjoy!

# Important Keyboard Shortcuts You Should Know

You can do just about any action in PowerPoint by hacking your way through the menus or clicking the correct toolbar button. However, you can sometimes work more efficiently if you know a few keyboard and mouse shortcuts. The following list details some of the most useful shortcuts and the areas where they are used:

✔ **Working with multiple windows:**

- **Ctrl+F6**: Moves you to the next presentation window

- **Shift+Ctrl+F6**: Moves you to the previous presentation window

- **Ctrl+F10**: Maximizes a presentation window

- **Ctrl+F5**: Returns a window to its normal size

- **Ctrl+F4**: Closes a document window

✔ **Editing:**

- **Ctrl+X**: Cuts the selection to the Clipboard

- **Ctrl+C**: Copies the selection to the Clipboard

- **Ctrl+V**: Inserts the contents of the Clipboard

- **Ctrl+Z**: Undoes the last operation

- **Ctrl+G**: Shows the guides

- **Shift (while drawing)**: Constrains objects

✔ **Formatting:**

- **Ctrl+B**: Bold

- **Ctrl+I**: Italic

- **Ctrl+U**: Underline

- **Ctrl+spacebar**: Return to normal format

✔ **Switching to other programs:**

- **Alt+Esc**: Switches to the next program

- **Alt+Tab**: Displays a list of running programs and lets you switch to another program

- **Ctrl+Esc**: Displays the Start menu

Another handy shortcut is to press Ctrl+S to save the presentation.

# Creating 35mm Slides

If you want to give your presentation using 35mm slides rather than over-heads or a computer projector, you'll have to deal with a photo lab (unless, of course, you have your own photo-processing equipment.) It isn't cheap (here in California, it costs $7 to $10 per slide), but the slides look great. *Really* great. They look better than anything other than what the most lav-ishly expensive computer projectors can achieve.

One way to produce 35mm slides from a PowerPoint presentation is to take the presentation files to a local photo lab with the equipment to create the slides. Call the lab first to find out the cost and to check on any special requirements it may have, such as whether you need to embed TrueType fonts when you save the file and how the lab prefers you to save the file.

To be safe, always embed TrueType fonts.

You can find photo labs that can produce computer output listed in the Yellow Pages under Computer Graphics, or perhaps under Photo Finishing. Call several labs, compare costs, and find out how quickly each lab can finish the job.

Choose PowerPoint File⇨Save As to save the presentation to disk. Take two copies of the presentation file — on separate disks — to the photo shop. Nothing is more frustrating than driving across town only to discover that something's wrong with your disk. Or you can always attach your file to an e-mail and send it to the photo shop; that is, if the shop is set up to receive files electronically. Or, if you have a CD burner, put the presentation on a CD.

Carefully proof your slides by using the PowerPoint Slide Show view. Run the spell check feature. At $10 per slide, you don't want any typos to slip past you.

If you can't find a local photo lab or print shop that will print your slides for you, you can use any of several companies that do the job over the Internet. All you do is connect to the company's Web site, upload your PowerPoint presentation and credit card information, and watch for the Federal Express truck.

The price of this service varies depending on how quickly you need the slides. If you can wait a few days, you can have slides made for $2 to $5 each. For rush deliveries, expect to pay more.

To find online slide production services, go to a search engine, such as Yahoo, and search for "presentation slides."

# Editing More Than One Presentation at a Time

Some people like to do just one thing at a time: Start a task, work on it until it's done, and then put away their tools. These same people sort their canned goods by food group and have garages that look like the hardware department at Sears.

Then there are people like me, who work on no fewer than 12 things at a time, would just as soon leave canned goods in the bag arranged just the way the kid at the grocery store tossed them in, and haven't been able to park both cars in the garage since before the kids were born.

Apparently, a few of the latter type work at Microsoft because they decided to enable you to open a whole gaggle of PowerPoint files at one time. Now we're getting somewhere!

To open more than one presentation, just keep choosing File➪Open. PowerPoint places each file you open in its own presentation. This presentation window is normally maximized to fill all the available space within the main PowerPoint window, so you can see only one presentation window at a time. But you can switch between windows by choosing the window you want from PowerPoint's Window menu or by pressing Alt+Tab to pop from window to window.

PowerPoint enables you to display the window for each open file in three ways:

- ✔ **Cascaded:** The presentation windows are stacked atop one another. This arrangement enables you to see the title bar of each window. To switch to a window other than the one on top, click its title bar or any other portion of the window you can see. This step sucks the window up to the top of the stack. To cause all presentation windows to fall into a cascaded stack, choose Window➪Cascade.

- ✔ **Tiled:** The presentation windows are arranged side-by-side. This arrangement enables you to see a small portion of each presentation, although the more files you have open, the smaller this portion gets. To arrange all presentation windows in tiled form, choose Window➪Arrange All.

- ✔ **Minimized:** The window shrinks down to a little title bar that is just big enough to show the first part of the presentation's name and the standard window-control buttons. To shrink a presentation window to a minimized window, click the window's minimize button. To restore the window, double-click the icon.

Even though you can open umpteen presentation windows, only one is active at a time. While you work on one presentation, the others lie dormant, praying to the ASCII gods that you won't neglect them forever.

To copy something from one file to another, switch to the first file's window, copy the object to the Clipboard (by using the normal Copy command, Ctrl+C), and then switch to the second file's window and paste (Ctrl+V) away. Or use the Edit menu commands to perform the same task.

Here are a couple of tips for working with multiple windows:

✔ You can open more than one file by choosing File⇨Open. Just hold down the Ctrl key while you click each file that you want to open or use the Shift key to select a block of files. When you click OK, all the files you selected open, each in its own window.

✔ Alt+Tab lets you cycle through all the windows that you have open on your desktop, whether those windows contain PowerPoint presentations or other documents. To constrain your window hopping to PowerPoint presentations only, use Ctrl+F6 instead of Alt+Tab.

✔ Some men especially love to use the Alt+Tab or Ctrl+F6 shortcut to flip from one window to the next. They sit there at the computer, beer in hand, flipping incessantly from window to window and hoping to find a football game or a boxing match.

✔ If you want to shut down a window, choose File⇨Close, press Ctrl+W, or click the window's close button. If the file displayed in the window contains changes that haven't been saved to disk, PowerPoint asks whether you want to save the file first.

# Stealing Slides from Other Presentations

What do you do when you're plodding along in PowerPoint and realize that you want to copy slides from an old presentation into the one you're working on now? You steal the existing slides — that's what you do. No need to reinvent the wheel, as they say.

To steal slides from an existing presentation, you get to use the Slide Stealer — oops, it's actually called the Slide Finder — feature. To use it, follow these steps:

1. **Move to the slide you want the stolen slides to be placed after.**

2. **Choose Insert⇨Slides from Files.**

   This step displays the Slide Finder dialog box.

3. **Click the Browse button.**

   This brings up an ordinary, run-of-the-mill Open dialog box.

4. **Rummage around until you find the presentation that you want to steal. Highlight it and click Open.**

   You return to the Slide Finder dialog box.

5. **Click Display.**

   The file opens and displays the first few slides of the presentation.

6. **Select the slides that you want to copy.**

   Click once to select a slide. When you select a slide, a heavy border appears around the slide so you'll know it's selected. You can select more than one slide by simply clicking each slide that you want to select. Use the scroll bar that appears beneath the slide images to scroll through all of the slides in the presentation.

   If you click a slide by mistake, click it again to deselect it.

7. **Click Insert to insert the slides you selected.**

   The slides are inserted into the document, but the Slide Finder dialog box remains on the screen.

8. **Repeat Steps 3 through 7 if you want to insert slides from additional presentations.**

9. **Click Close to dismiss the Slide Finder dialog box.**

   You're done.

Here are a few points to ponder as you drift off to sleep tonight, wondering in amazement that PowerPoint lets you plagiarize slides from other people's presentations:

✔ As the slides are copied into the presentation, they are adjusted to match the master slide layout for the new presentation. Embedded charts and diagrams are even updated to reflect the new color scheme.

✔ If you want to insert all of the slides from a presentation, you can dispense with Steps 5 through 7. Just click Insert All to copy all the slides from the presentation.

✔ If you find that you frequently return to a particular presentation to steal its slides, add that presentation to the Slide Finder's list of favorites. To do that, click the Browse button and open the presentation. Then, click the Add to Favorites button. Thereafter, you can click the List of Favorites tab to display your list of favorite presentations.

✔ Stealing slides is a felony in most states, and if you transmit the presentation across state lines by way of a modem, the feds may get involved — which is good, because it pretty much guarantees that you'll get off scot-free.

# *Exploring Document Properties*

PowerPoint stores summary information, known in Windows lingo as *document properties,* with each PowerPoint presentation file you create. Document properties include the filename and directory, the template assigned to the file, and some information that you can type, including the presentation's title, subject, author, keywords, and comments.

If you create a lot of PowerPoint presentations and have trouble remembering which file is which, the summary info can help you keep your files sorted. The summary info is also handy if you know that you created a presentation about edible spiders last year but can't remember the filename.

To view or set the document properties for a presentation, follow these steps:

1. **Open the file if it isn't already open.**

2. **Choose File⇨Properties.**

   The Properties dialog box appears.

3. **Type whatever summary info you want to store along with the file.**

   The Title field in the Summary info dialog box is automatically filled in with whatever you type in the first slide's title placeholder, and the Author field is filled in with your name. (PowerPoint asked for your name when you installed it, remember?)

4. **When you're done, click OK.**

5. **Save the file (Ctrl+S or File⇨Save).**

When you fill out the summary information, spend a few moments thinking about which keywords you will likely use to look for the file later on. Choosing descriptive keywords makes the file much easier to find.

Also, explore the other tabs on the Properties dialog box. You find all sorts of interesting information about your presentation there.

If you want to include summary information with every PowerPoint file you create, choose Tools⇨Options and check the Prompt for File Properties option on the Save tab. This causes the Properties dialog box to be displayed whenever you save a new file so you can type the summary information for the file.

# Using Passwords to Protect Your Presentations

If you're worried about bad guys getting in to your presentations, either to steal them, snoop for interesting information, look for juicy gossip, or to plant an insult aimed at the boss in the middle of the show, you'll be relieved to know that PowerPoint now lets you protect your presentations with passwords. You can use two types of passwords in PowerPoint: a Read password, which lets only those who know the password open the presentation, and a Modify password, which requires that you must enter a password before saving changes to a presentation.

To password-protect a presentation, follow these steps:

1. **Come up with a good password for the presentation.**

   Bad passwords are things like your name, phone number, or guessable words like "Password." The best passwords are random combinations of letters and numerals, such as 58dK33pJK2.

2. **Open the presentation that you want to protect.**

3. **Choose Tools⇨Options and click the Security tab.**

   The Security options appear.

4. **Type the password that you want to require when opening the presentation in the Password to Open text box.**

   As you type, your password does not appear on the screen. Instead, asterisks are displayed no matter what you type. This is to keep nosy neighbors from spying on you while you create passwords.

5. **Type the password that you want to require when saving the presentation in the Password to Modify text box.**

   Once again, the password is not displayed on the screen as you type.

6. **Click OK.**

7. **When a dialog box appears asking you to confirm a password, retype the password and click OK.**

   This is just a precaution to make sure that you didn't make a mistake when you entered the passwords in Steps 4 and 5 because you can't actually see the passwords as you type them.

8. **Write down the passwords you used so you won't forget.**

   Keep the passwords in a safe place — not on a yellow sticky note attached to your computer's monitor or stuck on your bulletin board.

Whenever you (or anyone else, for that matter) try to open or save a password-protected presentation, a dialog box appears asking for the appropriate password. Without the password, PowerPoint refuses to comply.

# Protecting Your Rights

PowerPoint 2003 has a new feature called Information Rights Management that lets you restrict access to your presentations beyond simple password protection. For example, you can specify that users can view but not copy a presentation. Or, you can place a time limit on how long a presentation can be viewed. Information Rights Management works in conjunction with Microsoft's Passport service to authenticate users. In short, a user must have a Passport account to access a protected presentation.

To use PowerPoint's Information Rights Management feature, choose File⇨ Permissions. This brings up a dialog box that lets you specify the Passport e-mail addresses of those users to whom you want to grant rights. It also lets you control options such as a presentation's expiration date and whether the presentation can be printed or copied. Note that the first time you use this feature, PowerPoint must download and configure some software from Microsoft's Web site in order to enable the Information Rights Management service. Fortunately, the download is small (about 360KB), so it should take only a few minutes.

# Organizing Your Files

My first computer had two disk drives; each drive held 360K of data. A year later, I had a gargantuan 10MB hard drive and wondered how I would keep track of two or three hundred files that I would store on the drive. (I never thought I would fill it up, either.) Today I have more than 40,000MB of disk space, with more than 20,000 files. It's a miracle I can find anything.

The key to getting control of the files on your hard drive is organizing them carefully. You must do only two things to organize your files, but you must do them both well: Use filenames that you can remember and use folders wisely.

## Using filenames that you can remember

One of the best things about Windows is that you have finally been freed of the sadistic eight-character file-naming conventions foisted upon you by the DOS moguls many years ago. With Windows, filenames can be as long as you want or need them to be (within reason), so instead of names like `cnexpo.ppt`, you can give your presentations names like `computernerdexpo99.ppt`.

The best advice that I can offer about using long filenames is to *use* them. I'm amazed at how many people are still in the habit of assigning short, cryptic names to their files. Breaking that habit takes some conscious effort. Using long filenames seems strange at first, but trust me: You get used to them.

Here are a few other things to consider when composing filenames:

✔ If your presentation includes notes, add the filename to the bottom of the page on the Notes master. That way, the filename is printed on each notes page, which makes it easier to find later.

✔ Be consistent about how you name files. If `2003 Arachnid Expo.ppt` is the presentation file for Arachnid Expo '03, use `2004 Arachnid Expo.ppt` for the next year's Expo.

> ✔ If you're going to store a file on the Internet, don't use spaces or other special symbols in the filename.

## *Using folders wisely*

The biggest file-management mistake that most beginners make is to dump all their files in the My Documents folder. This technique is the electronic equivalent of storing all your tax records in a shoebox. Sure, all the files are there, but finding anything is next to impossible. Show the shoebox to your accountant on April 14, and you'll be lucky if he or she stops laughing long enough to show you how to file for an extension.

Use folders to impose organization on your files. Don't just dump all your files into one folder. Instead, create a separate folder for each project and dump all the files for each project into its folder. Suppose that you're charged with the task of presenting a market analysis every month. You can create a folder named Market Analysis to store the PowerPoint files for these reports. Then you name each month's PowerPoint file by using the month and year: 2003 January.ppt, 2003 February.ppt, 2003 March.ppt, and so on.

Here are some tips:

> ✔ Every disk has a *root (or top level) directory,* which is a special folder that should not be used to store files. The root directory is kind of like a fire lane, which should be kept free for emergency vehicles at all times. In short, don't use the C: directory to store files.
>
> ✔ There's no reason why you can't store files that belong to different application programs together in the same folder. Each file's extension identifies the program that created the file. No need to segregate. Most Office Open dialog boxes filter by type anyway, so when you choose File⇨Open command in Word, you see only Word documents, and when you use File⇨Open in PowerPoint, you see only PowerPoint presentations.
>
> ✔ The My Documents folder is where Windows programs expect to find your documents. If you're going to create additional folders to organize your files, feel free to create those folders in My Documents.
>
> ✔ You can create a shortcut to a folder on your desktop by right-clicking an empty area of the desktop, choosing New⇨Shortcut from the menu that appears, and then following the instructions that appear in the Create Shortcut dialog box.
>
> ✔ Don't forget to clean out your folders periodically by deleting files that you no longer need. It also may be interesting to clean out your Recycle Bin — who knows what you have in there!

You have no limit to the number of files you can store in a folder, nor to the number of folders that you can create.

# Customizing PowerPoint's Menus and Toolbars

Hiding down near the bottom of PowerPoint's Tools menu is a command called Customize. Lurking within the dialog box that appears when you conjure up this command is the ability to improve PowerPoint's menus and toolbars. For example, if you routinely use a few specific AutoShapes, such as the Smiley Face and Lightning Bolt, you can easily add buttons for those AutoShapes to the Drawing toolbar so you don't have to wind your way through the AutoShapes menu to get to them. Or you can add a Smiley Face or Lightning Bolt command to the Insert menu.

To customize a toolbar or menu, choose Tools⇨Customize to bring up the Customize dialog box. (If necessary, click the Commands tab at the top of the Customize dialog box.) From the Commands tab of the Customize dialog box, you can add new buttons or commands to toolbars or menus.

The Commands tab lists all the commands that are available in PowerPoint, sorted into categories such as File, Edit, View, and so on. You may have noticed that these categories correspond to PowerPoint's menus and toolbars. When you select a category in the Category list on the left side of the Customize dialog box, the commands that are available for that category are displayed in the Commands list on the right side of the dialog box.

To create a new button on a toolbar, first select the category from the Category list, and then scroll through the Command list until you find the command that you want to add. For example, to add a Smiley Face button, first choose AutoShapes in the Category list, and then scroll down the Command list to find the Smiley Face command. After you have found the right command, all you have to do is drag it from the Customize dialog box to the toolbar location where you want the button to be inserted.

Adding a new menu command is similar. First select the category, locate the command, and finally, drag the command from the Customize dialog box to the menu you want to add the new command to. For example, drag the Smiley Face AutoShape command from the Customize dialog box to the Insert menu to add a Smiley Face command to the Insert menu.

To remove a toolbar button or menu command, choose Tools⇨Customize. Then, simply drag the button or command that you want to remove off of the toolbar or menu in which it currently resides. When you release the mouse button, the toolbar button or menu command vanishes.

When you've made all the customizations you care for, click Close to dismiss the Customize dialog box.

# *Setting PowerPoint's Options*

Like any good Microsoft program, PowerPoint has billions and billions of options that you can play with to affect the way PowerPoint works. Most of PowerPoint's options are consolidated into one mega dialog box known as the Options dialog box, which you reach by choosing Tools⇨Options.

To set PowerPoint's options, choose Tools⇨Options, click the tab that contains the option you want to set, and then choose the options you want to use. When you've had enough, click the Close button to dismiss the Options dialog box.

The Options dialog box has seven tabbed sections. The following paragraphs summarize the options that are available from each of these tabs:

- ✓ **View:** Options that affect PowerPoint's overall appearance, such as whether to display the task pane when starting up, whether to display a quick menu when you right-click an object, and whether every slide show should automatically end with a black slide.

- ✓ **General:** Options that affect PowerPoint's overall operation, such as how many recently opened files to display at the bottom of the File menu, as well as your name and initials.

- ✓ **Edit:** Options that affect how PowerPoint's editing features work. For example, you can turn off the Smart Cut and Paste feature or certain PowerPoint features, such as advanced animation or multiple masters.

- ✓ **Print:** Printing options such as how to handle TrueType fonts.

- ✓ **Save:** Options that affect how files are saved, including your default file location and whether automatic recovery information is saved.

- ✓ **Security:** Passwords and such.

- ✓ **Spelling and Style:** Options that control the spell and style checkers.

# *Using Macros*

Macros are a nifty PowerPoint feature that let you record a sequence of commands and then play them back at any time with the simple click of a mouse. For example, suppose that you're working on a presentation and realize that almost every new slide has used the Title and 2-Column Text layout. Wouldn't it be great if there were a button right on a toolbar somewhere that inserted a new slide and automatically applied the Title and 2-Column Text layout? As an added bonus, the button would leave the Slide Layout pane closed — a big improvement over PowerPoint's existing New Slide button, which inserts a new slide and opens the Slide Layout pane so you can apply a layout to the slide.

Macros to the rescue! With a macro, you can record the commands necessary to insert a new slide, open the Slide Layout pane, assign the Title and 2-Column Text layout, and close the Slide Layout pane. Then, you can place this macro on a toolbar as a button, so that you can insert a new Title and 2-Column Text slide with a single click.

To create a macro, follow these simple steps:

1. **Open the presentation you want to save the macro in.**

2. **Choose Tools⇨Macros⇨Record New Macro.**

   The Record Macro dialog box appears.

3. **Type a name for your macro.**

   Anything would be better than Macro1. (The name can't have a space in it, however.)

4. **Click OK.**

   A little Stop Recording toolbar appears to let you know that you are now recording a macro.

5. **Do that thing you do.**

   Do whatever commands are needed to perform the task you want to record in a macro. For example, to create the macro that inserts Title and 2-Column Text slides, follow these steps in sequence:

   • Choose Insert⇨New Slide.

   • Click the Title and 2-Column Text layout in the Slide Layout pane.

   • Click the close button (the "X") in the Slide Layout pane to close the pane.

6. **Click the Stop button in the Stop Recording toolbar.**

   The macro is finished!

To run the macro, choose the Tools⇨Macro⇨Macros. This brings up a list of all available macros, from which you can choose a macro to run.

To really get the benefit of macros, you should assign them to toolbars or menus. You can do that by choosing Tools⇨Customize. In the Command tab of the Customize dialog box, you'll find a category called Macros that lists macros you have created. Just drag the macro that you want to use from the Command list to the toolbar or menu on which you want it to live. (For more information, see the section "Customizing PowerPoint's Menus and Toolbars" earlier in this chapter.)

# Index

### • R •

### • S •

# Notes

# Notes

# Notes

# FOR DUMMIES®

**The easy way to get more done and have more fun**

## PERSONAL FINANCE & BUSINESS

**0-7645-2431-3**

**0-7645-5331-3**

**0-7645-5307-0**

**Also available:**

Accounting For Dummies
(0-7645-5314-3)

Business Plans Kit For
Dummies
(0-7645-5365-8)

Managing For Dummies
(1-5688-4858-7)

Mutual Funds For Dummies
(0-7645-5329-1)

QuickBooks All-in-One Desk
Reference For Dummies
(0-7645-1963-8)

Resumes For Dummies
(0-7645-5471-9)

Small Business Kit For
Dummies
(0-7645-5093-4)

Starting an eBay Business
For Dummies
(0-7645-1547-0)

Taxes For Dummies 2003
(0-7645-5475-1)

## HOME, GARDEN, FOOD & WINE

**0-7645-5295-3**

**0-7645-5130-2**

**0-7645-5250-3**

**Also available:**

Bartending For Dummies
(0-7645-5051-9)

Christmas Cooking For
Dummies
(0-7645-5407-7)

Cookies For Dummies
(0-7645-5390-9)

Diabetes Cookbook For
Dummies
(0-7645-5230-9)

Grilling For Dummies
(0-7645-5076-4)

Home Maintenance For
Dummies
(0-7645-5215-5)

Slow Cookers For Dummies
(0-7645-5240-6)

Wine For Dummies
(0-7645-5114-0)

## FITNESS, SPORTS, HOBBIES & PETS

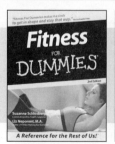

**0-7645-5167-1**

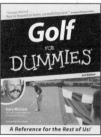

**0-7645-5146-9**

**0-7645-5106-X**

**Also available:**

Cats For Dummies
(0-7645-5275-9)

Chess For Dummies
(0-7645-5003-9)

Dog Training For Dummies
(0-7645-5286-4)

Labrador Retrievers For
Dummies
(0-7645-5281-3)

Martial Arts For Dummies
(0-7645-5358-5)

Piano For Dummies
(0-7645-5105-1)

Pilates For Dummies
(0-7645-5397-6)

Power Yoga For Dummies
(0-7645-5342-9)

Puppies For Dummies
(0-7645-5255-4)

Quilting For Dummies
(0-7645-5118-3)

Rock Guitar For Dummies
(0-7645-5356-9)

Weight Training For Dummies
(0-7645-5168-X)

**Available wherever books are sold.**
**Go to www.dummies.com or call 1-877-762-2974 to order direct**

# FOR DUMMIES®

## A world of resources to help you grow

---

## TRAVEL

**Italy FOR DUMMIES**
A Travel Guide for the Rest of Us!
0-7645-5453-0

**Hawaii FOR DUMMIES**
A Travel Guide for the Rest of Us!
0-7645-5438-7

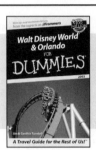

**Walt Disney World & Orlando FOR DUMMIES**
A Travel Guide for the Rest of Us!
0-7645-5444-1

**Also available:**

America's National Parks For Dummies (0-7645-6204-5)

Caribbean For Dummies (0-7645-5445-X)

Cruise Vacations For Dummies 2003 (0-7645-5459-X)

Europe For Dummies (0-7645-5456-5)

Ireland For Dummies (0-7645-6199-5)

France For Dummies (0-7645-6292-4)

Las Vegas For Dummies (0-7645-5448-4)

London For Dummies (0-7645-5416-6)

Mexico's Beach Resorts For Dummies (0-7645-6262-2)

Paris For Dummies (0-7645-5494-8)

RV Vacations For Dummies (0-7645-5443-3)

---

## EDUCATION & TEST PREPARATION

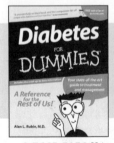

**Spanish FOR DUMMIES**
A Reference for the Rest of Us!
0-7645-5194-9

**Algebra FOR DUMMIES**
A Reference for the Rest of Us!
0-7645-5325-9

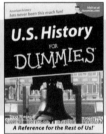

**U.S. History FOR DUMMIES**
A Reference for the Rest of Us!
0-7645-5249-X

**Also available:**

The ACT For Dummies (0-7645-5210-4)

Chemistry For Dummies (0-7645-5430-1)

English Grammar For Dummies (0-7645-5322-4)

French For Dummies (0-7645-5193-0)

GMAT For Dummies (0-7645-5251-1)

Inglés Para Dummies (0-7645-5427-1)

Italian For Dummies (0-7645-5196-5)

Research Papers For Dummies (0-7645-5426-3)

SAT I For Dummies (0-7645-5472-7)

U.S. History For Dummies (0-7645-5249-X)

World History For Dummies (0-7645-5242-2)

---

## HEALTH, SELF-HELP & SPIRITUALITY

**Diabetes FOR DUMMIES**
A Reference for the Rest of Us!
0-7645-5154-X

**Sex FOR DUMMIES**
A Reference for the Rest of Us!
0-7645-5302-X

**Parenting FOR DUMMIES**
A Reference for the Rest of Us!
0-7645-5418-2

**Also available:**

The Bible For Dummies (0-7645-5296-1)

Controlling Cholesterol For Dummies (0-7645-5440-9)

Dating For Dummies (0-7645-5072-1)

Dieting For Dummies (0-7645-5126-4)

High Blood Pressure For Dummies (0-7645-5424-7)

Judaism For Dummies (0-7645-5299-6)

Menopause For Dummies (0-7645-5458-1)

Nutrition For Dummies (0-7645-5180-9)

Potty Training For Dummies (0-7645-5417-4)

Pregnancy For Dummies (0-7645-5074-8)

Rekindling Romance For Dummies (0-7645-5303-8)

Religion For Dummies (0-7645-5264-3)

---

**Available wherever books are sold. Go to www.dummies.com or call 1-877-762-2974 to order direct**